The
BURNING
of the
RICE

A Cambodian Success Story

" 'The burning of the rice' marks the seventh month.
This is the season for harvesting the new rice, which is
brought to the South Gate and burned as a sacrifice to
the Buddha."

**(Chou Ta-Kuan, reporting on his visit
to Cambodia 1296-1297)**

DON PUCKRIDGE

Published in Australia by
Temple House Pty Ltd,
T/A Sid Harta Publishers
ACN 092 197 192
Hartwell, Victoria

Telephone: 61 3 9560 9920
Facsimile: 61 3 9545 1742
E-mail: author@sidharta.com.au

First published in Australia 2004
Copyright © Dr Donald W. Puckridge, 2004
Cover design, typesetting: Chameleon Print Design

The right of Dr Donald W. Puckridge to be
identified as the Author of the Work has been
asserted in accordance with the Copyright, Designs
and Patents Act 1988.

National Library of Australia Cataloguing-in-
Publication entry:
Puckridge, Don
Burning of the Rice
ISBN: 1-877059-73-0
326pp

"The commitment, undertakings and the sheer passion of the research and extension personnel is well reflected in this wonderful story."
Graham Blight, Australian Rice Grower and
Past President of the World Farmer's Federation

"This is an excellent account of an exciting saga which saw the bounce-back of Cambodian rice production after the devastating years of Pol Pot."
Tim Fischer,
Former Deputy Prime Minister of Australia

"This book documents with accuracy of detail and anecdote the restoration of food sufficiency in Cambodia."
Giles West, AusAID, Canberra

"A great book that provides excellent insights into the agricultural development work of an expatriate in a country like Cambodia"
Dr. Kwanchai A. Gomez,
Executive Director, the Asia Rice Foundation

"I think the real heroes are the Cambodian people, especially the researchers."
Bob Clements,
The Crawford Fund, Melbourne

*To the people of Cambodia and those who
helped their recovery*

*And with thanks to my wife
For her support through many years in Asia and her
patience with my fixation on the screen of a computer*

Foreword

The history of Cambodia during 1950-90 was one of immense misery and suffering. Pol Pot's Khmer Rouge practically eliminated all educated and technically qualified citizens of the country. Rice is the staple for the people of Cambodia and rice farming systems are the backbone of the food and livelihood security systems. It is in this context that the Peoples Republic of Kampuchea invited the International Rice Research Institute (IRRI) in 1985 to help that strife-torn country to rehabilitate and rejuvenate its damaged rural economy. I was then the Director General of the IRRI and our response was two fold.

First, we offered to train a cadre of young Kampuchean rice scientists, who could take up research and development in various aspects of rice improvement. Secondly, we proposed stationing of IRRI scientists to work with Kampuchean scholars and scientists in rebuilding the rice economy of that country. It was difficult to get support from donors to help Kampuchea at that time, since Vietnamese Government and soldiers were still controlling the politics and security of that country. However, the Govt. of Australia came forward with a generous support to IRRI to launch an Indo-China programme with special emphasis on Kampuchea. This project later came to be known as Cambodia – IRRI – Australia Project (CIAP).

I still recall the fear in the faces of the Kampuchean research scholars and scientists who came to IRRI for training in 1986, when my wife and I invited them to dinner at our home on the day of their arrival. When they returned after a few months of stay and training at IRRI they were indeed totally transformed human beings. It was a pleasure to watch the elimination of fear and the instillation of self-confidence and pride in them.

I am glad Dr Don Puckridge has chronicled the various phases of the CIAP programme for converting the food situation in Kampuchea from that of a begging bowl to one of a bread basket. This remarkable change in the agricultural destiny of Kampuchea came about through mutually reinforcing packages of technology, services and public policies. Don Puckridge has movingly described the political, social and scientific processes involved in this transformation. The book is written in a gripping style.

From the beginning of this IRRI - Cambodia - Australia collaboration Don Puckridge and Glenn Denning were actively involved. Later Dr Harold Nesbitt took over the leadership of CIAP. He became a friend, philosopher and guide for the rice scientists of Kampuchea. It is not therefore surprising that Prime Minister Hun Sen honoured Harry Nesbitt and Glenn Denning with gold medals for their outstanding service. I am also happy that Australia honoured Dr Nesbitt by appointing him a Member of the Order of Australia in 2003.

The project was transferred in August 2002 to the Cambodian Agricultural Research and Development Institute (CARDI). It is a tribute to the carefully designed withdrawal strategy of CIAP that the transition of the entire responsibility for leading this programme to CARDI has been very smooth and effective.

I would like to pay a particular tribute to Vice Minister Chhea Song and Minister Kong Som Ol for their extraordinary support to this programme. AIDAB also deserves our gratitude for rendering timely help to this unfortunate country. To me the success of the Cambodian programme gives particular pleasure since I worked hard during 1984-85 to bring young Cambodian scientists to IRRI and developed an IRRI - Cambodia partnership under difficult political circumstances. Fortunately the IRRI Gene Bank had a number of rice strains from Cambodia which would have been lost but for their conservation in this *ex-situ* genetic resources conservation centre. The strains preserved in the IRRI Gene Bank became the catalysts of subsequent breeding programmes, thus underlining the importance of such Gene Banks to the future of food security.

The Burning of the Rice is a moving and masterly account of the impact of science steeped in humanism. We owe Don Puckridge a deep sense of gratitude for this labour of love.

Prof M S Swaminathan,
M S Swaminathan Research Foundation, India

Contents

Chapter 1

*There is, moreover, a certain kind of
land where the rice grows naturally,
without sowing. When the water is
up one fathom, the rice keeps pace in
its growth. This, I think, must be a
special variety."
(Chou Ta-Kuan, 1297).*[1]

It seems that it was my fate to become involved with
Cambodia. It was by chance that I first visited 'The
International Rice Research Institute', or IRRI as
it is universally known, in the Philippines in 1965.
Two days later my plane from Manila to Singapore
touched down in Saigon and introduced me to Vietnam and the war that would soon engulf Cambodia.
It was a chance meeting in Adelaide with the Director General of IRRI twelve years later that provided
me with an opportunity to spend eight months
on a research project at IRRI headquarters at Los
Baños in the Philippines. That project eventually
led to employment with IRRI in Southeast Asia, to

---

1. The quotes at the heads of chapters are from a beautifully illustrated
book, *The Customs of Cambodia*, published by the Siam Society, Bangkok,
in 1997. The only description of Angkor near the height of its splendor is
to be found in Chou Ta-Kuan's *Notes on the Customs of Cambodia*. Chou
was assigned to a Chinese embassy in Cambodia for nearly a year in 1296-
1297 and wrote his account soon after returning to China. The Siam Society book was translated into English by J. Gilman d'Arcy Paul from the
French version by Paul Pelliot of Chou's Chinese original.

interaction with Cambodia through nearly twenty visits and to a small part in this story.

It was also by chance that in 2001 the person invited by Dr. Don Mentz, the Director of the Crawford Fund of Australia, to write an account of the Cambodia-IRRI-Australia-Project was unable to accept the work and referred it to me. Don Mentz then arranged for me to spend six weeks in Cambodia, the Philippines and Vietnam to meet with the principle characters and obtain an update of their history and work.[2]

In mid 1965 my wife and I had been looking forward to a relaxed return voyage to Australia after the stress of PhD studies at Reading University in England. But three weeks before the ship "Himalaya" was due to leave Southampton, a cable arrived from the University of Adelaide requesting me to return by air through the USA and the Philippines. My assignment would be to study research methods used by Professor Robert Musgrave and his team at Cornell University and to assess the possibility of adapting his techniques with maize crops to wheat research in Australia.

At the time Musgrave was on an exchange project in the Philippines and I was asked to first visit his co-workers in the USA and then travel to the University of the Philippines at Los Baños where he was working.

2.The Crawford Fund for International Agricultural Research was established by the Australian Academy of Technological Sciences and Engineering in honour of Sir John Crawford, who led the United Nations Food and Agriculture Program for a number of years. Its aims are to promote knowledge in Australia of the benefits derived from international agricultural research and to encourage greater support for international agricultural research from Australian organisations.

The cable left us two weeks to make the new arrangements and to program travel so that I could rejoin the family in Singapore for the remainder of the voyage to Australia. The time constraints also meant that after I departed on my first international flight Janice was abandoned to pack our many items of baggage and board the ship with two small children.

After visits to several research projects in the USA I arrived in the Philippines at the conclusion of an almost sleepless overnight flight from Honolulu. A friendly driver met me the Manila airport and took me on a fascinating trip along the western shore of the Lake of Laguna. The placid water of the lake was dotted with the bamboo poles of fish enclosures and along the road rice fields offset by stately palms linked small villages where children waiting by thatched huts for transport to school appeared as small clusters of black skirts and shorts topped by immaculate white shirts and smiling faces.

After about sixty kilometres we reached the foot of the richly forested Mt. Makiling, drove past the hot spring resorts that date from early Spanish times and entered the small town of Los Baños. After turning right the side road led us between small open-fronted shops and then through the arched gateway of the University before it continued its winding way through the dark green rain forest to a welcoming guesthouse in a peaceful compound of large western-style houses with immaculate gardens.

Soon after I had placed my belongings in a comfortable room of the guesthouse and eaten a snack in the spotless dining room Professor Musgrave and his two Cornell University post-graduate students arrived to take me to their field laboratory on the far side of the university grounds. There we spent most of the day as I was carefully instructed in the techniques of measuring photosynthesis of corn plants enclosed in clear plastic tents. That evening I was kindly invited to the Musgrave home for dinner. At their dining table, however, it was slightly disconcerting for me as an exhausted traveller when two maids entered the dining room, each carrying a dish of tempting food that they proffered to me before I had an opportunity to see what others at the table would select. I had no idea what would follow the first dish, but I was to learn that this polite procedure was not unusual for an expatriate dinner party in Los Baños.

My complete ignorance of the International Rice Research Institute (IRRI) was exposed next day when Professor Musgrave suggested a visit to the institute before I left Los Baños for Manila and Singapore. I soon discovered that IRRI was an impressive research centre a short distance from the university campus, along an avenue of trees and across the railway tracks that divided the institute from the university.[3]

The university had allocated around two hundred and fifty hectares of land to IRRI in 1960 when the Ford and Rockefeller Foundations, with the help of the Government of the Philippines, established IRRI as an international rice research and training centre. Much had been accomplished in its first five

---

3. The railway tracks doubled as a transport corridor for boys ferrying passengers to Los Baños town on small trolleys that they propelled along the tracks by pushing with one foot.

years. The substantial administration and laboratory buildings where I met research leaders looked across neat fields of dense crops of new rice varieties being developed for the irrigated areas of South and Southeast Asia. The fields were offset by a picturesque fringe of coconut palms and when the clouds parted the huge cone-shaped Mount Banaue, an extinct volcano, could be seen looming in the distance. Its shape, used on the IRRI logo, seemed a fitting symbol of the immense task of providing more food to millions of poor rice consumers.

As the American Airlines plane departed the Philippines next day I settled back in my seat, expecting a non-stop flight to Singapore and reunion with my family. Much to my surprise the plane landed at Saigon airport where transit passengers were ushered into a small room with a few seats and a souvenir counter. There I spent one US dollar on a small lacquer plaque inlaid with mother–of–pearl shell. It depicted a peaceful scene of a farmer walking home between rice paddies; perhaps an omen of my own future connection with rice in the region.

Outside, however, was not peaceful. The airport was packed with helicopters and military planes, and Saigon was in the midst of the war that would eventually engulf Cambodia and lead to its devastation. Ten years later the Khmer Rouge would overrun Phnom Penh and as the nation returned to 'year zero' townspeople would be forced out to the countryside where they slaved in the fields with little food and no reward except punishment while loudspeakers shrieked at them that 'rice means everything.'

Back in Australia I maintained my interest in IRRI through using its training materials and publications as a resource for my lectures on crop production. But although IRRI had impressed me with its research establishment and the dedication of its staff, the rice fields of Southeast Asia soon seemed remote.

Nevertheless, sixteen years later I stood in the middle of a pedestrian footbridge crossing over Sukhumvit Road in Bangkok, Thailand. As I stood there and looked at the grimy buildings and the dense pall of diesel smoke hanging over the road I pondered on whether I should accept an offer of work with IRRI on its regional deepwater rice project based in Thailand.

Two years earlier my family and I had spent eight months at Los Baños while I worked on a research project at IRRI. I was again impressed by IRRI's facilities, its surroundings, its research, and the atmosphere of urgency to improve the world's rice supply. When we left to return to Adelaide I had hoped for an opportunity to spend more time working in the pleasant surroundings of Los Baños, so it had been with some hesitation that I agreed to attend a conference in Bangkok to evaluate the offer to work in Thailand.

Bangkok was hot, humid and smelly, but the Thai rice scientists were friendly and hospitable, the deepwater rice project seemed interesting, and it was possible for me to take two years leave from my post with the University of Adelaide. But as I stood in the middle of that elevated walkway above Sukhumvit Road, looking at the traffic and the pall of smoke, I thought to myself, 'How will my wife ever be able to cope with this?' We found that it was not only a traffic problem. Three months later when she visited Bangkok to check out schooling and accommodation the same spot on Sukhumvit Road was flooded, with water lapping at the steps of the shops, after just three hours of rain.

Despite the conditions I accepted the position; Janice coped with the move and instead of two years we stayed for nearly sixteen. And after a few years of living in Bangkok we encouraged newcomers who found the city stressful by telling them that the first year they might hate it, the second year would tolerate it, and from the third year onwards they would probably not want to leave. For many people that was true.

The deepwater rice discussed at the conference is a fascinating crop. It is the only rice crop that can be grown on large areas of the flood plains of major rivers in tropical Asia during the high rainfall months of the year, the wet season. To survive the floodwater these remarkable plants must increase in height fast enough to keep pace with the increase in water level, which may reach over four metres in depth before the crop is ready to harvest. In the very deeply flooded areas it is also known as floating rice because of the way the foliage appears to float on the surface of the water. Some floating rice varieties can increase their height by as much as 20 cm in a day. They can do this because partial submergence in water stimulates production of ethylene gas within the plants. In deepwater rice plants ethylene promotes rapid cell division and cell elongation and the result is that the stems and leaves elongate quickly. Other types of rice lack this characteristic and are soon destroyed by deep water.

Most deepwater rice farmers broadcast seeds on ploughed soil at the beginning of the wet season. The seeds germinate with the rain and the plants grow for two to three months before floodwater enters the fields. Flooding can last for several months and the floodwater is usually deepest shortly before the rice plants flower. The water levels then start to drop and water has usually drained from the fields before harvest so that the plants lie prostrate on the ground with the panicles of grain on top of the straw. In some places where depressions in the landscape are slow to drain, particularly in India and Bangladesh, harvesting from boats may be necessary. In those places the water may still be two to three metres deep at harvest time.

Though the depth of water is in itself a challenge to working in deepwater rice fields, substantial barriers to improved grain production derive from the centuries of adaptation the plants have undergone just to survive. Because of this adaptation changing plant characteristics through plant breeding is a very slow process.

There are other challenges. When I saw a three-metre long cobra gliding through waist-deep water several times faster than it was possible for me to wade it occurred to me that using a boat could be a better way to inspect the crop, even in fields with shallow water. On the other hand, a colleague told me of his experience in Bangladesh where a snake decided that travelling by boat was a good idea and joined the passengers. Not surprisingly the human occupants quickly, but perhaps not wisely, jumped out.

IRRI's deepwater rice program was located in Thailand because there are no representative deepwater areas in the Philippines. Thailand has over half a million hectares of flood plains stretching north and northeast from Bangkok and its agriculture services provided good support for research on deepwater rice.. It was also more convenient to travel from Thailand to other deepwater rice areas of the region in which IRRI was involved. Those areas included the annually flooded valleys and deltas of the great Ganges-Brahmaputra rivers of India and Bangladesh, the Irrawaddy River of Burma and the Mekong River of Vietnam.

Cambodia, or Kampuchea as it was known under the Vietnamese supported government, was a missing link in the IRRI regional program for deepwater rice.[4] We knew from past reports that there had been over four hundred thousand hectares of deepwater rice in Cambodia, but the country was politically isolated and it was difficult to obtain permission to enter the country. Kampuchea had few contacts with Western countries and Thailand itself was viewed with suspicion by the Kampucheans because of its support for the Khmer Rouge and its allies in the guerrilla war against the Phnom Penh

---

4. The name Cambodia and the French version, Cambodge, are transliterations of the country's traditional name, pronounced Kampuchea in the Khmer, or Cambodian, language. The country has been officially the 'Kingdom of Cambodia' since Norodom Sihanouk was crowned king of Cambodia for the second time on Sept. 24, 1993. Under Pol Pot's Khmer Rouge from 1976 to 1979 the county was known as Democratic Kampuchea. The Vietnamese-backed government of 1979 to 1989 changed the name to the 'People's Republic of Kampuchea.' In this text Cambodia is used historically and for present day conditions while Kampuchea generally refers to the political situation. The author regrets any confusion that may result.

government. So in some ways it seemed that for us Kampuchea would just remain an obstacle around which Air France planes detoured on their weekly flight from Bangkok to Ho Chi Minh City (Saigon). However David Catling, one of my IRRI colleagues in Thailand, was not to be deterred and insisted that we should not neglect the annually flooded areas around Cambodia's Great Lake, the 'Tonle Sap,' and should continue to seek permission to visit the country, possibly through contacts in Vietnam.

IRRI researchers had maintained regular contacts with rice production in southern Vietnam through Dr. Vo-Tong Xuan, the Director of Research at Cantho University in the Mekong Delta. Some years earlier Vo-Tong Xuan had been a research fellow at IRRI, where he helped to produce a training manual for rice production. His interaction with IRRI was a long and fruitful relationship that culminated in his membership of the IRRI Board of Trustees. He was well known for his enthusiasm and innovative work. One year when insect pests destroyed thousands of hectares of rice in the Mekong delta Dr. Xuan arranged for the University to be closed, gave each of two thousand students a kilogram of seed of a new IRRI rice variety that was resistant to damage by the insects and sent them out to encourage farmers to test it.

David Catling and I first visited Vietnam in early 1983 for the start of co-operative work on deepwater rice with Xuan's staff and were surprised at the way the bureaucracy worked when we arrived in Ho Chi Minh City. The customs officials opened every piece

of our baggage and carefully examined each item of
the contents. It seemed that they were mostly curious because they asked questions like 'what do you
use this for,' 'what are you going to do with this,'
and so on. It was an interesting process that was
almost a social occasion. They also counted all the
money we carried, both on arrival and at departure.

I wondered about the money counting until on a
subsequent trip with my wife we were attracted by
some inlaid lacquer panels on display in a shop in
Ho Chi Minh City. The price was too high for us, but
the shop attendant told us that it was a government
shop and that the price, in US dollars, was the government price. She then added that if we came back
after five p.m. it would then be a private shop and
the price would be much lower. We returned later,
were tempted, and bought the panels for one third
of the original price! Unfortunately we did not know
that we should show a government receipt for the
purchase at the airport, and when the customs officer counted our money and found a deficit he said
rather forcefully that we did not have permission to
spend money. He then confiscated the panels.

After returning to Thailand I wrote to Air France
explaining the situation and a week later the panels
arrived in Bangkok with a bill of ten dollars only for
handling charges. It was impressive service. As the
years went by custom's procedures in Vietnam became more streamlined and less personal, so in some
ways the friendly curiosity and familiar faces of those
first customs checks in the arrival hall were missed.

It was a five to six-hour trip south through the

Mekong Delta from Ho Chi Minh City to Cantho, during which the road passed over more than fifty small bridges and two wide rivers that were crossed by ferry. In the next few years those waterways would be the means of transforming many thousands of hectares from one low yielding crop of rice a year to intensive agriculture with multiple crops of irrigated rice, fruit trees and other crops. The rapidity of those changes was indicated by the increasing amounts of rice grain spread to dry along the edges of the bitumen road.

Our travel by boat along the canals of the Mekong Delta to look at deepwater rice production provided fascinating and picturesque glimpses of waterside life — of farms, houses, communities and people. Men could be seen loading sacks of grain into barges. Slender women in traditional pyjama suits and conical hats stood to propel narrow boats by pushing on crossed oars; others with children by their side washed clothes and dishes in the canals. Children balanced on slender bridges with just one bamboo pole on which to place their feet as they crossed streams on the way to school. Small boats laden with baskets of squealing pigs, cages of crowded chickens, even a cage full of rats, and many other kinds of produce moved along the canals on the way to market.

At the time we didn't know that Vo-Tong Xuan directed a weekly TV program on agricultural technology for Cantho University. The program started soon after the end of the war in Vietnam and its aim was to instruct government leaders on methods that farmers could use to produce higher yielding rice crops. Most trained agricultural people had left

South Vietnam and the senior people in charge of the villages, districts and provinces were all recently returned military veterans.

Vo-Tong Xuan commented that after the war the number one worry was food security and the government was trying to mobilise everyone to contribute to that food goal. 'Brave soldiers those leaders had been, but technologically they were very limited,' said Xuan. However, he was neither a member of the communist party nor a government official and had no authority to tell the local leaders that they should follow the University suggestions. Consequently he negotiated with the Director of Cantho TV station to produce the rice program. He remembered the director saying, 'Ha, we can broadcast and make propaganda, but how can we do something on food security?' Xuan's reply was that 'You can do something if you let me do the propaganda. I can tell the farmers how to improve their production techniques and how to use the new technology that we have developed, especially that learnt during my time at the International Rice Research Institute.'

The success of the TV program extended across the Vietnamese border into Kampuchea where Kampuchean leader Hun Sen paid close attention to it.[5] Later Hun Sen insisted that the Vietnamese

5. Hun Sen was educated at a Buddhist monastery in Phnom Penh. In the late 1960s he joined the resistance Communist Party and soon became a courier for the local communist leader. He joined the Khmer Rouge movement, but during Pol Pot's regime, when the Khmer Rouge killed more than one million people (1975-79), he fled to Vietnam, joining pro-Vietnamese troops against the Khmer Rouge. He returned to Cambodia after the Vietnam-backed take over and led the country until the 1993 elections. He then became Co-Premier with Prince Ranariddh, but deposed him in the coup of 1997.

government send Vo-Tong Xuan to Kampuchea to discuss his rice production methods. So in 1984 Xuan started travelling to Phnom Penh where he learnt that the researchers he had known before the war had either been killed by Pol Pot's Khmer Rouge or had fled, and that Kampuchea had neither the tools nor the human capacity to do the work needed. Xuan said that Kampuchea was so technologically limited that when their vehicle went to outlying villages children would rush out and ask what it was.

After three missions to Kampuchea Xuan designed a program of rice improvement based on collecting promising rice varieties from farmers' fields. It was intended that seeds of the collected varieties would be multiplied and the best distributed to other farmers. However, before the program could start it was necessary to train the Cambodians on the methodology. The input costs were very small, but Kampuchea had no money for training and neither had Cantho University.

Xuan then submitted a proposal to the Mennonite Central Committee, a Non Government Organisation (NGO) that had aid projects in both Kampuchea and Vietnam. They provided a grant for six Cambodians to go to Cantho University for training and research in field plot techniques. Unfortunately, when the trainees returned to Kampuchea they could not carry out the program because they did not have any money for travel or for accommodation.

Vo-Tong Xuan realised that in the long run Cantho University could not help much. 'Finance and security issues were crucial,' said Xuan. 'I must confess that I was very worried about security. On each visit I had the same interpreter. Her mother was Cambodian and father Vietnamese. She told me to be careful, to never walk alone, but always go together with my Cambodian counterpart because although people in the daytime may be on Hun Sen's side, at night they might be on Pol Pot's side. It was very dangerous,. We had to be very careful and every time I went my wife was very worried.' [6]

Xuan therefore emphasised to government leaders that IRRI help was needed and the best option for Kampuchea was for them to approach IRRI directly. Not long after we started working with Vo-Tong Xuan I was fortunate enough to meet Fred Kauffman

---

6. It was an attack on the family village of Dr. Vo-Tong Xuan in Vietnam's Mekong Delta that provided a trigger for the Vietnamese invasion of Cambodia. He told me the story in June 2001 as we travelled towards Cantho from Long Xuyen, where Xuan is head of the new Angiang University. He said that towards the end of 1977 the threat of invasion by Pol Pot forces became very apparent. His father's village of Bachuc was in a mountainous area only 3 km from the border. In February 1978 one of his relatives came to Cantho and told about the awful things that they had seen. Pol Pot soldiers near the border had captured women and children, raped the women, speared them with bamboo and sliced apart the children. Every night after that the villagers climbed the mountain and took refuge in caves.

After nearly four months some people thought that it was now safe so they did not go to the mountain at night. But a few nights later people still hiding in the caves saw fire in the villages below and learned that Pol Pot forces had overrun the area. Many people ran to hide in bunkers built under temples for protection from bombing in the previous war, but the Pol Pot soldiers just tossed in grenades and killed everyone. They killed altogether more than four thousand villagers, including several of Vo-Tong Xuan's relatives. After three weeks the Vietnamese army reoccupied the area and collected the dead bodies and bones. The bones were placed in a genocide museum, but were thought to be very sacred and were stolen one by one. (At this stage in our conversation Dr. Xuan checked details with his driver, who had driven a truck to rescue people fleeing the Khmer Rouge.) The Vietnamese army did not stop at the border. 'We thought that if we continued to live that way our daily life would always be threatened. So the best thing was to go over and to fight Pol Pot,' said Xuan.

in Ho Chi Minh airport. Fred was the project leader of the Mennonite Central Committee humanitarian aid project in Kampuchea that had supported Xuan's efforts, and he promised to see how IRRI could be involved within the country. In early 1985 he wrote to inform the IRRI Director General:

> '*During March we met with the Minister of Agriculture, Mr. Kong Som Ol, to discuss various programs, including the possibility of translating some IRRI materials into Khmer. We suggested that an IRRI expert come to review the materials available and procedures for translation and printing them. The Minister showed interest in this possibility, but we have not put any project in writing ... The main objective is to re-establish the relationship between IRRI and the Kampuchean farmers. And perhaps the most workable first step is for an IRRI person to come here on a specific project and at that time explore other types of co-operation possible in the future.*'

Vo-Tong Xuan had also reported the Kampuchean situation to Dr. M. S. Swaminathan, the Director General of IRRI, who assigned Dr. Glenn Denning to find ways of providing the help needed. Glenn's main work at IRRI was focused on strengthening national rice programs and since much of the IRRI emphasis was then on Indochina it was a natural progression for him to become responsible for overseeing the program in Kampuchea.

Glenn's efforts added to those of Vo-Tong Xuan and Fred Kauffman prepared the way for direct Kampuchean government contacts with IRRI. Consequently when representatives of the Kampuchean

Ministry of Agriculture visited the Philippines they included IRRI headquarters in their itinerary and proposed to their government that IRRI be invited to send three staff members to Kampuchea to assess the situation.

It took several months to organise that first IRRI visit. Letters and telexes from the Philippines to Phnom Penh could only be sent through my IRRI office in Bangkok. From there they were taken to the UNICEF office in Bangkok for inclusion in the diplomatic pouch that was carried on the once a week Air France flight to Ho Chi Minh City. In Ho Chi Minh City they were transferred to a Red Cross charter-flight to Phnom Penh. As a result Dr. Swaminathan waited four months for his formal request for confirmation of the IRRI visit to pass through government channels in Kampuchea and the answer from Agriculture Minister Mr. Kom Som Ol to follow the reverse route through Bangkok to Los Baños. The Minister's reply of 30 November 1985 read in part.

> *'I am very pleased to inform you that following the visit of two of our agricultural technicians to IRRI ... the Government of the People's Republic of Kampuchea has fully approved the coming visit to Kampuchea of a group of 3 specialists from IRRI.'*

Arrangements for the IRRI group's visit to Kampuchea were made through UNICEF, the only organisation authorised by the Kampuchean government to do so. Those arrangements signalled the start of a new adventure in the science and practice of rice production. In less than fifteen years a starving nation learned to feed itself as a few expatriates and many Cambodians put their collective efforts to the task. This is their story, and as far as possible it is told in their own words.

The result is an inspiring example of how the lives of millions can be permanently improved by relatively few 'aid dollars' when governments, aid agencies and NGOs co-operate to support those efforts. It also demonstrates that providing practical help to the hungry through developing their ability to grow more food is of more lasting benefit than giving them food.

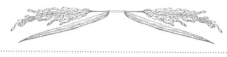

2

*'After crossing the frontier at
Chen-p'u, one sees everywhere close-
grown thickets of scrub forest; the
great estuaries of the Mekong cover
hundreds of miles; the heavy shade
of old trees and trailing rattan vines
forms a luxuriant cover.'*
(Chou Ta-Kuan, 1297)

Drs. Gurdev Khush and Glenn Denning from IRRI
headquarters joined me in Bangkok in January 1986
and we set out for Phnom Penh via Ho Chi Minh
City. Our purpose was to review the current agriculture situation in Kampuchea and to evaluate
possibilities for assisting the government to increase
rice production. On the first leg of the journey on
the Air France flight from Bangkok to Ho Chi Minh
City the female cabin crew seemed to be selected for
the coming severe conditions. In comparison with
the gentle cabin crew of Thai airlines they appeared
tall, angular and stern, with a 'sit down and be quiet'
attitude to passengers. One of them asked if I wanted
coffee with my lunch, but I asked if I could have
water instead. An imperious finger pointed to a very
small container of mineral water on my tray and she
said, 'Sir, you have water!' End of negotiation.

All travellers booked to travel on the Red Cross charter flight to Phnom Penh were required to take sixty nine dollars in cash to purchase their ticket at the Ho Chi Minh Airport. The charter plane was a two-engine Russian transport with drooping wings that gave it the appearance of a tired albatross as it waited on the tarmac. Passengers entered the plane by the rear ramp and were accommodated in the cargo hold, which had only two windows an each side of the cargo space and the old bus-type seats bolted to the floor were so close together that it was hard to squeeze in. More seats stacked in a loose pile at the rear of the plane were ready to leap about our ears if there was a sudden stop. They were accompanied by a variety of livestock of the feathered kind as well as loose parcels that slid back and forth on the floor with the turns of the aircraft.

It was only a short flight from Ho Chi Minh to Phnom Penh. Vietnam is a long and narrow country and Cambodia — then named Kampuchea — is only about 450 kilometres from north to south and 580 kilometres from east to west. Cambodia is enclosed on three sides by forested mountains; the Cardomen and Elephant Mountains on the south-west and west; the Dangrek mountains along the northern border with Thailand and the Central Highlands of Vietnam on the north-eastern border. Forests provide building materials, timber for export and firewood for cooking. Besides logging, firewood collection is a necessary activity of most farmers and forests close to populated areas are rapidly diminishing.

A brief glance through one of the two windows as we neared Phnom Penh revealed the broad brown expanse of the silt-laden Mekong River winding majestically southwards across the flat central plain to the border with Vietnam. The Mekong is over four thousand kilometres long from its source in China to its mouth. It flows through the eastern part of Tibet, forms part of the international borders between Myanmar (Burma) and Laos and between Laos and Thailand and then crosses Cambodia and southern Vietnam before discharging into the sea to the south of Ho Chi Minh City. It joins the Tonle Sap river at Phnom Penh.

The Mekong's mean annual flow in central Cambodia is about fourteen thousand cubic metres per second, but the flow is much greater during the wet season from mid-May to early October. Then the water level rises approximately nine metres and an enormous volume of water flows backwards up the Tonle Sap River for nearly one hundred kilometres to the Tonle Sap (The Great Lake). This annual backflow expands the lake surface area from around 3,000 square kilometres to more than 8,000 square kilometres. The process is reversed in the dry season and the water drains back into the Mekong and so to the sea.

Pochentang airport outside Phnom Penh was almost deserted when we arrived. There were sixteen people on our plane, the only flight for the week, and immigration clearance was little more than filling out a form and watching that form and our passports move along a row of officials, each of whom studied them seriously and made notes on another form. Customs examination was not nearly as detailed as in Ho Chi Minh City and was smoothly handled except for our package of rice seed that was erroneously labelled 'Democratic Republic of Kampuchea' instead of 'Peoples Republic of Kampuchea.' The 'Democratic' Republic consisted of the very undemocratic Khmer Rouge who had taken refuge along the Thai border, so the wording had to be hastily changed.[7]

Mr Ith Nody and two colleagues from the Agronomy Department of the Ministry of Agriculture and a representative of UNICEF met us at the airport. After greetings and a brief outline of our program for the day they took us into the city of Phnom Penh where we checked in to the Samaki Hotel. The front yard of the once elegant four-storey hotel was occupied by a few four-wheel drive vehicles belonging to the Red Cross and World Vision and the rooms allocated to us by Red Cross staff at a cost of nineteen US dollars per night were available only because their regular occupants were out of the country.

The 'Samaki' (solidarity) hotel had graceful traditional Khmer architecture and lots of atmosphere, of rather a gloomy sort, and some hints of its glamorous past. It was featured in the film 'The Killing Fields' released two years earlier. The huge kitchen was eerily

---

7. The airport staff had an air of authority, but with so few outsiders entering the country they were friendly and I soon learnt that they remembered regular travellers. Once an Agriculture Ministry employee worried for three days about whether it was safe to give me a letter to post to his relatives in Melbourne, but eventually did so. At the airport security check one of the officials gave me a searching look and asked 'letters?' I shrugged my shoulders and looked non-committal, so after a moment's hesitation he reached into his pocket and dropped a letter into my bag. Then the other two officials did likewise, pleased to have a reliable mail delivery service.

empty, so we had to eat out at the very few restaurants in the city frequented by foreigners. When returning to the city in 2001 to update information for this book it was fascinating to walk through its refurbished buildings. It had been restored to the splendid 'Le Royale,' where the 'Jackie Onassis Suite' cost nearly one hundred times the price that we had to pay.

The Samaki and the Monorom hotels held the offices and accommodation of all the non-Soviet-bloc organisations, and their personnel lived either in the hotel rooms or in bungalows in the grounds behind the Samaki. We learnt that with such confined living and very few opportunities for relaxation that most expatriate personnel stationed in Phnom Penh went out of the country for a rest and recuperation break after every two or three months.

The purpose of our visit was to work with Ministry of Agriculture personnel to assess the potential for increased rice production, but it was the dry season and we did not see much rice growing in the fields. The Ministry's statistics for wet season rice crops indicated that average yields for Kampuchea were about 1.1 tonnes of rice per hectare, possibly little different to rice yields during the pinnacle of Khmer civilisation a thousand years earlier. There were few resources available to increase it. Just to provide a subsistence rice ration for its seven million people meant that approximately 1.3 million hectares of rice crop needed to be planted and to do so required around seventy five thousand tons of rice seed and two hundred and thirty thousand plough oxen and buffaloes. Huge areas of cropland had been abandoned due to war and the danger of anti-personnel mines in rice paddies and to insecurity in isolated areas. Irrigation systems had become unusable and over ninety percent of the rice crops depended solely on the variable monsoon rains for their growth.

We were told that there were only eleven graduates left in the Ministry of Agriculture. One of them was Vice-Minister Chhea Song, whose visit to IRRI had initiated our trip to Kampuchea. Their daunting challenge was the restoration of an agriculture system devastated by Pol Pot's Khmer Rouge. The population was still on the edge of famine and the tools for assisting in crop recovery − experiment stations, equipment, records and supplies − had all been destroyed by the Khmer Rouge.

An example was the Prey Pdau Experiment Station forty kilometres from Phnom Penh where the buildings had been destroyed and only one technician of twenty was able to return. On the road leading to the station rusted car bodies recorded Pol Pot's decision to go back to the primitive. Our translator, Mr. Ngak Chhay Heng, who was also head of plant protection services in the Department of Agronomy, pointed out that one of those cars had belonged to him.[8]

---

8. Mr. Ngak Chhay Heng had never completed a university degree but had a thirst for knowledge, particularly of languages, and spoke Khmer, French, English, Russian, Japanese, German, Thai and some Filipino. 'Heng' told us that when he and his family were driven out of Phnom Penh they pushed their car eighteen kilometres. 'When we abandoned the car we were ordered to cut up the tires and take the pieces to make sandals,' he said. 'We could not use money so at the next village we bartered sarongs to rent an ox-cart to carry the small children and our few belongings up country.' Starting at 5 am, they travelled thirty kilometres, stopped for the night, then travelled about the same distance the next day to another village where they were forced into farming. 'We worked all day, attended compulsory meetings at night, and lived under the Khmer Rouge for 3 years, 8 months and 20 days,' said Heng.

The Prey Pdau station was being restored by a Belgian aid organisation. It had a new wooden office, a few fibreglass tanks for storing seed, and an old pump at the nearby river to supply irrigation water to the fields. The fields showed the benefit of using irrigation water in association with modern rice varieties and fertiliser. Some rice crops had recently been harvested and two contrasting mechanical threshers were threshing the grain from the straw. One was a large engine driven machine that had been manufactured in Vietnam from a design produced by IRRI engineers. The other was a simple machine operated by a foot pedal, rather like an old style sewing machine, where spikes on the outside of a rotating drum beat the rice grain from bundles of stalks held against the drum. It was one of several donated by India. At the nearby village four small children in the care of their slightly older sisters jostled on the cement surround of a hand operated village pump, enjoying the vital source of clean water provided by a UNICEF well drilling program.

During our visits to three provinces outside of Phnom Penh we were guarded by five Kampuchean soldiers. At Prey Pdau they posed proudly in front of the flagpole, three with automatic rifles and the other two with an arsenal of rifle grenades strapped around their waists. They were fascinated by the threshing machines. The threat of trouble did not seem to be taken too seriously and they appeared to be enjoying an escape from the tedium of their usual army duties. When we stopped for a snack in a local restaurant, an open fronted shop-house with a few tables and chairs and a supply of noodle soup and tea, they casually leant their rifles against the wall. A group of young and old quickly gathered on the street to see the foreigners, the majority of them young girls carrying siblings on their hips. The small children laughed at the sight of a camera.

On another trip, to Prey Veng province, we crossed the Mekong by ferry to Neak Luong, a town mistakenly flattened by 'friendly' bombs during the war against the Khmer Rouge. Thatched huts on the flat ground along the edge of the river were almost numberless. Some dwellings appeared to be floating on the river, while others were of such light construction that it would be a simple matter to move them to higher ground as the river rose. Even so, it seemed odd to see houses right at the river's edge while a boat was being constructed higher up the bank. On one occasion that week the road was blocked by a moving house of the same type. About thirty people were carrying it, the thatched roof and matting walls all still in place as it was moved to a new location.

We ate lunch in the town, though raw turtle eggs on plates of ice and meat served almost raw did not appeal to my taste. After lunch Glen Denning upset a Vietnamese army officer by taking a photo of a motley group of soldiers on trucks waiting to cross the river. The officer seemed a little over sensitive, but we learned that guerrillas had attacked soldiers in the area a few days previously.

No doubt each of those soldiers had his own fears

and memories to haunt him in later years. While updating information for this book I interviewed a Vietnamese ex-soldier, Mr. Nguyen Tan Viet, in Hanoi. He had been stationed close to the Cambodian border in 1972, when they were in theory allies of the Khmer Rouge. But he said that even though Vietnamese soldiers helped Cambodia, the Khmer Rouge were still hostile and the Vietnamese soldiers were miserable. 'The Khmer Rouge could fight against us any time, but we could not fight back,' said Mr. Viet. On one occasion two of his comrades went to try to retrieve a stolen gun from the Khmer Rouge. The Khmer Rouge killed both of them, cut them up and threw the pieces into the Mekong River. He could not find the right words to express how terrible it was to live near the Khmer Rouge. 'We could grow vegetables, but not plant trees, especially mango trees. The Khmer Rouge said that if the shadow of a mango tree growing on the Vietnamese side of the border fell on the Cambodian side the Vietnamese were trying to take their land.' Perhaps it was not surprising that Vietnamese soldiers were sensitive about photographs.

An enduring memory of Prey Veng province was of a narrow dusty road on the bank of a canal drawn straight across the landscape. It was a typical example of Khmer Rouge changes to rice culture in which they dug canals to follow grid lines of a map without reference to the topography. A few diminishing pools of water along the bottom of the canal were a reminder of the futility of trying to keep the dry season drought at bay. Another more fortunate canal was half full of muddy water, with a bamboo fence placed across it to trap fish as the water level dropped. Nearby were four substantial wooden houses on stilts, scattered as if they avoided associating with each other. Conical stacks of straw near each house were being undermined by bites from cattle taking respite from the dry and almost barren fields.

We stopped at a group of huts and saw an orphan girl of about sixteen years of age tending an earthen fireplace in the open, boiling sugar palm juice in a large wok to make palm sugar, a common ingredient in cooking for those who could afford it. Seeing this girl and other orphans in that place made more impact when we learnt that Prey Veng had over 34,000 widows and 10,000 orphans in a population of about 700,000. Seventy percent of the men had died under the five years of Khmer rouge rule and sixty five percent of the remaining population was female. Kampong Speu province had 17,000 widows and 7,000 orphans, Kampong Chhnang province 15,000 widows, and so on. In the sixteen to forty-five age group of Prey Veng province females outnumbered males by about three to one.

This disproportionate ratio of the sexes resulted in social disruption and lack of male muscle power for heavy farm work. Consequently women were often obliged to perform tasks that were traditionally done by men, such as land preparation and application of farmyard manure and chemical fertiliser to crops. The loss of animals due to the effects of war, widespread disease and over-work took their toll as well. People without animals had to hire them, with payment usually in rice or labour, or to do the work by hand. On one occasion we even saw a young woman with a yoke over her shoulders straining to pull a plough while an old woman behind it guided the blade in the furrow.

A social survey a few years later found that such women had less access to animals and other resources, were the major borrowers of informal loans and had less access to information. Even though they may have been the only adult in the family there was still the cultural perception that they were not farmers, but were helpers and housewives. In families without cattle or buffaloes for ploughing and raking of their fields it was the women who were almost always the ones who repaid the labour owed as payment for borrowed draught animals. One morning of ploughing and raking was usually repaid by a full day of pulling seedlings and transplanting. Women who did not own animals also provided labour in exchange for cow manure for use as fertiliser on their fields and they were often exploited because they lacked cash or other assets.

The Vietnamese-backed government gave high priority to primary education and had also reopened secondary schools and institutions of higher education. However, knowing the urgent need for more trained agriculturists to cope with rice production problems, it was rather sobering to visit the Institute of Agriculture on the outskirts of Phnom Penh. Pol Pot's Khmer Rouge forces had converted the

University into an ammunition dump and dynamited it when they departed and it was still to recover.[9] A dusty road led past newly whitewashed buildings, but there were few other resources. The Director was the only one of the ninety-four Kampuchean staff with a college degree, so seventeen instructors from the USSR were teaching at the institute. Consequently all the students had to learn Russian before starting their course work.

Red flags and portraits of Marx and Lenin were displayed in the classrooms and apart from a few books in French and Russian there was little to be seen of science or agriculture in the university library. A prominent display in a passageway outside the library contained titles such as 'Lenine', 'Youri Andropov', 'Union Sovietique', 'Hiroshima', 'Terrorisme … USA'. The Russian lecturers we met were friendly and one professor showed us a live snake squirming in a preservative bottle. He did not have much else with which to teach, though he spoke excellent French, a valuable asset in the community.

Historically, French had been the official language of the Cambodian government and commerce and for older Cambodians was still the main means of communication with foreigners. The French influence was also subtly emphasised by the long golden bread rolls stacked in cane baskets for sale by clusters of women vendors seen squatting on the ground at the edge of

---

9. The Khmer Rouge also shut down a college of agriculture at Prek Leap across the Tonle Sap River from Phnom Penh. In 1986 students there were taking courses in agronomy, veterinary science, fishery, water management, agricultural mechanisation, and forestry, but laboratories were not equipped and teaching was supplemented by visiting lecturers from Vietnam.

a road, chatting with their neighbours, feeding babies, or just patiently waiting for customers to come by.

The French moved into Cambodia in 1863 to prevent British and Siamese (Thai) expansion threatening their access to the Mekong River. Cambodia later became an 'autonomous state within the French Union' but was controlled by France until it gained independence in 1953. During the colonial period the French built hundreds of kilometres of paved roads, established thousands of hectares of rubber plantations and operated some large-scale mechanised commercial rice farms. By 1940 Cambodia was the third largest rice-exporting country in the world with a large proportion of the exported rice originating from the commercial farms in the northern province of Battambang. However, rice research and extension services for the peasant farmers in the rest of the country were virtually non-existent. They grew rice using traditional methods on their small farms and their rice yields had remained stagnant at around one tonne per hectare.

The French influence was more obvious in the wide streets and gracious buildings of Phnom Penh. Legend has it that Phnom Penh was established in 1372 after a Lady Penh retrieved from the river a floating tree that contained four Buddha statues. In celebration of her find she built a small hill (Phnom) crowned by a temple and the surrounding area became known as Phnom Penh. The city grew to be the capital of the country as a result of its convenient defensive and trading location at the junction of the Mekong and Tonle Sap rivers.

Phnom Penh has many lovely buildings, especially the impressive residential villas, some of which were beginning to be restored. I noted that the upper stories of substantial buildings in a street near the river still maintained the cream paint of past times, but lower walls and pillars were stained with water and the plaster fretted. The main roads were quiet during the daytime, but thronged with cyclists in the morning and evening. In contrast many side streets were still almost deserted, with shop fronts barricaded with sheets of corrugated iron attached to rusting iron grills. A few lonely pot plants graced the balcony of one shop house and the occupant's washing was suspended on poles balanced on the backs of three chairs standing in the street.

Some long streets had only two or three 'cyclos' — tricycles with two wheels at the front supporting a padded seat under a canopy for passengers or goods — or bicycles moving along them. Dense weed growth on the footpaths indicated the absence of pedestrians. On one such street three small children were enjoying a bonfire of leaves. Nevertheless it was still hard to imagine that two days after the Khmer Rouge entered the city on 17 April 1975 over two million people had been driven out into the country, leaving only a few thousand needed by Pol Pot and his Khmer Rouge. Everywhere we were reminded of Pol Pot and the Khmer Rouge, verbally or otherwise.

We were fortunate while in Phnom Penh to be invited to a cultural show presented in honour of a visiting Lao government delegation. The show presented traditional and modern versions of Kampuchean dance with superb footwork, timing and rhythm. Some dances were almost identical in costumes, hand movements and music to Thai dancing, but from her shape it was evident that the lead dancer would soon retire to fulfil her role in replenishing the population. A traditional dance where evil characters in black were banished by the handsome hero while rescuing the distressed maiden could well have had political implications. The jugglers and gymnasts had been trained in Russia. One had a marvellous comic routine of legs and face combined with first class juggling while another was a lovely lissom lass who spun hula-hoops around her waist as she used her feet to pick others off the floor and work them up her body and over her head.

The performance was in a huge theatre built in 1965 and for some reason not destroyed by the Khmer Rouge. It seemed no one could understand their motives. For example the reception hall in Prince Sihanouk's palace was perfectly preserved, but everything in the adjoining kitchen was smashed.

Sunday was the official rest day, a day to visit the palace and museums. The palace was built in traditional Khmer style in 1930 and the main features we saw were the beautiful audience hall and some restoration work in the Silver Pagoda. At the cultural museum the formal central courtyard provided an air of serenity not found elsewhere. Four rectangular lily ponds separated by a cross of straight paths focused attention on a central 'sala' sheltering a seated Buddha while strategically placed palms completed the peaceful setting. Consequently, though the museum focused on the historical past with its statues and other artefacts, its serenity seemed completely divorced from the recent turbulent times and its untouched state another enigma of the Khmer Rouge.

A unique feature of the museum is that its roof is home to hundreds of thousands of bats. As they fly out at dusk every evening they form a dark cloud of fluttering shapes against the evening sky, seemingly symbolic of the souls of those who lost their freedom, their families and their lives while under the dark shadow of Pol Pot.

The obligatory visit to the Tuol Sleng Genocide Museum that followed provided a stark contrast to the serene atmosphere of the cultural museum. Formerly a high school, Tuol Sleng was turned by the Khmer Rouge into a prison where over fourteen thousand men, women and children were imprisoned and tortured. All but five died in the prison or in the killing fields at Choeung Ek, fifteen kilometres out of Phnom Penh, where they were thrown into mass graves. There among the peaceful fields in which cattle contentedly grazed we saw a few holes in the ground surrounded by bones and pieces of cloth, mute testimonies of the fate of the several thousand humans whose skulls were displayed on racks nearby.

Of the thousands of photos the Khmer Rouge kept of their victims now displayed on the walls of Tuol Sleng, probably the most haunting to me was an assembled family group of an engineer with his wife, three daughters and son. He had worked for the Khmer Rouge, but he and all his family were destroyed.

Fifteen years after that first visit I was taken to dinner at a small restaurant opposite the walls of Tuol Sleng. It gave me an eerie feeling to pass the gate and I couldn't help but glance across to the buildings and wonder how such a thing could have happened.

We found that resident members of the few international aid organisations represented in Phnom Penh were very helpful, an indication of the valuable co-operation with IRRI that would come later. Their presence was also a reminder of the help the country desperately needed. The humanitarian assistance from voluntary organisations and the United Nations Children's Fund (UNICEF) supplemented assistance from Soviet Bloc countries and from India. Besides more general aid India donated cloth for school uniforms, cotton thread, sewing machines and copybooks for school children.

The various contributions of other countries and organisations from the time that the Khmer Rouge retreated to the border in 1979 until our visit in 1986 make an extensive list, but were in total a very small amount of aid that could not meet major needs.

Czechoslovakia provided Kampuchea with textiles, hospital equipment, medicines, cranes, trucks, spare parts and water cleaning equipment and assistance for reconstruction of a tire factory and the operation of a Phnom Penh power plant. Some Kampuchean students were receiving free education in Czechoslovakia.

East Germany provided medicine, medical equipment, food, textiles, lorries, bicycles, sewing machines and teaching aids for schools. It also supplied lorries, spare parts and maintenance specialists to Kampuchea under the United Nations Relief program. By the end of 1984, more than five hundred Kampucheans had started training in East Germany.

Hungary supplied electrical instruments and appliances; medicine and medical instruments and textiles as well as pharmaceutical raw materials, copybooks and office supplies. Hungary also completed an orphanage in Kandal province. There were fifty-eight Kampuchean scholarship holders at Hungary's vocational training schools and higher education establishments.

The Government of the Mongolian People's Republic provided goods to fill basic needs and Kampuchean students were being trained at Mongolian institutions of higher education.

Bulgarian grant aid consisted of medicines, foodstuffs, fabrics; machines, school aids, electrical equipment, office equipment and building materials and the restoration and equipping of a Phnom Penh hospital. By 1985 there were twenty Kampuchean students in Bulgaria, including Mr. Men Sarom, future Director of the yet to be established Cambodian Agricultural Research and Development Institute (CARDI).

Poland provided a loan for the reconstruction of shipyards on inland waterways, equipment for agricultural technical services and help for the protection of monuments such as Angkor Wat. The Polish Red Cross had given assistance each time the Kampuchean people were faced with natural disasters.

From 1980 to 1985, the Soviet Union had provided grant aid and long-term interest free credits for work on fifty projects. The projects included restoration of the ports of Kampong Som and Phnom Penh, the thermal power station in Phnom Penh, a Phnom Penh hospital and a higher technical institute. The USSR also gave aid to restore rubber production and equipped a rice selection and seed growing station. Aid included oil products, fertiliser, trucks, tractors, paper and fabric. University training in Moscow included Ms. Chan Phaloeun, whose role in CIAP is an essential part of this story.

Vietnam's friendship treaty with Phnom Penh committed it to around twenty-five million dollars in annual aid, much of it supplied through a system of twinned provinces.

In addition to help from the countries above a few international voluntary agencies working in Phnom Penh co-ordinated their activities with UNICEF and the International Committee of the Red Cross.

The American Friends Service Committee had a staff of five, including two physiotherapists and a veterinarian. A main activity was the making of artificial limbs and rehabilitation of amputees[10] with technical support from 'Operation Handicap International'. They also contributed equipment and supplies for health and education and a project for animal vaccination.

Church World Service had an administrator, two veterinarians, a mechanical engineer and an agronomist. Projects covered field and laboratory training in veterinary services, heavy equipment repair, training for hydrologists and maintenance of facilities, development of a research and seed multiplication station for vegetables, public health and nutrition and agricultural services and supplies.

Redd Barna from Norway contributed funds for agriculture and supplies of fertiliser and insecticide.

In 1984 'S.O.S. Enfants du Cambodge' started work for the care of children, particularly those in orphanages, with an allocation of two hundred and fifty thousand US dollars. Their one staff representative, a qualified nurse, managed the project.

---

10. From 1998 to March 2001 there were nearly 3,000 new victims of land mines exploding. Harvesting of crops, searching for firewood and travel all contributed to land mine injuries. Most casualties occurred in March when people went into the forest to forage and collect wood. The continued worry of mines was illustrated by an experience of IRRI consultant Greg Wells. On one trip he asked the driver to stop the vehicle so that he could relieve himself. But the driver said he could not stop because they were crossing Khmer Rouge guerrilla territory. From then on the passengers became very interested in activities in the surrounding countryside. A few kilometres further down the road the driver stopped and said that now the passengers could get out. But as Greg was about to walk into the bushes on the side of the road (being a modest fellow), everybody shouted 'Don't step off the bitumen!'

The World Council of Churches (WCC) had one representative in Phnom Penh and supplied pharmaceutical machinery and raw materials for medicines, and agricultural and industrial machinery.

World Vision, with two administrative staff, a hospital team of five persons and a public health nurse, helped restore the National Paediatric Hospital in Phnom Penh and established orphanages. It set up a 'Re-hydration, Immunisation, Nutrition and Education' programme and gave support to the Faculty of Medicine and to the city water works. Their earlier projects included rice production, animal feed factories, a soap factory, milk factory, oxygen factory, animal breeding and fisheries. From 1980 to 1985 World Vision spent over eighteen million dollars in Kampuchea.

Other voluntary agencies sent regular missions to Phnom Penh. Among these was the French group 'Association pour le developement des relations avec le Cambodge' (ADRAC), which helped to rebuild the medical research 'Institute Pasteur' in Phnom Penh.

The International Committee of the Red Cross provided administrative and logistical support to three national Red Cross teams in Kampuchea. The French Red Cross supported a doctor and one lab technician working in tuberculosis control. The Swedish Red Cross supplied two doctors and a nurse to the Provincial hospital in Kampong Chhnang and donated surgical instruments, vaccines, an electrical generator, and construction materials to the hospital. The Swiss Red Cross team consisted of three doctors, one nurse and one lab technician. It donated supplies for the repair and construction of hospitals and maintained a clinic in Takeo.

Co-operation Internationale pour le Developement et la Solidarite (CIDSE), a European catholic relief organisation, showed us their project near Phnom Penh. At peak river levels during the wet season they impounded water in a natural lake with barriers across the lake's entrance channel. They were growing good crops of rice that were irrigated with water allowed to flow back into the fields during the dry season until the level was too low, after which pumps were used.

The CIDSE project manager, Ms. Oneste Carpene, told us that the government strategy of increasing the land under cultivation and making fertiliser available through co-operative groups was largely unsuccessful due to the lack of water control in the wet season. Her CIDSE group considered the emphasis should move to more intensive farming techniques, including proper irrigation, the careful use of fertilisers and improved rice varieties. Their six hundred hectare project included ten villages with a population of 3,659 inhabitants in 806 families. (In comparison, a modest one family wheat farm in Australia could be over nine hundred hectares in area.) The CIDSE project aimed to increase rice production from one tonne per hectare to three or four tonnes per hectare. Its success would ensure self-sufficiency in food for its people and produce a surplus for sale to surrounding districts.

The conditions of employment offered by CIDSE provided compensation for the difficult living conditions in Kampuchea. Salary, air travel, accommodation and insurance were all provided. Holidays, including public holidays, were twenty nine days a year. In addition, two rest breaks of one week each with return ticket to Bangkok were considered essential.

Such voluntary organisations and UNICEF were doing a great job with the resources available to them, but none had the necessary support, expertise and training needed to help the Ministry of Agriculture restore the rice farming systems and ensure food security for the country as a whole.

Rice alone is not an adequate diet and we were informed that fish products provide about three-quarters of the population's animal protein intake. Natural fish are important in rice fields, rivers and lakes and before we left Cambodia we were taken by boat to inspect a fishing operation on the Tonle Sap River. 'Houseboats,' consisting of floating platforms with thatched huts, were moored in lines across the river with nets strung between them to catch fish that move up and down with the flow of water as the Tonle Sap Lake fills and empties. On the houseboat that we boarded men were struggling to lift a heavy net to empty thousands of tiny fish into a boat already filled to nearly overflowing. We were told that the fish catch in the river — sixty thousand tonnes in the three month season — was less than half of that in the past and plans were being developed for better conservation and improved production. Some three hundred species of freshwater fish have been identified in Cambodia, of which two hundred and fifteen are in the Tonle Sap.

The lake is a great reservoir of biological diversity that includes fish, birds and wild animal species of international as well as national importance and the periodically flooded areas around its edges play a key role in maintaining and renewing its productivity. The areas of 'flooded forest,' alternately dry land and deeply flooded as the lake water level rises and falls about nine metres each year, are key breeding and feeding habitats for the fish and other forms of life. The productivity of the lake is among the highest in the world due to its combination of high water temperature, annual flooding and the supporting role of the inundated forest in stimulating the development of microorganisms which are a major source of food for aquatic species. However, wood gathering has caused extensive deforestation in the inundated areas and the loss of the flooded forest as well as over-fishing is a direct threat to the lake's productivity. [11]

---

11. Cambodia ranks fourth amongst the world's top freshwater capture fisheries, but unfortunately a focus on profits rather than sustainable resources has seen uncontrolled degradation of spawning and nursery habitats, destruction of mangrove swamps and over-fishing. 'The Cambodian Daily' in May 2001 reported the immediate challenge was to control the one million people fishing the Lake waters, of whom very few cared whether there were Fisheries Department patrols or not. As many as 50 boats using illegal equipment fish Tonle Sap waters, and 'if the destructive fishing goes on uncontrolled for just three more months, some fish species will disappear.' At Chhnok Trou town on the western shore it was estimated that nearly 100 tonnes of small fish are brought in for sale daily. On the other hand family fisheries on rice farms produce in total more fish than the large-scale fisheries, so development of improved rice-fish farming systems has a huge potential.

Sitting and watching the action on the houseboat was a Vietnamese soldier attired in a green uniform and green pith helmet. Standing nearby was a smiling girl, barefoot but also dressed in Vietnamese army clothes. A soldier? Our translator said that if the Vietnamese soldiers had money they bought fish, otherwise they hoped for a handout. Most local Cambodians preferred to ignore them and in Phnom Penh itself Vietnamese soldiers seemed very relaxed, often walking around alone unarmed.

Along the edge of the river small boats were nosed into the mud and barges and larger boats were moored side by side. The red Cambodian flag with its yellow depiction of Angkor Wat flew on large boats with double decks that were usually packed with people and produce. On the roofs of some there were baskets or trees in pots, on others a parking lot for bicycles. A red flag with a yellow star identified a Vietnamese wooden boat with patched planks, a motley collection of boxes adorning its stern platform and earthenware jars its top deck. Hundreds of people waiting to buy fish to take up country were scattered at random in makeshift camps further up the bank— the muted colour of their clothes appearing to merge into the bare earth. Close to where we landed two small children played in the dirt while their mother sorted tiny fish, placing some into large earthenware pots for fermenting into fish sauce.

In Cambodia the fish, crabs, shrimps, edible insects, and frogs that inhabit the lowland rice fields are all used for food and people seem free to take fish from any rice field that they choose. Rice fields have two main types of fish, small white herbivorous fish and black carnivorous fish. The black fish are air-breathers that can be carried live to the market and if not sold can be carried home again and returned to the water. At the onset of the rains each year both types of fish appear from seemingly nowhere and populate areas that a few weeks before were completely dry. At the end of the wet season they move from drying fields to deeper water where they can survive until the next season. Farmers drain shallow ponds and depressions in the rice fields and catch the fish by hand, or use 'jump traps.' The jump traps consist of a bamboo screen that blocks fish migration along a channel and the fish are caught in a dry pit when they jump over or around the bamboo obstruction.

The reason for involving IRRI was, however, not related to fish. It was because of its worldwide reputation for increasing food production from rice-based farming systems, particularly through breeding new rice varieties.

At the time of IRRI's establishment in 1960 the traditional tall rice varieties used by most South and Southeast Asian farmers had low grain yields. Attempts to improve production by application of fertilisers resulted in more vigorous growth but less grain than without fertiliser because the plants became too leafy and fell over.

IRRI plant breeders made an immediate start on developing new rice varieties for the tropics that had similar characteristics to the short, high yielding crops of Japan and Taiwan. They concentrated on varieties for irrigated areas and the most famous of the first releases to farmers was named IR8, meaning 'International Rice Number Eight', which could produce up to ten tonnes of rice per hectare. IR8 was not popular in many parts of Asia because of its poor eating quality, but one farmer in India named his son IR8 in appreciation of its contribution to the well being of his family. Rapid farmer adoption of other new rice varieties as they were released enabled national programs, such as in India, Indonesia and the Philippines, to meet the demand for more and more rice as populations grew.

Research scholars, mostly from developing countries, attended training courses at IRRI and learnt traditional and new approaches to rice production under supervision of IRRI scientists. The goal was to help farmers grow more rice on limited land with better water control, more efficient use of labour, fewer chemical inputs and, despite some opinions to the contrary, to do so without harming the environment. A major IRRI thrust was the development of varieties that reduced farmers' dependence on chemical pesticides and other purchased inputs.

Kampuchea in 1986 needed more than just new rice varieties. The country depended on traditional methods of rice production and had insufficient labour, insufficient draught animals, limited supplies of essential fertilisers, and a disproportionate ratio of women to men. The food situation was critical, and the Ministry of Agriculture did not have enough trained people to help farmers learn improved methods of production.

In order to achieve anything worthwhile it would be necessary for IRRI to put in place a fully integrated team with sufficient funding to undertake a full-scale research and training program. Before that could be done it was essential to obtain financial support, and in the meantime to focus on what might be achieved in the next two or three years.

Our conclusion was that IRRI could most rapidly and effectively assist by training Ministry of Agriculture staff as technical specialists in rice production in a 6-month training course to be held at IRRI headquarters in Los Baños. The course was expected to be practically oriented with a minimum of classroom lectures and a maximum of sixteen trainees could be possibly be catered for in the following year provided two translators were available. Our first interpreter, Mr. Ngak Chhay Heng, would have been the ideal person to accompany the trainees. It was expected that basic IRRI rice publications, such as *'Field Problems of Tropical Rice'* and *'A Farmer's Primer for Growing Rice'* could be translated into Khmer and provided to all rice trainees. Upon their return to Kampuchea they could then use the information that they had gained to train agricultural officials and farmers in different provinces.

We returned to Bangkok and met with Dr. Tatsuro Kunugi, special representative of the UN Secretary General for co-ordination of Kampuchean Assistance Programs, to discuss the general aid situation and possible sources of donor support. Then Glenn Denning returned to Los Baños to start the search for money. His first approach would be to request approval to use money from the Australian funded Indochina project that already provided support for IRRI assistance to Vietnam and Laos. In the meantime other IRRI staff would make short term visits and it was agreed that I would return regularly to Kampuchea to maintain contacts with the authorities and to start some field work in deepwater rice areas.

3

> *'Cambodia is an excessively hot*
> *country and it is impossible to get*
> *through the day without bathing*
> *several times. There are no bath*
> *houses, no basins, no pails; every*
> *family, however, has a pond — or,*
> *at times, several families own one*
> *in common ... There are no shops*
> *in which the merchants live; instead,*
> *they display their goods on matting*
> *spread upon the ground. Each has*
> *his allotted place.'*
> *(Chou Ta-Kuan, 1297)*

For the next trip from Ho Chi Minh City to Phnom Penh five months later the Red Cross charter flight was upgraded to a Russian passenger plane instead of the 'tired albatross' cargo plane with its rear ramp and stack of loose seats. My wife Janice and Keith Moody, an IRRI weed control specialist, accompanied me. It was the beginning of the wet season and we could see the brown waters of the Mekong River winding across the flat landscape. Annual deposits of silt brought down by floodwaters had built the banks up higher than the surrounding countryside and large trees almost obscured the winding roads linking the ribbon of houses strung along the bank.

Further from the river some fields were already green and water was accumulating as muddy lakes. Close to Phnom Penh many fields were just expanses of pale murky water with only the low banks defining borders of the fields visible. Others had already vanished under the spreading water. Parts of the landscape were scarred by bombs of ten years earlier, with as many as 200 craters to be seen in one frame of my camera viewfinder.

The Agronomy Department in Phnom Penh had arranged a two-day field trip to deepwater rice areas near Prey Yutka, a small village close to the border with Vietnam. We found the road south a fascinating cross-section of rural Kampuchea, though not necessarily a comfortable ride. The once smooth bitumen surface of the road to Takeo was just a memory. It was filled with potholes, making our vehicle pitch, bump and groan, and the modern 4-wheel drive vehicle loaned by the Red Cross took nearly three hours to travel 70 km to Takeo. Cyclists and oxcarts avoided the bitumen altogether, preferring the sandy soil beside the road. The oxen plodded slowly along, the carts distinctive with high narrow wheels and a centre pole between the animals that curved upwards to the sky. Other curved pieces of wood extended from the axles to the front and rear of the cart like an archer's bow, strengthening the frame and protecting the wheels. An occasional buffalo drawn cart lumbered along, the pair of gentle beasts emphasising their huge and fearsome horns by the movement of their heads from side to side.

Cameo-like scenes of the countryside came into our view and faded as we passed by. Beside the road a woman knee deep in a muddy pond was washing clothes, her thatched hut sheltered by the trees behind her. We saw two men bathing in a pond while a third filled a kettle with water from the same pond to take back to his house. Ten cyclists riding in single file towards the road on a track from somewhere in the distance gave movement to a scene of straggly trees and misshapen pools of water. A barefoot woman in a black skirt and purple top and with woven baskets suspended from a springy bamboo pole padded along a narrow path beside a canal, her backdrop a green rice field and a collection of bushy palms.

A group of thatched shacks signalled a market, vendors avoiding the deep dark puddles edging the road, their meagre wares displayed on mats or on low bamboo benches. Further on a mini-market consisted of just four ox carts, the proprietors displaying a few melons and pumpkins on the ground. Next a more substantial market adjoined a rare smooth part of the bitumen road, the thatched houses and shelters attracting cyclists, but no motorised vehicles were in sight.

In an open field two cows and a calf tethered near a 30-metre wide bomb crater were peacefully grazing on the few green plants appearing after the rains. The deep pools in bomb craters served as both water resources and fishponds, but there must be a cheaper and friendlier method of excavating ponds.

Palm fronds fixed to frameworks over each of three loaded buffalo-drawn carts provided the occupants some shelter from the blazing sun as they lumbered along. Inside the concrete framework of a roofless once-beautiful pagoda, the upright poles provided supports for the roofs of three thatched cottages. Beyond it a passenger lorry was stopped by the roadside, surrounded by vendors with trays of fruit raised to their shoulders: apparently a regular refreshment stop on the shuddering journey to Takeo. [12]

The provincial town of Takeo was reached at last and we ate lunch at the only café in the town. Flies were so thick on the floor that it changed colour when they flew away. Afterwards we referred to it as the "Fly Café". The main item on the menu was rice with chopped chicken and ginger. It was quite appetising if one ignored the flies. After lunch we met with local agricultural officers who briefed us on the local situation and provided a guide for the next stage of the journey. [13]

The road southward from Takeo wound on sandy tracks through wooded areas linked by open fields.

---

12. A passenger lorry is a marvel of packing people, people inside the canopy over the rear tray, some hanging on to the back and some on the roof. On another occasion the way was blocked at a wooden bridge where a large passenger lorry leaned precariously towards the canal, its nose in the air and a wheel poking through broken planks. Bicycles accumulated. Two carried a dozen live fowls, the bird's feet tied to the handlebars and their heads hanging down. A resigned crowd watching the action, or lack of it, stood with hands on hips, hands behind backs, resting on bicycles or talking. People with red hats, straw hats, chequered headscarves, grey cloth hats, round hats and the occasional Vietnamese conical hat, all waited to continue their journey.

13. On another trip we arrived in Takeo late one night and the only food available was at a food stall where even with candlelight it was almost too dark to see the pork and rice. A black and white pig pushed its way under the table to forage for scraps. Suddenly loud indignant pig squeals followed by yelps signalled that a dog that tried to get a share of the spoil had lost to its larger competitor. Pigs are commonly pets as well as produce.

In one village we came upon a wedding party in the street. The groom wore an open necked white shirt, a grey suit with coat sleeves far too short and trousers too long and a red rosette above his left pocket. The round-faced bride was resplendent in a striking red dress embroidered with yellow stars. Her piled up hair was adorned with a silver tiara and several cloth rosettes. On her wrists, upper arms and ankles she wore thick gold bangles. Her attendants were attired in a range of best dress with coloured blouses and dark shirts, down to the inevitable little girl with her only garment an oversized black skirt drooping from her hips to her ankles. On a later visit I was able to find the same house and photograph the bride's parents proudly holding a mounted copy of a photograph of the wedding that I gave them.

In a densely wooded area further along the track a thronged village market was separated from the road by an almost impenetrable wall of parked bicycles. The bicycles had undoubtedly originated in Vietnam, but I still wonder how the people in their recent absolutely destitute state had managed to find the money to buy them. Another market was a jumble of bicycles, people and ox carts surrounding rough thatched shelters. Children looked wonderingly at our vehicle as we drove past. Markets seemed to pop up everywhere. One country market was by a path between fields with about 25 women sitting or squatting on the ground in the shade of trees, their smiling faces and relaxed manner suggesting a degree of contentment. They wore headscarves and skirts of various colours, though cloth hats giving an appearance of coloured fur seemed to be the latest fashion. A pretty young woman with a brown head scarf over her long black hair was carefully weighing out two medium sized fish by adjusting the weight on a hand held beam balance, three shallow baskets of small fish on the ground in front of her. Vegetables, papaya and other fruit were displayed in bowls and baskets of various shapes and sizes.

That colourful and happy scene was in a very deep flood area where the thatch houses of the nearby village were nestled along the built up road, the rear of the house supported three metres above the field level by poles and the front of the house at road level. The crop system would change in the next few years, but the flood would still come and the villagers would still need to be prepared.

We stopped to buy green coconuts for drinking water since ordinary water was not safe. Our guide slashed off the tops of the nuts with a machete, and then it was a matter of juggling a nut larger than one's head to drink without spilling the contents on our shirts. The coconuts were large and we could not drink all of their water so shared them with watching children. One little girl, with a large pink curler holding her hair in the middle of her forehead, produced a smile almost as big as the coconut as she hugged it closely.

Further south we came to open plains with fields divided by small bunds (banks) which had the dual purpose of dividing the land and retaining rainwater. A few sugar palms with tall trunks topped by fans of foliage were dotted across the plain, standing like stark sentinels saying 'make a living here if you can.'

Near the track three tan-coloured cows with legs folded under them lay sleepily on a dry part of the field, their attitude indicating that this day they had found enough to eat from the sparse grass in the fields. But we also saw little girls whose stomachs bulging over their skirts indicated a deficiency of protein in their diet.

The isolation as we moved into the open plains of the deepwater rice areas was accentuated by a lone man trudging barefoot along the track. He wore his jacket over his head to shelter a sick child in his arms as he headed for the only village in the area with a nurse. Far behind him a solitary tree waved its tufted foliage against the clouds like a flag on a pole, the clouds enhancing the blue of the distant southern mountains. We were told that Khmer Rouge guerrillas operating from those mountains would make the area unsafe for us late in the day and our guide repeated his request to return to Takeo early in the afternoon.

As we neared the village of Prey Yutka we came to fields turning green with young rice plants and early floodwater flowed across a low spot of the track. Near the village a dense crop of short-stemmed rice almost ready for harvest was growing in a wet depression in one of the fields. We were told that the rice was the IR42 variety from IRRI, but at the time I did not realise that it was a forerunner of crop systems that would displace much of the deepwater rice and greatly increase rice production in the area.

Prey Yutka village was on ground slightly higher than the surrounding plains and straggly low trees surrounded its houses. It was a homely village despite the dilapidated state of the thatched roofs and matting wall panels on some of the houses. Young children were playing in front of the houses, the small boys naked and the little girls topless with handed-down skirts drooping from waist to ankle and, quite unexpectedly, one little girl with a bright pink balloon in her hand.

Janice's attention was drawn to women busily weaving, but the products were not to be seen on the children or the village women themselves. The equipment was simple. One woman was winding red yarn on a large wooden wheel with six spokes, the axle simply a wooden peg supported in an upright post. Under a low roof another woman was weaving on a simple wooden framed loom. She used foot treadles to operate a cross bar and moved the shuttle by hand. As she sat on a bench of bamboo slats and concentrated on her work, a small white piglet snuffled the ground by her bare feet.

Russian-built tractors and ploughs from a government tractor station had ploughed the area around the village at the end of the dry season. As soon as the tractor drivers finished ploughing they had moved on to the next location and the farmers had broadcast seed in the fields by hand. Those seeds had already germinated and within a few months the fields would be a waving carpet of rice foliage above floodwater a metre or more deep.

We could only stay one hour at the village before security concerns made it necessary for us to return to Takeo. There we stayed the night in the only accommodation available for official travellers, a three-storey building in a picturesque setting of sugar palms and eucalyptus trees on a small island about two kilometres from the town. It had once been the country retreat of Khmer Rouge general Ta Mok and was reached by crossing a causeway between a lake and the Takeo River. The sleeping accommodation was a single long dormitory, bare except for two rows of beds protected by mosquito nets, with no segregation of the sexes. Two members of the Swiss Red Cross team operating a local medical clinic lived upstairs in slightly more comfortable conditions. But even for them the three wood and rusted galvanised iron toilets about 50 metres from the main building made for a lonely trip on a dark night.[14]

As we left the town of Takeo next morning we stopped to watch some three thousand men and women digging a canal to bring water from the Bassac River to irrigate rice fields. The canal was about twenty metres wide at the top, five metres wide at the bottom and three or four metres deep. When finished it would be twenty-five kilometres long. The work-

---

14. Three years later Dr. Ram Chaudhary, Men Sarom, Chan Phaloeun and others arrived late and tired at this isolated 'guesthouse' outside Takeo. Since the only restaurant in the town was due to close at 7 p.m. they planned to hurry back there for dinner and buy some green coconuts to provide water for drinking, shaving and brushing teeth next morning. As they entered the upstairs dormitory with its rows of beds, the guesthouse keeper was looking towards the ceiling with a stick in his hand. Without taking his eyes off from the ceiling he murmured worriedly to Men Sarom, 'I can't find the snake sir!' At dusk he had seen a poisonous snake slither into the dormitory and thought that it had either entered one of the beds or moved up to the ceiling. Rather frightened, they beat the coconut mattresses and around the beds with a bamboo stick, to no avail. They were careful to pull their mosquito nets well under the mattresses and none of them ventured out that night in answer to nature's pressing call.

ers could be seen toiling away far into the distance as they dug soil with hand tools and filled scoop-shaped baskets. The baskets were carried by other workers up the bank of the excavation to where it was dumped on the mound at the top. The canal was a project under a food-for-work program where people were paid in rice according to the amount of soil they excavated.

Our journey to Kandal town in the next province took us across a wooden bridge over a tributary of the Bassac River. The bridge was then five metres above the water, but later in the wet season I saw that same bridge two metres under water, a graphic demonstration of the annual rise and fall of the river levels and emphasising the need to build houses on high ground or on stilts. Fishermen in narrow boats were casting circular nets that created spreading ripples on the tranquil surface of the water. One man at the stern of each boat propelled the craft with sweeps of a single oar pivoted on a short upright post, while a second man stood on the narrow front seat to cast the net, an occupation that obviously needed practice and a good sense of balance.

Along the banks of the Bassac River the land was more productive than that we had seen on the way to Prey Yutka, with large trees, banana palms and crops of tobacco and corn. Cattle were larger and sleeker, wooden houses more substantial. Children looked healthier and better dressed; though in poorer villages elsewhere house yards were also neat, tidy and swept clean.

In Kandal town the streets were thronged with

bicycles, and 'remokes' for hire. In contrast to the cyclos in Phnom Penh these 'remokes' were a two-wheeled trailer attached to the rear of a bicycle; effective for carrying goods, but less comfortable for passengers. Bicycles, remokes and cyclos were carryalls; for men and women, chickens and pigs, vegetables and fruit, grain, wood, huge earthenware pots and furniture. At times a moving car-sized conglomeration of baskets seemed to be moving without guidance until a head could be seen just visible among the mass. Women on bicycles were transporting full sacks larger than themselves by balancing one on each side of the frame, the riders barefoot or wearing plastic sandals. Locally made, long chequered scarves were draped over their heads and around their necks to provide protection from the sun. Headscarves curled to form a cushion were very common for those who carried water jars, baskets or sacks on their heads.

We met local agricultural leaders in their office, an open wooden building with bamboo slatted benches and a low railing around the raised floor. The railing provided a convenient leaning place for the local children and their elders to watch us strangers, particularly the foreign woman. The agricultural office provided extensive statistical data on the population and crop production of districts and the province. The outcome of our discussions was a plan to conduct field experiments in the next season, using introduced deepwater rice varieties that were expected to be more productive and to have better eating quality than the local varieties. It was already too late in the season to plant anything in farmers' fields, but I was asked to return towards the end of the wet season to see the local crops when they were approaching maturity.

The follow-up visit at the end of the wet season was in November. From the air the landscape near Phnom Penh that had looked like a series of isolated lakes in June now appeared to be spreading green islands in an inland sea. Much of the silt and mud in the floodwater had settled and from the air the water had a bluish tinge, a marked contrast with the muddy brown of the rivers.

The Agronomy Department staff had arranged three days of travelling for my week in Kampuchea. The first trip was from Phnom Penh to Takeo and then eastward. In contrast to the barren fields of earlier in the year the landscape along the road was now covered with green rice crops, though in many fields the plants were widely spaced and looked to be deficient in fertiliser and affected by a water shortage earlier in the season. An exception was where some enterprising farmers had planted rice in a disused Pol Pot canal. The rice was greener and more vigorous than in the main fields, making use of accumulated runoff and showing what was possible with extra water and more fertile conditions.

We travelled one hundred and fifty kilometres until we came to the end of the road, and then continued by boat for five kilometres down the Takeo River to the border of Vietnam. A powerful car engine balanced over the stern to drive the extended propeller shaft of the narrow 'long-tailed' boat moved us faster than we could travel on many roads. It was mid afternoon, the sun was shining brightly, lovely clouds floated in the sky and white birds flew lazily over the vivid green vegetation of the marshes. Occasionally we saw black water buffalo at rest near isolated greyish-brown thatched houses on higher ground. It was picturesque, relaxing and officially work. Then when we seemed to be away from all human habitation we saw a solid two-storey building standing brooding on the plain, the erstwhile 'country mansion' of another Khmer Rouge general. Its isolation and tiled roof, high windows and balcony posed unanswered questions on its history and purpose.

As we neared our destination of Borer Chat Sar on the Bassac River, a red-tiled building became visible through a gap in spreading trees, the smooth water reflecting the building and clouds, forming a seemingly idyllic setting. It was a local government building and as we turned around the next bend to where the Takeo River joined the Bassac we came to a mass of sampans — long boats with a curved roof in wood or bamboo — that hugged the shore. These and a straggling selection of rough huts on the riverbank were the homes of fisher-folk, mostly Vietnamese that had travelled up the river. When the Vietnamese children saw foreigners they came running and crowded around, much more assertive than their Cambodian counterparts who had watched carefully from a distance. After a lot of persuasion they were convinced to sit still long enough for me to take their photograph, though I noted that the Cambodian district official who relayed the request was quite uncomfortable with the closeness of his group to the Vietnamese.

A further fifteen-minute boat ride took us into deepwater rice fields where the water was about two metres deep. It would be another two months before the plants were ready for harvest and on each side of the boat the waving foliage of deepwater rice stretched as far as we could see. Unfortunately field rats were major pests in the area, and later I learned that they had destroyed many of the crops that we saw. In deepwater rice fields the rats bite off the stems of rice plants and use the stems to build small floating rafts to rest upon. Then they use the rafts as a base from which to swim through the fields to eat both stems and grain. In some field experiments in Thailand where we grew several deepwater rice varieties in adjoining plots it was obvious that rats were very selective, completely destroying some plots and leaving others. In an attempt to find out the reason I chewed stems of the different varieties and found that the variety with consistently more damage than others had the sweetest stems.

We did not reach Takeo again until about two hours after dark, though this time the locals did not seem worried about being late. On the other two days we saw some good rice crops where farmers had access to irrigation water and fertiliser, but for most of the area the rains were late and transplanting had been delayed until October. Yields were expected to be low and farmers told us that they would be short of food for at least two or three months the next season.

Back in Phnom Penh I had difficulty in trying to track down the fate of the small packages of deep-water rice seed I had sent from Thailand for immediate planting. The intention was that the harvested plants would provide enough seed for use in experiments the following year. At one experiment station someone told his co-workers that it was too late to plant deepwater rice, so the seed had been put in the cool store for next year, which was not much help. At another station the seed was sown in the lowest field, where floodwater rose too quickly and only three plants survived.

It was frustrating to see wasted opportunities, but on the other hand it was encouraging to see the enthusiasm of some local leaders. I was told that another lot of seed was planted at a third site. After reaching the site we removed our shoes and walked half a kilometre through water and slippery mud over rough ironstone gravel to find five good plots of rice. Three of the four were Thai rice varieties, but the seed had come from Dr. Vo-Tong Xuan's program in the Mekong Delta of Vietnam.

The next Thursday I nearly missed the plane to Ho Chi Minh City, which would have meant another week in Phnom Penh. My guide came to collect me in the early morning so that I could visit the market on the way to the airport, but I discovered that my passport had not been collected from the UNICEF office. That office was not yet open but luckily Emma, the Filipino woman responsible for passports, lived in the same building. Emma had forgotten to get my passport from the Ministry of Foreign affairs and I had forgotten to ask for it. We rushed to the Ministry building and were again fortunate that they started early. Stout Emma rushed up the stairs, then ten minutes later came running down again to suggest that we leave her there and go to the airport, where eventually my passport caught up to me.

A five-hour delay in the Ho Chi Minh airport allowed me to write most of my trip report before I arrived back in Bangkok. On Saturday my Thai secretary worked overtime to complete the reports and letters so they could be sent to IRRI with a trainee the following morning. She told me that she had given her husband enough money to buy beer so that he would happily look after their two children while she worked.

By the time of the next visit in February, well into the dry season, Kampuchea was hot and dry and for three excruciatingly hot days in a row I travelled with Agronomy Department staff in dry provinces. Most rice fields had been harvested, but women were seen bending in a field, cutting stems of rice plants with a curved hand sickle and then forming sheaves of the harvested material by twisting straw around the bundle. At the edge of a field a water jar, a rolled up skirt and two pairs of pink sandals waited patiently for their owners. A farmer trotted out of another field, the heavy load of sheaves suspended from a springy bamboo yoke over his shoulders bouncing up and down as he scurried along.

Ox carts stacked high with bundles of rice sheaves brought their loads to a row of houses, to add to the piles ready for threshing on the flat area outside the houses. Oxen would be driven around in circles on the spread out sheaves to tread the grain from the straw. A woman standing on a wooden platform poured a steady stream of threshed rice from a basket, so that the wind blew away the chaff and pieces of straw before the grain reached the heap on the ground. A second woman handed up a re-filled basket to her as the first was emptied. In that locality the houses were spaced in treeless isolation along a barren road. In such areas where did people find fuel for cooking if they did not use the straw?

One day we left Phnom Penh at 6.00 a.m. in a vehicle loaned by the Red Cross and spent nearly thirteen hours bouncing on rough, dusty roads, returning well after dark. At 11.00 am that morning we had had once again reached the small village of Prey Yutka near the Vietnamese border. This time we asked the village leaders if they could conduct two field experiments in the coming wet season. Each experiment was designed to have four plots of each of four different varieties of deepwater rice, sixteen plots in all.

We sat down in a thatched-roof shelter and laid out packets of seed, some string and a tape measure on the table. Then the village chief made notes in his book as our translator Mr. Sokchea relayed suggestions for planting the seed. When asked if the experiment was too complicated his answer was 'no problem'. However, after a lengthy discussion with Sokchea he asked for money to pay someone for full time care of the experiments. 'How much?' After more discussion they decided that the rate should be the same as the salary of Government workers, which was then 200 riels per month. Since that was less than two dollars a month I also had 'no problem' in deciding that our budget could provide that much support.

After completing the arrangements we ate lunch of biscuits and fruit brought with us, and as we did so about forty children stood at the front of the shelter watching us. Fortunately I had enough boiled sweets and biscuits in my bag for such an occasion and handed out a sweet to each of the larger children and a biscuit to each of the small children. They all appeared quite happy with their small gifts and I felt better about eating my lunch in front of them. We stayed in the village for less than an hour, and then headed back to Phnom Penh. Government workers were still not supposed to be out later than 4 p.m. because Khmer Rouge guerrillas were sometimes seen in the area at night.

Meanwhile at Los Baños Glenn Denning had put considerable effort into gaining financial support for a major project. Australia already provided financial support for rice research work in Laos and Vietnam, so Glenn requested inclusion of Kampuchea as part of an overall Indochina project. However, it seemed that establishing a large scale IRRI project based in Phnom Penh would be difficult, even though it was a unique opportunity to participate in a project of great humanitarian significance.

The Australian Development Assistance Bureau (ADAB) was the government organisation responsible for management of the Australian Government overseas aid programs. In later years it became known as AIDAB and was then again restructured as AusAID, a name that will be used henceforth. Its major focus was on administration, health, education and training, agriculture, rural development and infrastructure. Investment in agriculture and rural development was considered essential because most people in developing countries lived in rural areas and obtained a living from farming. Australia's strategy for development assistance to Cambodia thus recognised the importance of agriculture as the starting point for sustainable economic development.

In September 1986 the Australian embassy in Manila informed the IRRI Director General that ADAB considered that IRRI's initial emphasis should be on training and provision of technical publications. Increasing production on rice farms was the primary objective, so the success of the whole Kampuchean project would depend on trained personnel working with farmers. An essential first step was therefore to train local scientists and technicians in research and in extension, the process of transferring information to farmers.

That year less than 700,000 Australian dollars would be allocated to the whole three-country Indochina program and funds for future years were not likely to be much more. The suggestion therefore was for IRRI to develop its long-term program as frugally as possible. It should delay setting up a representative office in Kampuchea and use the available funds for training and publications. Other activities could be started through short-term visits of IRRI staff. The long-term view was still for a five to ten year project that would provide technical assistance and training for researchers and farmers, but a lot more money would be needed. ADAB wanted a more comprehensive proposal.

Agriculture Vice-Minister Chhea Song was adamant that his government's highest priorities were for a resident IRRI scientist in Phnom Penh and the training courses for Kampuchean researchers at IRRI. He told me that his Ministry had already made an agreement with Cantho University in Vietnam to train 40 people a year in a four-month course in rice production, but asked me to leave that information out of my trip report. His Ministry did not want to jeopardise the possibilities of IRRI training in the Philippines.

Glenn Denning was forced to postpone the training course and delete equipment and office supplies from the budget because ADAB decided it could provide only half the proposed amount for the first year activities. The postponement of the training course was not entirely unforeseen because the dormitories and classrooms at IRRI were already committed for other courses.

Kampuchea was at the time under an aid embargo from Western nations because the Vietnamese army had remained in the country after it forced the Khmer Rouge to retreat to the Thai border. The situation was politically difficult, but IRRI could operate because it was a non-government organisation and though internationally funded was accepted as being politically independent. Even so there was considerable International pressure against Australia providing such aid to Kampuchea. The Australian Foreign Minister recalled that the US Secretary of State was particularly abrasive, and that China and a few other countries weren't happy about the plans either. It meant that Australia had to be very careful and look for ways around the diplomatic issues.

Some other countries were sympathetic to the urgent needs of Kampuchea, but the attitude of most potential donors was that no substantial support could be provided until the political situation was resolved. For example Mr Yookti Sarikaphuti, the Director General of the Thai Department of Agriculture, could only write that his government was:

> '… *particularly aware of the problems facing the people of Kampuchea due to the events of the past two decades. Thailand has collaborated with IRRI ever since its foundation, and we have seen the benefits of the flow of technology in both directions. We are therefore pleased to support in principal the research activities of IRRI in the Indochina program, although until the current political situation has been resolved, we will not be able to take a more active part.'*

Australia agreed to support a first training course and preliminary work, but it was a further eleven months before the Australian Embassy in Manila informed IRRI, in October 1987, that Australia had agreed to a more extensive IRRI project in the country as part of the Indochina program. The Cambodia-IRRI-Australia Project (CIAP) developed from that agreement. Other help did not eventuate, and Australia maintained the project throughout. [15]

Although Glenn Denning had been making good progress towards getting support for the larger project, it was obvious that the limited inputs and short term visits of the first year and a half would make negligible impact. The next step was to place an IRRI representative in the country. As a temporary measure it was decided to employ a consultant who would spend several weeks at a time in Kampuchea.

Dr. Greg Wells was contracted for a total of six months as the consultant. He was an Australian who had worked on research projects with multiple crop-ping in the Philippines and on improving the stand-ard of living of people in the northern highlands of Thailand. Greg reached Kampuchea on 2 April 1987 and stayed for six weeks in his first assignment. He held discussions concerning the proposed IRRI training course and on printing of publications and visa arrangements. He visited Prey Pdau research station to discuss the program for that season and helped compile a list of Kampuchean rice varieties that had been collected by the staff. Small samples

15. The second phase, from March 1988 to June 1991 at a cost of $A2.31 million marked a shift in focus of Australia's agricultural aid to Cambo-dia. It confirmed its partnership with IRRI in developing 'from a very low starting level' a national rice research and extension infrastructure. Third and fourth phases were added in later years and AusAID recommended that low-income rice-farming households should be directly targeted, particularly the approximately 25% of households headed by women. To-tal project cost over 14 years was Aus$29.27 million, of which Australia provided over 90 percent. The Swiss Agency for Development and Co-operation and the United States Agency for International Development (USAID) contributed some money in the later stages of the project..

of the seeds were prepared for safekeeping in the IRRI long-term cold storage germplasm bank at Los Baños. He visited development areas at Sri Ampil, Tonli Bati, and Day Eth and the Soviet sponsored Kap Srau mechanised seed multiplication station, as well as a cotton research and production station and Kandal rice experiment station.

Facilities for development and evaluation of modern rice technology were extremely limited. For example Prey Pdau needed a new irrigation pump and a proper pumping station. The existing pump needed constant repairs and once it was installed on the river three people were needed to guard it day and night. There were concerns about security and after his first two weeks in Kampuchea Greg reported:

> *'A bomb exploded in the parking area of Orosay Market last Thursday. No one to our knowledge claimed responsibility but one person died and eight were hospitalised with injuries. I happened to be at the market that day but some hours after the event. I didn't stay long! We're having a lot of power cuts at the hotel now which is making life difficult.'*

Greg remembered his months in the Monorom Hotel as spartan. His bedroom, room 308, was also used as the IRRI office because there were no other rooms available. Sometimes he had no water for a shower in the morning, which made the rest of the day pretty grim in the hot climate. However the dining room had reasonable food and opportunities for talking with people of common interests. The hotel menu was always pork chop and chips, chicken and chips, or fish and chips, which became tedious after a few months. Rice was a request item. Costs were interesting. A good pork steak with potato chips and vegetables cost 61 cents at the hotel, less than the cost of a can of 7-up in the market. Greg said that he occasionally cooked noodles over a portable electric ring placed on the floor in one corner of his room. 'The noodles were accompanied by a wonderful crusty bread roll from the stall around the corner.' Occasionally, his electric cooking ring would explode but they were cheap to buy.

Greg made his bedroom/office at the Monorom reasonably homely by adding pot plants and Khmer paintings. A chair and an antique wooden table with carved legs next to the bed defined the office, a clay pot at the end of the table the base for a broad-leafed vine twisting upwards. A low table nearby supported a portable computer, its small monochrome 3-inch by 10-inch screen supposedly the ultimate in such equipment.

Greg said that all the expatriates in the hotel got on very well together, but apart from the odd bear hug his communication skills were put to the test with the Russians!

Hotel residents sometimes ate at a restaurant by the river where a dish called 'Happy soup' was on the menu. It was rumoured to contain marijuana, but Greg said that no side effects were ever reported. A year earlier my wife and I had visited the same restaurant for a romantic riverside dinner, which we had to finish and get back to the hotel before the curfew. It was very enjoyable until a bone in the chopped chicken broke off one of my teeth and provided more work for our Bangkok dentist.

From the Monorom it was a short walk to the

"Number One" restaurant. The Number One was classed as a "good" eating place where foreigners could expect a white cloth on the table and where in the interests of hygiene chopsticks were placed in long paper sleeves before they were placed on the tables. At lunch one day I watched three women staff members busily engaged in that task. To open each paper sleeve they put it up to their mouth and blew into it!

Rooms in the Monorom were not as spatially grand as at the Samaki hotel and bed bugs were sometimes unwanted companions. I found that spraying under the one sheet with insecticide carried for the purpose could solve that problem.

As the demand for rooms increased Western country expatriates were permitted to stay at the nearby Sukalay Hotel. The rooms were reasonable, but on my first stay there the bathroom floor looked as though the workmen had just finished it. The tiled floor was brown with dirt and for interest I cleaned one square with some soap and water. What was brown then became white, so I tried again with my shoe brush and soap and water. Experience was enough to see what was possible, so I showed the room boy what I had done. He rushed out and brought back a stone to rub the floor, but of course it did not work on uneven tiles and I demonstrated the brush. He looked at the brush, turned it over, examined the bristles and looked to see how they made contact with the floor and then decided to scrub the whole floor. The brush must have been used several times that week, because by time that I left the whole floor was white.

It was, however, somewhat a disadvantage that my room was on the seventh floor of the Sukalay. There were no lifts, the hotel had tall ceilings and there were 183 large steps to the top. Food for breakfast at the Sukalay was not appetising, so I had a morning walk down those 183 steps, across the street to the Monorom, up 120 steps to the 6th floor, eat breakfast, back down 120 steps and up 183, then down 183 again. Ready for the day — apart from being almost exhausted.

A Japanese volunteer group had organized a plane trip to Siem Reap and the opportunity to visit Angkor Wat, one of the world's great monuments, was too good to be missed. Visibility was poor during the flight, but it was still possible to see the landscape around the northern section of the great Tonle Sap lake as we approached Siem Reap. It helped me to relate the scene to satellite pictures of the famed deepwater rice areas around the lake that we could not visit because of security problems.

Angkor Wat is a few kilometres to the north of the town of Siem Reap and is the best known of many temples scattered over an area of several square kilometres. The area is one of the world's most celebrated archaeological sites. Building of Angkor Wat commenced at the beginning of the tenth century and the adjoining city Yasodharapura remained Cambodia's capital until it was abandoned in the 15th century. Over the centuries the temples have been subjected to the ravages of weather and war, and have in recent years been extensively vandalized by robbers who have removed heads and other items for sale.

We approached Angkor Wat by a massive stone causeway across one of the wide moats that surround the temple and symbolized the ocean around the world. The grandeur of the tower over the main entrance was somewhat diminished by the apparent truncation of its summit and it was festooned by bamboo scaffolding where workers applied their modern skills to restoration of the ancient stones. An imposing portico, a covered walkway with its stone roof supported by stone columns, stretched for 500 metres from each side of the entrance. In the shade of the massive portico young women labourers in colourful skirts, sarongs and shirts were dwarfed by the massive structure as they waited for their next task as part of the restoration team. They beamed smiles as we passed.

There was only a short time available in which to marvel at the magnificent stonework of craftsmen whose only record is the grandeur of their work. Inside the entrance an intricate array of balustrades in rectangular design set off massive buildings with ornamented facades and windows barred with slender stone columns that looked like the supports for banisters on a staircase. The central temple is surmounted by five gigantic, heavily ornate lotus-shaped towers of multiple levels tapering to a point. Outside, the hundreds of metres of wall decorated with scenes of battle and mythology in bas-relief are extraordinary. Rich relief sculptures on the walls, many once painted and gilded, depict exploits of

Hindu gods and celestial nymphs. Although ancient, the major bas-relief of the 'churning of the sea,' showing two groups pulling in opposite directions on the great snake could also be visualized as symbolic of the struggle between opposing forces that were still tearing at Kampuchea.

A step on a high tower looking over the courtyards of Angkor was a peaceful place to sit and ponder the historical journey of nearly a thousand years since the building of Angkor. Political events had shaped the lives of Cambodia's people long before the Khmer Rouge dictatorship dragged it back into the shadows of 'the year zero'. After a thousand years of turbulent history were the shadows of the past fading? Was there an aura of hope for the future? What events in Cambodian history would have prepared the stage for the government of Pol Pot and his Khmer Rouge? What support would the country now get in its endeavours to improve the lives of its people? And how would agriculture gather enough resources and expertise to remove the threats of famine?

Two outstanding kings were builders of Angkor and their power and authority over the people, considered 'the king's children' was absolute. Both came to power when Cambodia was seriously fragmented by internal and external conflicts and each 'god king' tried to outdo his predecessors in making war to maintain power or in building monuments.

The first of the two, King Suryavarman II, started building Angkor Wat at the beginning of his reign but did not live to see its splendour completed in

1150. The second was King Jayavarman VII, who reigned from about 1181 and directed a program of building and public works that involved hundreds of thousands of people. He was relentless in his pursuit of glory for his people and his empire. He believed his task was to deliver himself and 'his children,' from suffering and he began to modernise Cambodia through public work projects.

After Jayavarman's death about 1220 the Khmer Empire began to contract, though Angkor remained wealthy enough to impress the Chinese visitor Chou Ta-Kuan, the source of the quotes at the heads of chapters in this book. Chou's account of a bustling city in which the king still went forth in great pomp and ceremony is the most detailed description of the Khmer capital that has survived, supplementing the bas-reliefs of the temples.

By the time Chou Ta-Kuan arrived at the gate of Angkor from China in 1296 the Khmer Empire was already in decline. Internal conflicts among Khmer rivals, along with repeated invasions and attacks from its powerful neighbours in Siam (Thailand) and Vietnam led to the downfall of Angkor and its abandonment in 1431 as the Khmer capital. Angkor's city of over a million people suddenly became a ghost city — a parallel with the Khmer Rouge driving out the population of Phnom Penh in 1975. Some of King Jayavarman VII's ideology of ancient Cambodia has also been compared with that of Pol Pot. Both wanted radical changes for Cambodia's society. Both were extremely powerful in their own time. But whereas Jayavarman VII unified and then built a great nation under his tight reign, Pol Pot divided, tortured and murdered his people and ruined Cambodia.

Cambodia fell alternately under the dominion of Siam and Vietnam as it tried to play one neighbouring country off against the other. In the 1620s a Cambodian king declared independence from Siam and sought assistance from the Nguyen overlords of southern Vietnam. In exchange for that support he married a Nguyen princess and allowed the Vietnamese to take over Khmer territory near present-day Ho Chi Minh City, a loss that is not forgiven by present day Cambodians.

Cambodia survived as a separate country in the 18th century mainly because the Thai wars with Burma, whose armies destroyed the Thai capital of Ayutthaya, limited their incursions into Cambodia. However, in exchange for placing a refugee Cambodian prince on the Cambodian throne in 1794, the Thai's appropriated the Cambodian provinces of Battambang and Siem Reap, including the abandoned ruins of Angkor. Those provinces were not returned to Cambodia until 1907.

But it was the present situation that demanded attention, and back in Phnom Penh Greg Wells turned his efforts to arranging clearance for trainees nominated to attend the first rice production training course at IRRI. Unfortunately, for reasons undisclosed, the translators were not given a security clearance to go to IRRI. The absence of translators was a serious matter because most of the trainees could not speak English.

Greg quickly arranged a two-week English course in Phnom Penh with the assistance of several enthusiastic NGO personnel. Jennifer Ashton of the Joint Australian NGO Office in Phnom Penh had previously written to me that 'We had a banquet on Saturday night at which conversation was quickly turned to English language training for students going to IRRI in July. There is already an interested group of volunteers here willing to donate teaching time. Do think about this, as we are only too willing to help.'

It was the first English training course for Kampuchean government personnel. Those who participated thought it most worthwhile, but were of course nowhere near fluent in English and the lack of translators was still a major obstacle. Fortunately eleven of the thirteen Cambodian trainees who eventually arrived at IRRI could converse in French and IRRI engaged a French translator. Despite language difficulties the rice production course was successful and on their return to Kampuchea the trainees quickly put their new knowledge into operation. One of their most dramatic achievements was in Takeo Province where trainees Mr. Kim Choen and Mr. Hong convinced farmers to use water from a nearby lake to grow rice during the dry season for the first time.

A second training course at IRRI the following year had even more problems in getting trainees cleared by the Ministry of Interior. They had to obtain visas through Philippine representatives in Hanoi and only two had received approvals when it was nearly time to travel. Our main contact, Mr. Kong Thay Bunthan of the Ministry of Agriculture, had almost given up on the arrangements. Nevertheless they eventually reached IRRI and a positive report in the 'Bangkok Post' newspaper informed readers in Thailand that the training course would help Kampuchea regain self-sufficiency in rice production. The article noted that the group included three women, and that about 60% of the time was spent in lectures and the remainder in applying the principles learned to field work. The 'Post' also reported a shortfall of 200,000 tons of rice that year and the Kampuchean government's appeal to the international community for more aid.

On their return to Kampuchea the trainees had very few resources for putting their new knowledge to work. Providing information and assistance to farmers was a government responsibility, but the few extension workers available to distribute seeds and fertilisers or to supervise seed production and conduct periodic farmer training lacked even the most basic information. There were no applied research programs to provide them with technical recommendations for crop production and they had little or no transport. Many did not even have a bicycle and lack of mobility was critical since Kampuchea had such a low ratio of extension workers to farmers. They had no television network to spread information in rural areas, limited radio and a dysfunctional telephone system. There was really no foundation on which to build increased rice production in the shattered country.

The absence of training and reference materials in the Cambodian language was a serious problem.

Fred Kauffman of the MCC had already requested a supply of IRRI training materials, but very few people could read English. Subsequently IRRI agreed to translation of its *'Field Problems of Tropical Rice'* and *'A Farmers Primer on Growing Rice'* and to publish them in the Khmer language. Both booklets had clear photos or diagrams and would be of immediate use to extension workers.

Mr. Kong Thay Bunthan translated the captions for *'A Farmers Primer on Growing Rice'* and the Khmer text was drawn by hand onto illustrated pages provided by IRRI. Publication was delayed when some questions arose and the Ministry of Agriculture decided to review the whole manuscript. Then it was delayed again when Vice-Minister Chhea Song was given a copy of the translation for his approval and asked for a different foreword. He knew that many people in Kampuchea did not know anything about IRRI, so requested Dr. Swaminathan to write a new foreword to emphasise IRRI's work, its good relations with Kampuchea and joint efforts to improve rice production.

Greg Wells imported twelve and a half tonnes of paper from Singapore and thirty thousand copies of the *'Farmer's Primer'* were printed. The Khmer language translation of IRRI's *'Helpful Insects, Spiders, and Pathogens — Friends of the Rice Farmer'* was also completed and five thousand copies printed for distribution to agricultural colleges, extension workers, and farmer organisations.

When Greg met me at the airport on my next visit to Kampuchea I was first informed that the Agronomy

Department expected me to stay for two weeks and secondly that the UNICEF messenger had not brought my visa to the airport. After an hour the visa was organised and later the schedule was re-arranged so that I would be free to leave after a week.

Next day we visited Day Eth research station to collect seed, and then travelled to Prey Veng where we had an appointment with the Vice-Governor. At the only restaurant in town we met six Russian lecturers from the agricultural university near Phnom Penh and learnt that they were also meeting with the Vice-Governor. The local officials requested us to wait until 2pm for our meeting and we waited while the Russians were taken to their meeting. Then they waited until we arrived, then we waited and watched while the Vice-Governor communicated with the Russians through their translator. Eventually we had our discussion with him at 4.30 p.m.

In the meantime a messenger arrived from Phnom Penh, a three-hour trip, to tell us that Prime Minister Hun Sen wanted to borrow the IRRI vehicle we were using, a new blue Toyota Land Cruiser. The replacement was an old Red Cross vehicle without air conditioning, and since we needed the windows open to combat the hot weather we were soon covered in dust. Such combinations of dust and heat and rough roads, once taking thirteen shaking hours in the new four-wheel drive vehicle to cover less than 300 km, made it easy to conclude that improved country roads would be a great contribution to Kampuchean agriculture.

4

*'In Cambodia it is the women who
take charge of trade. For this reason
a Chinese, arriving in the country,
loses no time in getting himself a
mate, for he will find her commercial
instincts a great asset.'
(Chou Ta-Kuan, 1297)*

One Wednesday in July the following year I went home early from the Bangkok office to buy supplies for yet another trip to Kampuchea and Vietnam. Nothing unusual happened on the flight to Ho Chi Minh next day other than to note that the cabin crew on the Air France plane were courteous and pleasant and that the food was exotic and delicious, a marked contrast to the half sandwich and five grapes of earlier years.

At Ho Chi Minh airport the plane was delayed for two hours, waiting for the weather to clear in Phnom Penh. I was quite content to avoid bad storms around airports, though for the third time in a row there was no visa approval waiting for me at Phnom Penh airport. Sokchea, who had been quite ill and was looking very miserable, suggested that he should go back into the city to find it, but I pointed out that it was after 5 p.m. and where would he find the approval? Luckily, after a bit of pleading, the officials at the airport decided to put a second stamp on the visa I had used in March.

A field trip was planned for the next day to check on trials in Prey Veng province. We were late starting and were further delayed by the usual extravagant lunch with the local chief of agriculture. Both field experiments were a bit of a disaster and unlikely to provide any worthwhile information. Our plots were not sown until nearly two months after the farmer's fields and many seeds had not germinated.

One excuse offered for the delay was that the men responsible were sent with the army to clear forest near the Thai border. Another was that the farmer did not want to miss sowing the crop on his other piece of land as a result of working on our experiment. This was understandable, but one of my colleagues had rejected the local agriculture chief's suggestion that we provide compensation to the farmer for work done. It looked like a bad decision. Providing a small amount of money had been very effective at other sites in the previous year and as the project expanded it was found to be essential. For the cost of our lunch we could have paid the farmer to prepare the field and maintain the experiment for most of the season.

The following Monday we headed south to Prey Yutka again. This time our group included two young women from the Ministry of Agriculture, Miss Chan Phaloeun and Miss Socheata. Some stretches of the road were rougher than before, though at one spot a

dozen or more people were swarming over a tractor
and trailer as they filled holes in the road with soil
and gravel. It took nearly six hours to travel 130 km,
but the sights were again thought provoking. The
village markets still displayed their meagre wares
on the ground. In front of some thatched houses
children with the distended stomachs of malnu-
trition watched silently. Beside an open stretch of
the road a lone spreading tree protected the small
thatched shelter of a roadside food stall where cyclists stopped for refreshments and chat.

Near the border with Vietnam green tinged fields
reached towards the distant hazy blue hills and beneath a solitary tree a lone figure watched over five
grazing cattle, a tuft of foliage at the top of the tall
tree providing him a tiny moving patch of shade.

The road edging across the plain was wet and slippery, with the last three kilometres into Prey Yutka particularly challenging. We were unsure as to
whether we could continue forward, but knew that
it would be difficult to turn back on the narrow track
so it was a relief to approach the edge of the village.
The feeling of relief vanished as our four-wheel
drive vehicle slid to a stop in the middle of the last
pool on the track. Two deep trenches, carved out by
the narrow wheels of ox-carts, were hidden by the
muddy water and our vehicle came to rest on the
centre ridge as the wheels lost traction and spun
uselessly.

A member of our group went to the village to
seek help, but soon returned to report that the government tractors had moved to other parts of the

country when ploughing around Prey Yutka was finished. Luckily we found a log of wood nearby and I persuaded our team leader, Mr. Leng Tek Seng, to borrow two hoes so that we could place the log in a trench and use the winch and cable to pull our vehicle out. As officials didn't normally expect to perform manual labour Mr Leng Tek Seng looked around to find someone else to carry the log. The best help he could find were two little girls of about ten who managed to get the log onto their shoulders and set off, staggering under the load. I said to Leng Tek Seng that it was too heavy for them, but since they were already carrying the log it seemed a good photo opportunity. Unfortunately they saw my camera, dropped the log and ran. It was then my turn to carry the log. Leng Tek Seng and driver Mr. Sarath dug a shallow trench across the track in which we laid the log, covered it with soil, hitched on the winch cable and, as the locals watched this entertainment, the log and luck held and the vehicle crept out.

Beyond Prey Yutka village the low-lying fields between the village and our experiment were already flooded. Phaloeun and Socheata were wearing ankle-length black skirts that were deemed appropriate for young women travelling in the countryside, but were quite unsuited to wading through deep water. Consequently they had to be content with watching from the distance as the men waded through a canal and walked across the fields to be rewarded by visiting an experiment with good plots of different varieties of rice. However, both young women were later pleased to pose for photos with a background of green fields, blue hills and floodwater their evidence of almost attaining the goal.

This trip was my first acquaintance with Chan Phaloeun, a determined young woman who was destined to become a leader, first in the CIAP program and then in the Agriculture Ministry's research institute, even though at that time she could speak only a few words of English.

On a trip north from Phnom Penh to Kampong Chhnang two days later Phaloeun and Socheata were better prepared. They wore jeans and showed an obvious determination to wade through whatever water was not over their heads (about 150 cm for Socheata).

That day we travelled only halfway to Kampong Chhnang before we had to turn back. A truck had broken through the wooden planks of a narrow bridge and blocked the way. While waiting in hope that the bridge would be cleared we walked out into the fields where I photographed a lone woman transplanting rice. Leng Tek Seng talked with her and we learned that she was a widow with three children whose father, mother and husband had been killed by Pol Pot's Khmer Rouge. She seemed to be a capable, cheerful woman and I thought how hard it was to be a widow in a harsh land, and that it must be doubly hard to be a widow as a result of a cruel and deliberate political policy.

She told us that there were one hundred and fifty people in her *krom samaki*, which was a 'solidarity group' or collective production unit. One hundred were female, about the same ratio of males to females as reported in the southern provinces. Men of the *krom samaki* did the ploughing and field preparation and women like her did all of the transplanting.

On my next visit to the area I took one of the photographs to give to her, but when we showed it to people in the same fields they all said that they did not know the woman. Consequently the photo of her that graces the cover of this book is a tribute to an unknown woman, a representative of the many heroines of Cambodia.

The Vietnamese backed Kampuchean government had assigned farm families to such solidarity groups after the Khmer Rouge retreated. The collective owned the land and production units were each farmed jointly by ten to fifteen families that shared the products according to the number of people in each family. Collectivisation was not strictly enforced and a whole range of management styles developed. A typical style involved shared use of labour, implements and plough animals within the group.

Private land tenure was re-established in 1989, a year after our stop at the bridge, and the communal lands were then divided between families. Village administrators tried to allocate land fairly so that each family received a balance of productive and less productive land. Consequently a farmer's land allocation could be dispersed in as many as five to eight plots of a few hundred square metres each. Some would be in drought prone 'high' fields and others in the more reliable 'middle' and 'low' fields, with the result that farmers needed to grow several different rice varieties to suit the quite different soil and water conditions.

It was not a good day for bridges. Unable to continue on to Kampong Chhnang we decided to return to Phnom Penh and visit experiments in Kandal Province instead. We left Phnom Penh just after lunch, but were delayed at a bridge under repair and on the return journey found that half of the bridge had been removed and that it was closed for the night. Luckily our provincial guide knew of a detour, though he had to negotiate passage at two roadblocks that were also closed for the night before we arrived back in Phnom Penh at 8.15 p.m.

The experiment we saw was better than that in Prey Veng, but germination was also poor and our plots were not looking nearly as good as the surrounding farmer's fields. Sowing had been delayed due to late arrival of the seed, and the poor germination may have been partly due to insect damage while the seed was in storage since local authorities had no appropriate storage facilities.

The road to Kampong Chhnang was open next day, which allowed us to complete the journey and visit the site of our deepwater rice trial.

The young woman who had been assigned by the local agricultural office to conduct the experiment was a recent graduate from high school with no previous research experience. With just a few diagrams and translated verbal instructions she had efficiently established a trial designed to identify which of four different varieties of rice was the most productive.

The plots were precisely laid out with even rows of plants; each plot was labelled with the name of its rice variety and she had supervised construction of a fence of wooden poles linked by thin rails to keep foraging cattle away from our plants. She was very attentive and carried her well organised notes of the experiment in a coloured folder that matched the long-sleeved blouse protecting her arms from the sun. Her example indicated that with the right training the local agricultural officers would be a vital link in the search for food security in Cambodia. Her only request was for us to provide a bicycle so that she could make more visits to the site. Chan Phaloeun and Socheata, were impressed by her work.

The experiment had started well with good early rainfall, but the flood had not yet reached the site. There was not even a trickle of floodwater, whereas we had expected there to be about 50 cm of water. Towards the end of the previous crop season the floodwater had been nearly two metres deep in that field.

Thirteen years later Chan Phaloeun remembered those arduous trips to Prey Yutka and Kampong Chhnang. 'It was the first time that I had worked with foreigners,' she said, 'and I was very excited. Cambodia was a socialist country, so it was difficult for government staff like me to have contact with foreigners, especially those from non-socialist Western countries. I felt that I would have a chance to do research and improve my knowledge by working with rice scientists more experienced than myself."

Like nearly everyone else in Cambodia, Phaloeun

had been forced to work in rice fields under the Khmer Rouge. It was in the northern part of the country, in an area we could not visit in 1988 because of security concerns.

'I was in Banteay Meanchay province, in a village we called Kandaul. Beyond the village were a lot of rice fields, but before I was there they were just high grass areas. The Khmer Rouge commanded us to cultivate that area. The grass was tall with big flowers and could be used to make brooms. It was difficult to cultivate because the roots were very strong and deep and we had to pull them out. We had to work every day. Pol Pot ran the group by the age of the people. The young children under five were one group, the kids under twelve were another group, twelve to eighteen were a group, and married people were a different group.'

Phaloeun' experiences clearly indicated difficulties faced by individuals in Kampuchea during Khmer Rouge time. She became so ill with malaria that she was unable to walk and for three months after the Vietnamese intervention was too sick to return to Phnom Penh.

'In 1978 we had very little rice, and when they counted the number of sick in the village, thirteen of us were seriously sick and they sent twelve to the hospital," said Phaloeun. 'Under the Khmer Rouge regime people sent to the hospital were expected to die. There was no medicine, no pills; they just stayed in the hospital. I was number thirteen, but I was left in the village because the head of the medical service thought I would soon die and they would not need to collect me from the hospital. However, before people died they were allowed to have some extra rice and some sugar palm juice. When I received rice and sugar palm juice every day I felt better and I got stronger. I was also given two fish heads every day and I could share what I had with my mother and my younger sister. This went on for two months and so we survived, but the twelve who went to hospital all died.'

Phaloeun returned to Phnom Penh by army truck. 'A lot of people could not travel by truck because they had no money,' she said. 'I still had a little gold, very little, and I paid the truck driver. I had nothing to eat but paid the driver, because I could not walk.'

After such experiences it was surprising that Chan Phaloeun made agriculture her choice of a career. When I asked her about that decision she said that her hobby as a child had been to plant vegetables and fruit trees near their house. She was able to make use of that experience in the Pol Pot camp because she had access to a plot of land. She planted many things, but she still became sick and she said that a lot of her friends died from lack of food and effects of disease.

After recuperating in Phnom Penh, Phaloeun returned to high school, graduated in 1980 when she was 22, and was awarded a scholarship to go to Vietnam. She refused to take it. Vietnam was still recovering from its war and according to Phaloeun there was no point in going there because the conditions there were no better than in Cambodia. She then worked for one year as a teacher before getting a scholarship to go to Russia. Two other Khmer students that she knew also studied agriculture in Moscow, but when they came back to Cambodia they did not want to work in agriculture. One went to the Ministry of Planning and one to the Ministry of Tourism. Phaloeun selected agriculture because she did not want to work in an office.

Phaloeun's first month in Russia was very stressful. She did not understand any of the language and when she went shopping she used only bank notes, not coins, because she could not understand when told how much an item cost. By the end of the month she had used all her paper money and still did not know how to use coins, even though they were different in shape and colour. One day she gave a cashier all her coins to count and the cashier kept the lot and she had no money left.

Phaloeun has vivid memories of her first language training. The college had planned a class for students who could speak French, but since the French speaking teacher had not yet arrived Phaloeun was placed with the Arabic-speaking students. The teacher could speak only Russian and Arabic while Phaloeun spoke only Khmer and French, so she had no means of verbal communication with the teacher, none at all. Her only communication was by waving her hands and drawing in the notebook she carried. The teacher just took Phaloeun's hand and pushed her in the direction required, though it was obvious that she felt bad about doing so.

'One day the class moved to another building, but I did not understand the directions,' said Phaloeun.

'After lunch I went back to our previous classroom to wait for the teacher, but my teacher was not there and I could not understand the new teacher in the room. So for two weeks I just waited outside the classroom until lunch each day, and then went back to my room. I felt very uncomfortable about this so I went to the Director's office in the University — but they could not understand me there either.'

Phaloeun knew that her teacher's name was Marie, but a lot of Russian women had the same name and Phaloeun was very lonely because none of the teachers could speak Khmer. However, when the French-speaking teacher arrived at the school the problem was solved and Phaloeun was happy. She said that the new language teacher was very good, with excellent communication skills and a lot of materials for study during the six months of the course. Phaloeun said that in the year after the Khmer Rouge she had felt that her brain would not work any more, but in high school and Russia she found that she could succeed.

At the time of those trips to Prey Yutka and Kampong Chhnang, negotiations for to obtain IRRI staff housing outside the hotel and an IRRI office had already continued for over two years without success. Greg Wells had advised the Agriculture Ministry in Phnom Penh that Australia had agreed to fund the project and that three IRRI scientists would soon arrive. IRRI's request was to rent two of the many large villa-style houses in Phnom Penh, one as combined office and living quarters for the team leader and another for the other scientists and their families. The Agronomy Department was still trying to find suitable buildings, but negotiations had became more difficult and time consuming due to the increased influence wielded by officials making political and security decisions.

In June, Greg reported that there was still no decision and Glenn Denning requested me to follow up again when I returned to Phnom Penh in October with Dr. Ernie Nunn, an American specialist in research station development. Ernie's responsibility was to develop a master plan for a research institute so that IRRI could approach prospective donors for money to establish the institute. All parties had agreed that a well-equipped institute with trained staff would ensure the long-term success of agricultural research. Ernie's mission was, unknown to all, the start of a long and involved saga that continued for thirteen years before establishment of the Cambodian Agricultural Research and Development Institute (CARDI). [16]

When Ernie and I arrived in October, Mr. Leng Tek Seng of the Agronomy Department told us that his department had located a building for the IRRI residence. He also said that ten military families were prepared to use force to get the building and that

---

16. Glenn met me at Ho Chi Minh airport to hand over a computer and laser printer for Cantho University in South Vietnam before he continued on to Hanoi. After a five-hour trip to Cantho it was soon set up and being used. A bit incongruous, a $10,000 computer system being operated by university staff members who received a salary of around two dollars per month. At Cantho we held a two-day research meeting on deepwater rice and made revised plans for collaborative projects. At the meeting 'muesli bars', bought in Australia were handed around, with sultanas and cinnamon the most popular flavours.

it was difficult for the Agronomy Department to protect it without an immediate decision from IRRI. When he took us to inspect it we saw that it was a three-storey structure with a lot of style on a nice street. That was the good news. The bad news was that construction had stopped 14 years earlier and the potential IRRI residence was just a concrete shell covered by vines. It lacked doors, windows, plumbing and most of the roof.

The cost to complete the structure and convert it into apartments and a couple of offices was estimated to be around US $60,000. It would be quite a challenge, but I promised to get a response from Glenn Denning as soon as I returned to Bangkok. We also inspected a room on the ground floor of the Agronomy Department building that was proposed as the IRRI office. It had been used as a storeroom and had patched grey walls, oil on the floor and an atmosphere of gloom, but it was solid, four metres wide and eight metres long. Though dark and cheerless it could be brightened up and had the advantage of being in the same building as the Agronomy Department staff.

As soon as I returned to Bangkok and working telephones I contacted Glenn Denning with the details. He did not hesitate. He realised the urgency and lack of alternatives and fortunately had enough money available that he could give immediate approval to go ahead. Ernie Nunn had remained in Phnom Penh so a message was relayed to Ernie asking him to confirm IRRI's acceptance of the Agronomy Department offer and to arrange for completion of the building. The building was eventually converted to three apartments and became known as the 'IRRI Villa'.

Phaloeun was assigned to help Ernie Nunn while he remained in Phnom Penh to prepare plans for the research institute and oversee construction of the IRRI housing and office. At first they had a difficult time communicating but Phaloeun said that Ernie liked the way she worked. She was well aware of her English language limitations. 'I could only read the name of a day and some numbers and I could not say much else,' said Phaloeun. 'If Dr. Nunn asked me something I just pointed with my fingers.' When her supervisor, Mr. Leng Tek Seng, asked Phaloeun if her work was satisfactory she said 'You can ask Dr. Nunn,' because she did not know whether her work was good or not. Ernie told him that Phaloeun was a very good assistant, but Leng Tek Seng then asked Phaloeun how could she be a very good assistant if she could not communicate or translate.

'I told him I was not a translator, only a guide,' said Phaloeun. 'The driver took us to a place; I made an appointment, and asked if they had a translator to help Dr. Nunn.' The second week Leng Tek Seng was still doubtful and asked again, but Ernie Nunn asked him not to change her and said that he would like Phaloeun to work with him for the next three months. So Phaloeun helped Ernie with supervising construction, contacted electricity and water companies and the municipal authorities, advised the post office and obtained approval from the Ministry of Health for water from the well at the site of the research institute to be tested for use in the proposed laboratories.

The following month Dr. Harry Nesbitt, the newly designated team leader for CIAP, and his wife Betty arrived in Phnom Penh and were introduced to the Ministry of Agriculture, the IRRI Villa, Ernie Nunn and Phaloeun. It was the beginning of a long and fruitful association during which Cambodia moved from famine to rice sufficiency and then to surplus rice production.

5

*'Should a Chinese, newly arrived,
wear cloth with two groups of
flowers, it cannot be charged against
him, for he is "An-ting pa-sha
(min-ting bhasa)," a man who does
not know the rules.'
(Chou Ta-Kuan, 1297)*

As soon as approval was received from Australia for the in-country research program IRRI advertised for three expatriate senior researchers who would all be stationed in Kampuchea. Outstanding scientists were needed and the advertisements were placed in the UK published 'The Economist', the American 'Agronomy News' and 'The Weekend Australian'. The Agriculture Ministry in Kampuchea had insisted that any IRRI scientists located in Kampuchea should be practical, familiar with agricultural equipment, capable of organising people to get things done, patient and co-operative.

The lead position was for a Farming Systems Agronomist/Team Leader to collaborate with Kampuchean researchers in design, implementation and analysis of on-station and on-farm experiments. Qualifications specified were a Ph.D. in agronomy or a related field and seven years experience in farming systems research and development. Fluency in French and project management experience was stated to be advantageous. The candidates for the other two positions of 'Plant Breeder' and 'Technology Transfer Specialist' were expected to have a similar standard of qualifications. The advertisements attracted nearly one hundred applications and it took a long while for IRRI management to sift through the applications, check references, arrange interviews, evaluate qualifications and personalities and assess willingness of families to live in Cambodia.

Harry Nesbitt was eventually chosen as team leader. An Australian with a Ph.D. from Murdoch University in Western Australia in 1979, Harry had travelled much of the world. He worked for two years as a horticultural technician in Zimbabwe and then measured road compression in South Africa. He wandered through Germany, England, Scandinavia, North Africa, Turkey and Afghanistan. While travelling through Central and South America he managed to sleep through much of a civil war battle waged in a village in Guatemala. His work experience included two years as a research agronomist with a Philippine-Australian Development Assistance Program where he was responsible for the management of a research program in rice and upland crops and for the training of Philippine staff and farmers. He also worked for three years on projects in Thailand, assisting the Department of Agriculture to review research, provide information for the extension departments, and prepare research results and co-ordinate equipment provision. He had a lot of relevant experience and was judged personally well equipped to cope with the challenges of Kampuchea.

When Harry was offered the position as team leader he was invited to undertake a one-week visit to Cambodia with his wife to preview the situation before finally accepting the appointment. He visited the Bangkok IRRI office with Glenn Denning on the way to the airport early on the Thursday morning that they were scheduled to leave for Kampuchea, but Harry was not in an appropriate state of mind to absorb information concerning the logistic support that Bangkok could provide for the Kampuchean program. His problem — his wife was missing somewhere in Bangkok.

Soon after Harry and Glenn Denning arrived from the Philippines the previous evening Glenn had telephoned me at my apartment to ask if I had heard anything from Elizabeth Nesbitt. 'Betty', five months pregnant, had been expected to travel from Perth and stay at the Imperial Hotel before meeting Harry and Glenn for the trip to Phnom Penh, but the Imperial Hotel had no record of her. Other hotels were contacted, but she was nowhere to be found. So when Harry could not concentrate we gave up talking and went out to the airport to search for her there.

We could not find any record of Betty at the airport. Harry went upstairs to the Qantas office where he learned that Tuesday's records had already been erased from the computer. I tried the airport's hotel booking counter, but the helpful Thai girl behind the counter said that there was no record of an Elizabeth

Nesbitt. Searching the crowd for Betty was difficult for Glenn and me because Harry was the only one who knew what she looked like! Glenn then went upstairs for a second visit to the check-in counter, and when Harry and I rejoined him we found that Harry's search was over.

Betty told me that she had expected to find a message from Harry when she arrived at Bangkok airport, but there was none. 'I didn't know what to do, so I thought I would go to a hotel and we would meet again next day,' she said. 'It was ten o'clock at night, the airport was packed and at the hotel desk they said that only the Royal Orchid Hotel had rooms available. I knew that was very expensive, but then I thought, it's too late, I can't stay at the airport, I will go there.'

Next morning Betty's taxi was delayed in the inevitable Bangkok traffic jam and it took a long time to get to the airport. She found the flight counter, but Harry had the plane tickets and she could not see him anywhere. 'There I was, looking around, pushing my trolley, five months pregnant, without an air ticket,' said Betty. 'I was afraid I might be stuck in Bangkok without knowing where anybody was. Then this bearded man came up to me and said, 'Excuse me, but are you Betty Nesbitt?'' Betty said she had never met Glenn Denning, but when he found her she simply collapsed in tears on his shoulder. A few minutes later Harry showed up and they set off to see Cambodia for the first time.

Harry had been forewarned that living conditions in

Phnom Penh were difficult. He had been told about the city's lack of reticulated water and its shortage of electricity and limited medical support; that it was difficult to work with the Government; that the country was isolated and all westerners were required to live in hotel rooms. Nevertheless after reading the project design documents he could see that given sufficient time the project had the potential for making a huge impact on Cambodia's economy and signed a 20-month contract as team leader. 'My vision was to set the project up to be managed by somebody else, having little thought of remaining in Cambodia for longer than a couple of years,' he said.

Betty Nesbitt was somewhat taken aback when they arrived in Phnom Penh. To her it did not look much like a capital city at all, 'it had the feel of a sleepy, dusty town.' The people seemed extremely poor, and she was amazed how many chickens and pigs were in the streets. Completion of the IRRI Villa under the supervision of Ernie Nunn and his helper Chan Phaloeun had only just commenced. The cover of tropical vines had been removed and Betty said she was glad she didn't see the numerous frogs and snakes that had previously occupied the building.

The plan was to convert each floor into one or two apartments. Betty had worked as an engineering draftsman in Canada, so Ernie Nunn found her a drafting board and asked her to draw up plans. 'It was quite funny looking around the skeleton of the structure,' said Betty, 'but it had possibilities. They asked me to draft up floor plans of how we wanted the apartments laid out, where to put kitchens and so on. We wanted it to be comfortable because it was so isolated working and living in Cambodia and Harry said that a home must be comfortable enough that you enjoy coming home, otherwise you are never going to stay.'

Locally available products, such as the floor tiles, were to be used in construction, but equipment like stoves and refrigerators and hot water systems had to be imported on the once-a-month ship from Singapore.

It would take another six months to finish the apartments, so until then they would need temporary accommodation at the Samaki hotel. 'But we thought the community was wonderful,' said Betty. 'Apart from the Russians there were less than 100 expatriates. All were living at the two hotels and it was a lovely warm feeling of community. We felt that everybody would help each other. But when I went out into the provinces one could really see that the families of subsistence rice farmers were really poor. The kids had fat tummies and skinny legs.'

After their week in Kampuchea Harry returned to the Philippines for eight weeks of orientation in management and rice production and Betty returned to Australia to await the birth of their baby.

A second member of the team, Dr. Ram Chaudhary, joined Harry at IRRI. Ram was a very energetic plant breeder whom I had met beside a flooded field in India several years earlier to discuss a Ford Foundation project with deepwater rice. At the time Ram was a professor of plant breeding and co-ordinated the work of rice scientists in four regions in the state of Bihar. He was later a visiting scientist at IRRI and was working for a World Bank supported project in Nigeria before he joined the Kampuchean project to lead the plant-breeding program.

Harry and Ram moved to Kampuchea in early January 1989 and Harry appreciated the preliminary work accomplished by Glenn Denning and others, particularly the documents that laid out plans for the project. His previous experience in the Philippines and Thailand convinced him that the project's major contributions would be to provide training and develop facilities that could be operated by local personnel. On the other hand, the whole Ministry of Agriculture in Kampuchea had only eleven agricultural graduates with whom to start. They included three women, one of whom was Chan Phaloeun.

Most were recent graduates from eastern-bloc universities with limited experience in practical agriculture and negligible experience in research. They needed training in rice production and all the technologies associated with it. Overriding this was the necessity for English language training so that they could communicate with expatriate scientists, read technical reports on crop production, and travel abroad to obtain further experience.

The next two IRRI team members to arrive were Richard Lando and Margaret Jingco. Richard was an American who had been working with rice in Thailand. His responsibility was to help develop a national system for transfer of information to farmers. Margaret, a Filipino, was expected to stay for a year to help Harry set up the office and the administration system and then return to Los Baños. At the time the Department of Agronomy had no record system and computers were just being introduced to Kampuchea. As a senior secretary coming from the training section of IRRI Margaret knew the whole IRRI system. She became a great help to Harry in organising training activities and maintaining contacts with the training section at Los Baños. Eventually many of the training staff from IRRI spent some time assisting with training in Cambodia.

Margaret's first impression of Phnom Penh was a sense of having seen it all before. She said that the short trip from the airport to the hotel made her feel like she was an eight year old girl again, as if she had come out of a time machine and travelled thirty years back to old Manila. The Pochentong Airport on the outskirts of Phnom Penh had a single runway, passengers walked in the heat across to the concrete building where they collected luggage from a cart and then lined up to watch their passports move from hand to hand for inspection, recording and stamping. The streets abounded with roundabouts, yet motor vehicles were a rarity. The pedal operated three-wheeled 'cyclos' with passengers sitting under a canopy or loaded with goods reminded her in some ways of the horse-driven carriages that transported goods and people in old Manila. To her the apartment buildings seemed to have been forgotten by time, 'they were wanting of a good scrub and a repainting job but the flowering trees lining roads on the way to the hotel were beautiful.'

For Margaret's first few months, Room 308 of the

Monorom Hotel, vacated by Greg Wells, was the IRRI office by day and her bedroom at night. As the project was extended phase by phase, Margaret's one year assignment stretched to seven and a half years.

The expatriate staff soon discovered that the stories about working in Cambodia were true. Living conditions were basic; the few public eating-places were filthy and the project staff worked long hours for six days of the week. Sunday was 'survival day.' However, despite the problems, Harry felt that the country had a wonderful atmosphere that inspired confidence in the future. When Betty returned to Phnom Penh in April 1989 with lots of luggage and baby Jessica they were accommodated behind the Samaki Hotel in what had been an unused bungalow. 'It was really a quite depressing building,' said Betty. 'It had never been renovated like the UN or the World Vision ones. It had black tiles on the floor and grey barred windows. It was just a square with a toilet and a kitchen on one side and half a wall that hid the two beds.'

Despite the limitations of the bungalow Betty enjoyed living behind the hotel and the friendship and advice that could be gathered just by stepping out the door. 'There were always kids to see and women to talk to and it had a very nice atmosphere,' she said. 'A huge tree covered the open area between the hotel and the bungalows, so it was nicely shaded. Somalie, the girl who helped me with the housework, would take baby Jessica out in the morning, sit with the other nannies and rock her to sleep on the swing. When new people or a visiting delegation came to

Phnom Penh there would be a welcome dinner, and it was so cheap to entertain that most people invited everybody, including kids. So we would all get together around the pool with its green water, have a meal and be introduced to the people coming in.'

Harry had first met Betty in Kathmandu at the start of a seven-month trip across Asia and Africa to London, on what was to be his last big trip before settling down in a steady job. Betty had quit her engineering drafting job in Canada and planned to travel with a girl friend to Africa and find work there. But she had always wanted to visit Asia so the two women booked a trip from Kathmandu via Africa to London, thinking that they would return to Africa afterwards. Betty said that she got to know Harry really well on the trip and that before he left London for a two-month contract in Thailand he asked her to visit him on her way back to Canada. Harry proposed marriage the evening before Betty was to leave Thailand so she went to Bangkok and bought an engagement ring and two tickets to Canada. They were married in Moose Jaw in December, with the outside temperature a very cold minus 30 degrees Celsius. A few months later they were in tropical Cambodia with its daily temperatures of over 30 degrees.

Harry and his CIAP team members immediately set about developing a network of crop trials and training people how to manage them. ADAB strongly supported the project and Harry felt that given enough time and a concerted effort from all team members the achievement of the project objectives was not just a possibility but a certainty. There was no doubt in his mind that it was possible to significantly increase the production of rice farming systems in Cambodia and at the same time develop a long term national agricultural research capacity.

When they had still not moved to the office by March Harry finally conceded defeat with the building contractor and engaged another. In April there was another problem. 'The office was just finished and we had started installing furniture,' said Harry. 'A guard who normally slept near the front of the office had just walked around to the back of the building at five o'clock in the morning, when someone lobbed a grenade at the window. It fell off the window onto the pavement and exploded, blowing the glass out of the windows and scattering it to the end of the building fifteen metres away. The blast cut big chunks of concrete out of the ceiling below the overhanging balcony. What could we do? We just got the glass repaired, filled the holes with plaster, and started work again.'

By May things at the office were looking better; the electricity supply was good, the guards and maid were excellent, three of the four telephones were connected and working, though as yet they didn't have numbers, and the imported and locally made furniture had been installed.

In contrast with his experience with the builder at the office Harry found that workmanship on the IRRI Villa apartments was truly professional. Construction was finished in July and when personnel from other organisations saw the completed building they also wanted housing outside the hotels. The authorities then decided to rent houses to approved organisations; at a cost of US$500 per month per bedroom for houses that still needed to be renovated and provided with their own electricity generator.

Betty Nesbitt furnished their apartment with cane furniture, including beds and side tables and lounge suite with coffee tables, for only three hundred US dollars. Food was extremely cheap, but there was little to choose from. There were no supermarkets and the only refrigerators were those in foreigner's houses. Baby Jessica adored the Khmers (Cambodians) that she knew well. As she grew older and developed her language skills the staff at IRRI Villa practised their English with her. A child did not intimidate them, and 'Jess' would say words over and over again until the person was satisfied that they had the pronunciation right.

Their second daughter, Jillian, was born in Thailand. There were no international standard medical facilities in Phnom Penh so Betty travelled to Bangkok where she stayed with my wife Janice before and after the birth. Harry arrived a week before the due date, then waited a further ten days for Jillian to show up.

Since CIAP was the first organisation to have a house the Nesbitt's often entertained. Harry said that British guests would arrive at 7 p.m., the Australians at 8 p.m., the Americans at 8:30 p.m. and the French at nearly midnight. At one party John Holloway, the recently arrived Australian Ambassador, was sitting out on the balcony when a woman from a refugee organisation saw him sitting there and asked him who he was. He said, 'I'm John.' She asked 'What do you do here?' 'Oh, I work at the Embassy,' he replied. 'So, I hear there is a new Ambassador in town,' she said. 'What's he like, is he a bit of a …' 'Of course everyone was waving hands in the air trying to stop her,' said Harry, 'while John was sitting there with a big smile on his face waiting to see what would happen.'

As time went on other organisations held more functions. In 1993 the Australian Embassy held a reception for Prime Minister Paul Keating. 'The Embassy imported wonderful food from Australia — including crocodile fillets, Sydney rock oysters, lamb cutlets and meat pies,' said Harry. 'The diplomatic staff members from different countries ate the fancy food, like oysters, but the resident Australians consumed the meat pies because they had missed them so much.'

The government did not mind if expatriate spouses worked and expatriates could always teach English because Cambodians wanted to learn English and there were no University courses available. Betty Nesbitt didn't want to work while she had a new baby, but she took on the task of ordering supplies from Singapore. Twice a year the expatriate community imported items that were not locally available, such as toilet paper, dishwashing detergent and diapers. The Red Cross brought in a weekly food box for its own staff and other organisations brought in supplies each time a staff member returned from a trip. Betty was also the Parent Teacher Association chairperson at the International School for one year and a Board member for two years, but she felt she was burnt out dealing with International School issues and eventually found a job in accounting at the British Embassy.

For logistical support the team in Cambodia relied on backup from UNICEF, the Red Cross, and IRRI headquarters in the Philippines and the IRRI office in Bangkok. In-country and international communication was difficult and travel from Phnom Penh to the outside world was restricted to the one flight a week to Bangkok through Ho Chi Minh or a trip overland to Ho Chi Minh City.

It took at least 6 weeks to obtain a Kampuchean visa. The visas were issued at the airport on arrival in Phnom Penh but a traveller could not depart Bangkok for Ho Chi Minh until advice had been received from Phnom Penh that the Kampuchean visa had been approved. There were no banks in Kampuchea and traveller's cheques and credit cards could not be used. Payments for plane tickets and hotel bills were in US dollars and it was necessary to have a supply of $20, $10, $5 and $1 US notes. The notes were not accepted if torn or repaired and had to be dated no earlier than 1975.

Harry wrote to me in Bangkok soon after his arrival in Phnom Penh. 'Time is running out for the mail to be submitted to UNICEF and some of this information should have been sent by cable a couple of days ago. A couple of things are needed from Bangkok. A stone went through the windscreen of our Toyota land cruiser station wagon last week. We've replaced it but require another to be shipped here. The 18,000 BTU air conditioners quoted are very large. Please also request quotes for 9,000 and 12 thousand BTU units. We also require three 240-volt stoves with four hot plates plus oven. Obtain quotes for single phase and three-phase electricity. Please arrange for Richard Lando to bring an extra $10,000 over what he has in his possession. Could you also be prepared to bring in $20,000 to $30,000 cash yourself in March.'

My US$20,000 in bundles of $100 notes was transported on the flights to Phnom Penh via Ho Chi Minh in my usual carry on bag. It was not a good bag to leave unattended on the airport terminal floor.

In March of his first year Harry advised that all flights in and out of Phnom Penh and Ho Chi Minh City were fully booked to the end of April, but one way or another he would travel to IRRI for discussions during the next month. In May the Red Cross diplomatic pouch was lost between Bangkok and Phnom Penh for a few days, much to the horror and disappointment of the resident expatriate population. But the work went on.

Harry reported in May that Richard had put a tremendous effort into an extremely successful one-week training course and was then on an equipment-buying trip to Hong Kong. Ram Chaudhary had his program well under way and was not suffering from homesickness as much as previously — his family had remained in India where the children were attending school. By July Ram and his Cambodian counterpart Mr. Men Sarom had visited all of the major rice producing provinces in Cambodia. There they conferred with agricultural staff members and provincial administration and research centres. Others were involved in organising training courses and setting up methods of transfer of information to farmers.

By August Ram and Harry were travel weary and sunburnt, but Harry reported that the research was shaping up really well. Margaret was always busy. The office was filled with co-opted Cambodian staff and was regularly frequented by locals and consultants alike. By October there were sixty-one rice variety trials at twenty-five locations in nine provinces being conducted with Cambodian co-operators. Crop rotation trials, fertiliser response trials, and evaluation of green manure species had been initiated in several research centres. Training and instructional resource development had started and some IRRI rice training modules had been translated into Khmer.

By the end of Harry's first year the project was also well advanced into its dry season research program despite the fact that some sites were inaccessible due to the continuing war. Margaret Regnault, a director of AIDAB (later AusAID), visited Cambodia and expressed very high regard for the efforts of Harry and his co-workers under very difficult conditions. She especially commended the CIAP team on their co-operation with NGOs, some of which were also supported by AIDAB. Support of the Cambodia project for at least another three years and expansion of the IRRI team seemed likely.

Weather conditions made research difficult during the second year. Heavy rains and floodwaters from the Mekong River caused flooding south of Phnom Penh and around the Tonle Sap Lake. Other provinces were afflicted with drought and the country was racked with political instability and insecurity, but some good progress was made. Maps of many rice areas were completed together with detailed maps of the provinces and a larger scale map of Cambodia. The baseline surveys conducted by Richard Lando and his counterpart Ms. Mak Solieng during the previous year were printed for distribution. Especially good news was confirmation that Australia would provide A\$1.5 million a year for the next four years.

CIAP continued to make good research progress during the next two years, although continuing political instability limited progress and forced the abandonment of some projects. Sparse end of season rains over much of the country also made it difficult to interpret results from poor crops. The rice variety improvement program continued with twelve new varieties recommended to farmers. Nearly three thousand five hundred rice varieties from Bangladesh, India, Indonesia, Malaysia, Sri Lanka and the Philippines were evaluated for Cambodian farm conditions. Two 'germplasm' catalogues of collected rice varieties were prepared during 1992 and duplicate samples of all the rice varieties that were stored in deep freezers in Phnom Penh were sent to IRRI headquarters for long-term storage.

CIAP researchers became aware of many research needs from their own experience, from annual planning meetings and from people 'walking in off the street'. There were also many requests emanating from provincial agricultural offices and other organisations working in rural development for CIAP to undertake specific research projects. Putting priorities on research was essential.

Such progress would not have been accomplished without the support of the Cambodian government leadership, of whom Ministers Kong Som Ol and Chhea Song were prime examples. The Minister of Agriculture, Kong Som Ol, was considered one of the most capable members of the government and was especially helpful in the first stages of the project. He was articulate, knowledgeable and very supportive of the project. Vice-Minister Chhea Song was another very powerful person who provided good support. He was the first Cambodian to see the possibilities of an IRRI-Cambodia project and in later years, when he was Under Secretary of State for the Ministry of Agriculture, all the major project decisions had to pass through his office. Chhea Song had the final say on what occurred in nearly all agriculture Departments and while it appeared that he worked quite slowly he was very thorough and solicited the opinions of everybody. His management style was generally for the decision to be made before he made the decision himself and he looked at all the options until the best one floated to the top. [17]

---

17. The early death of Chhea Song before the project was completed was a loss to the country that affected many. Chan Phaloeun had worked with him at the Cabinet of Agriculture when he was a Vice-Minister and found him warm and friendly. She said that she talked with him every day, though she was a just a junior staff member of the documentation office. 'Most of the staff at MAFF thought that I was a relative of his,' said Phaloeun. 'But I was not, though I thought of him as my uncle. When I worked with CIAP, he was always pleased to see me. The day he died I was very, very sad.'

The following year was devastating for many Cambodian farmers. Some areas were at first badly affected by drought and then flooded in early August from higher than usual rivers. Many of CIAP's deepwater rice breeding experiments were destroyed and other trials would need to be repeated. Despite these setbacks, Harry was able to report that other things were going well. The progress report for AIDAB had been submitted and 'AIDAB are still happy with us.' The Annual Research Report was also completed and though a huge time consuming job it was essential for all agriculturists working in Cambodia. Agriculture Minister Kong Som Ol praised CIAP for its progress and added, 'This country runs on the farmers' stomachs. If they are empty of rice all else is useless.'

Harry had soon realised that more resident expatriate staff would be essential if the project was to make a lasting contribution to Kampuchea's rehabilitation. A crop protection specialist, a soil scientist and an agricultural engineer would round out the team. More money was needed and when the Australian Embassy opened in Phnom Penh in 1993 Harry was assured that CIAP was almost certain to have its funding increased. To ensure that increased funding Glenn Denning encouraged Harry to visit AIDAB headquarters in Canberra to promote the project, having been told that there was no better way to bring a project to the 'top of the pile.'

A crop protection program was needed to train farmers in methods of limiting damage to their crops from insects and diseases and other pests

such as rats. The program had some input from IRRI
headquarters, but was without a long-term leader
until Gary Jahn, a young American entomologist
who had been working in Thailand, joined the program. Harry said he would have preferred someone
with more experience, but was correct in thinking
that Gary would make a good impression in the
community.

Gary's work required a lot of travelling in the countryside and he needed to be careful because there
had been several kidnappings and the Khmer Rouge
were offering ten thousand dollars for the head of
an American. To get over this problem Gary's Cambodian counterparts would usually tell people that
he was Dutch. There were exceptions. On one occasion a farmer invited him into his house for a
meagre meal of rice and boiled chicken. The farmer
asked Gary his nationality and on learning that Gary
was an American he became quite excited. He went
outside and brought back a bomb case that he had
found while ploughing his field. On the fin of the
bomb was written 'USA'. The farmer was not angry
about the bomb, just excited to learn that Gary was
an American and curious to know if Gary's father or
some other relative had dropped it. Some members
of the farmer's family had worked at various times
for Prince Sihanouk's government, the Americans,
the Lon Nol Government, the Khmer Rouge and the
Vietnamese government. So at different times people in his family were working with or against each
other, but that was not unusual for the time.

Gary said that his work in Cambodia was quite

different from research projects he had experienced elsewhere. In other countries he had found trained scientists with whom to collaborate, whereas in Cambodia probably eighty percent of what they did was helping people to learn how to do the work. He tried to avoid the word training, because that implied a specific training course. There were training courses but much of what CIAP did was not really formal training. It was just working with people day to day. Simple things like learning to make and maintain an insect collection were essential. When Gary started working in Cambodia the national collection was just a few insects in a cigar box and the Cambodians did not even realise the need to improve it. Without one they could not properly identify pests and start doing research.

Gary knew that he had to accomplish his objectives in a short time. "In six years my position would be over,' said Gary. 'I was trying to work my way out of a job. You find things to do, figure out how to do them, and then find people who can do them instead of you. And that is more or less what we did in Cambodia. Probably eighty percent of what we did was helping people to do it themselves.'

The next CIAP staff requirement was for a specialist in soil fertility and plant nutrition work. Harry was informed that a likely candidate was Peter White, a recent graduate of the University of Western Australia who had worked with soils and fertilisers in both Western Australia and in Syria. Peter was just finishing a post-doctoral degree when a telegram from Harry asked him to apply for the position in Cambodia. Since Peter was interested in tropical agriculture and development work and had learnt a lot about international agricultural research systems from his work in Syria he considered that it would be a good opportunity for him. However, when he went to Phnom Penh for an interview and stayed at the Monorom Hotel his room appalled him. 'It was shocking. There was mould on all the walls, the bathroom had no hot water and cockroaches were everywhere. It was disgusting,' said Peter. But next morning when he met Harry for the first time he said that the hotel was fine because he thought Harry might just be testing him for the living conditions in Cambodia.

Peter White and his co-workers worked hard to produce practical soil and fertiliser management recommendations that the government and provincial agricultural services could provide to Cambodian rice farmers. They produced a soil map of the Cambodian rice growing areas and a new soil classification method that was later distributed as a printed manual for use throughout Cambodia. Peter gave two reasons for the new simplified soil classification. The first was to help researchers be more effective in conducting on-farm or research station experiments. They had previously made no distinction between different soil types, so whatever they did in one place they would try to do everywhere. They could make more appropriate recommendations to farmers if they knew what soils were in their region. The second reason was to get people to think more about soils and to identify the important characteristics of soil that influenced its management.

Another staff requirement was for an agricultural engineer who could provide a better understanding of the physical conditions in farm fields and methods that would lead to more efficient ploughing, water control and other cultural operations. Harry and Glenn Denning decided that it would be best to employ a consultant for three months before proceeding with a long-term appointment.

Glenn contacted Joe Rickman, an Australian that he knew had worked on similar assignments in Vietnam and Laos. At first Joe was not keen to be involved, but Glenn persisted and Joe arrived in Phnom Penh in April 1994. When I talked with him seven years later Joe was enthusiastic about what had been accomplished. He said that the 'adventure' started when he met Mr. Meas Pyseth, his Cambodian counterpart engineer, and they travelled over nearly all the rice-growing areas of Cambodia during the three month consultancy. Joe could hardly believe the potential he saw and when Glenn asked him to accept a long-term position he did not hesitate, even though it was a big career change and he had to say goodbye to his career in Queensland.

Joe noted that by the end of a dry season the soil in most Cambodian rice fields is extremely hard, which made him think that the power requirement to plough a field was the main problem. But it soon became evident that farmers could not control water distribution in their fields. Even in small fields there was about twenty centimetres difference between the lowest and the highest spots, so at the beginning of the wet season some parts were still dry while in other parts the water was too deep. Consequently his CIAP staff group started work on levelling fields. They did not know if it was going to make much difference, but they soon found that level fields used water more efficiently and produced much more rice than fields that were not level.

There were other personnel changes. Ram Chaudhary moved to a separate program at IRRI headquarters in 1993 and was replaced by Edwin Javier, a senior plant breeder from the University of the Philippines at Los Baños. Edwin had regular contacts with IRRI before starting with CIAP and had also worked for two years at a rice station in Sri Lanka. He said that it was easy for Filipinos such as himself to live in Phnom Penh. 'Southeast Asians have similar cultures and behaviour and we could understand the body language,' said Edwin. 'Sometimes when people said yes they meant no, and I knew that it meant no. For people who do not belong to these regions it is difficult to understand. Sometimes it is difficult to say no, so they do not say no, but they give you some inkling that they mean no. That is Cambodia.'

When asked about his time in Cambodia Edwin said that he would do the same again, 'The thing about working in Cambodia was that you could teach so many people, counterparts and co-operators.' said Edwin. He considered that his greatest challenge after he arrived in Cambodia was learning the best way to train counterparts and co-operators who had language difficulties and a lack of formal education. He could quickly identify good rice varieties and developed effective interaction with farmers. On-farm trials stimulated demands for seed of new rice varieties provided through the CIAP program and farmers gave good feed back on the deficiencies and merits of the varieties tested. 'Although the farmers were talking in the Khmer language, their faces showed their appreciation,' said Edwin. 'But even though it was satisfying to develop improved varieties, the most rewarding was the ability to teach many people. That was our greatest joy — and the most challenging. But the roads were so bad — after travelling all day one needed a good rest.'

Mayette Nadal was a Filipino secretary who joined Margaret in Phnom Penh for a short period. Margaret had been asked to go to Laos to help set up an administrative office for the IRRI Laos project but her visa was never approved. So for three months Phnom Penh had two expatriate secretaries. In contrast to Edwin Javier, Mayette did not feel at home. She felt that there was something depressing about the place, not in the office where they all knew each other, but whenever she went out of the office or the IRRI Villa. She thought that maybe it was the look on the Cambodians faces, that they all had a sober look as if they were not used to smiling. 'And they always said yes, even if they didn't understand you. The Cambodians in the office were all willing and helpful, but by the end of my stay I was so depressed that I really wanted to go home.'

Mayette was lucky to go home alive. On what was expected to be an uneventful trip to Battambang the Khmer Rouge ambushed two passenger trucks a short distance ahead of the vehicle in which she was travelling with Ram Chaudhary and Men Sarom. Bullets were fired at their vehicle and a rocket grenade exploded on the road a short distance in front of them. It was just the quick action of Ram Chaudhary in telling the driver to reverse the vehicle that saved them from being hit. A few hours later, after government soldiers had cleared the road, they were able to continue their journey. That night in Battambang as Mayette lay in bed she could hear the artillery from near the Thai border. When she heard it the day's events came back to her and she could not sleep for thinking about what might have happened.

Other expatriates worked with CIAP at different times. Peter Cox, an economist from the Queensland Department of Primary Industries, encouraged CIAP researchers to ensure that farmers were fully involved in the design and conduct of research on improved cropping practices. One example of successful involvement was a successful rat control program developed with staff of a Catholic Relief Services project for farmers in Svey Rieng province that also pointed the way to reducing rat damage in other provinces. Peter Cox conscientiously attended Khmer language classes and became fluent in the Cambodian language.

Dr. Sahai was a plant breeder who took leave from his institute in India to work with CIAP on the classification of rice varieties. 'We were lucky to have Sahai, who was a hard worker in the field.' said Harry. Another Indian plant breeder, Siddhu, was also with CIAP for a couple of years. He wore a turban, which was a subject of some amusement for the

Cambodians. Siddhu was a very hard worker who spent long hours in the glass house area. He tried to push the Khmers to work harder also, but one day a Khmer counterpart pushed back and Siddhu landed in the glass-house pond.

Siddhu was held up at gunpoint one afternoon when he was walking down the street near the IRRI Villa. He handed over fifteen dollars and talked about the event for weeks afterward. Harry said that Siddhu did not talk about the danger or the robber, only about 'What is the man doing with my fifteen dollars.' Another Indian plant breeder was with the project for a year, but unfortunately became very ill and died within a month of returning home.

'It was an absolute joy working with my expatriate colleagues leading the research,' said Harry as he neared the end of his assignment in Cambodia. 'Adoption of improved technology is spreading rapidly among farmers and there is no turning back.'

6

'Cambodia has a language of its own.
Though the languages of the people
of Champa and of Siam seem to us to
have similarities of sound, they can-
not understand each other.'
(Chou Ta-Kuan, 1297)

The expatriate staff of CIAP would have accomplished very little without the help of their Cambodian counterparts from the Ministry of Agriculture. Counterpart assistance in translating, contacting government ministries and provincial officials and supervising research was essential to the success of the project. Ms. Chan Phaloeun was seconded to work with Harry and Mr. Men Sarom with Ram Chaudhary when they first arrived in Cambodia. Phaloeun and Men Sarom were officially assigned full time to CIAP though they still had other duties with the Ministry that included lecturing at Prek Leap Agricultural College and office duties in the Department of Agronomy. Richard Lando was without a counterpart for two months until Ms. Mak Solieng was assigned to work with him. 'The delay was possibly a lack of staff, though at first the Ministry didn't think that we needed many people to work with us,' said Harry.

The lack of trained scientific staff and general

expertise in Cambodia was one of the worst legacies of the Khmer Rouge attempt to set the Cambodian clock back to 'year zero.' A new generation of technicians and scientists such as Phaloeun, Men Sarom and Mak Solieng had to be trained, but though they had passed through a period of intolerable stress they were determined to succeed.

Although Phaloeun's experience while studying in Russia and her work with the Ministry of Agriculture had partially prepared her for such a position, there were new language and administrative problems to contend with. 'When I started to work with Harry I was pleased that I had an opportunity to learn new technology from a foreign counterpart, but in the first month it was difficult to communicate. Harry expected me to speak clearly and I felt troubled because I did not understand his English. When we went to the fields we needed a translator. It was so difficult to manage the work and communicate with the people that I told my supervisor that if I had nobody to support me, to translate and facilitate, I didn't want to work with IRRI any more. So Mr. Hieng Sokchea was asked to translate for us. After four months I felt more confident because I could talk more easily with Harry. We knew each other better and had a more friendly relationship.'

Phaloeun said that Cambodians working with foreigners during that early period had to be careful because they were monitored by the secret police. Though they worked under the Ministry of Agriculture they also had to report to the Ministry of the Interior where officials were suspicious that

Westerners had come as spies. When the Director of the Department of Agronomy first asked Phaloeun to report on Harry's work she had to tell him that she could not understand much, so how could she report anything?

It was also a problem for Phaloeun if Harry went alone to appointments or on field visits while she stayed in the office. Her Director asked how could she know what Harry was doing if she did not go everywhere with him? So Phaloeun complained to Harry about going alone and said that if he did so he should write a report that she could translate for her boss. 'Harry was upset with me and asked me why I needed a report,' said Phaloeun. 'I told him it was because I had to report monthly to my boss and to the Ministry of Interior.' Harry was even more upset and asked, 'Why do you report to the Ministry of Interior, are you a secret policeman or something?' Phaloeun told him that she was not, but it was the policy for Cambodian counterparts to regularly report to the Ministry of Interior. Otherwise their officials would come to the office and ask directly. 'If I did something wrong they might send me to jail,' said Phaloeun, 'but I did not do anything wrong, so I did not have any problem.'

Phaloeun added that in the long run they worked well together and that Harry was a strong leader and an excellent person for the task to be accomplished.

Although English was an initial constraint Phaloeun had no problems with her work. On one occasion she was attending a short training course at IRRI when a delegation from the Cambodian Secretariat of State for Women's Affairs visited there. The visit was organised by Glenn Denning, who requested Phaloeun to give a short talk on her work with CIAP in Cambodia and her training at Los Baños. Glenn later reported to Harry that Phaloeun spoke to the Cambodian visitors in Khmer with real confidence and authority and the delegation was impressed. That visit of the women's group influenced Glenn to consider including a 'Women in Rice Farming' component in CIAP in order to enhance women's opportunities and assist them to try out new technologies that could be of direct relevance to them.

Despite her great contribution to CIAP over the years Phaloeun told me that she was somewhat disappointed with her own lack of opportunity for graduate study. 'As the CIAP work expanded and other Cambodians joined the project there was competition between the old and new staff,' said Phaloeun. 'I lost face because of my poor English and I felt bad when my Ministry boss asked me why I had not gone to study abroad. Harry organised a scholarship for me in 2000, but I felt it was too late for me. I think research scholarships are only good for those under thirty five years of age'

Men Sarom, Ram Chaudhary's counterpart, is now the Director of the Cambodian Agricultural Research and Development Institute (CARDI). He said that he knew very little about the project when he started working with CIAP. 'I just knew that people had come from IRRI to conduct a kind of survey on where the future Institute was going to be,' he said.

'I went with Dr. Nunn to Kap Srau on one occasion and although my English was very poor, I heard through translation that Kap Srau was not a good place to have a future institute. The soil was unsuitable because it had been deeply ploughed and levelled with big tractors under a Russian mechanised farming project.'

As a child Men Sarom had lived in Phnom Penh and under the Khmer Rouge was sent to a district about twenty kilometres from Phnom Penh, not far from his parent's birthplace. There he worked long hours in the rice fields with little food, and scant rest, comfort or hope.

"I was 15 years old," said Sarom. "My mother had died when I was three, but there were many relatives. At first they put me into a children's group and later into a youth organisation. We built canals and several dams, big and small. The rice yield was reasonable because the dams protected the fields from water outside the dam and everything was irrigated within the dam. I remember that Pol Pot ordered us to use only semi-dwarf varieties of rice plants that came from China. Those plants were high yielding, but the problem was that we were told to use only one variety for the whole area, and in some areas the water was too deep and damaged the crop. We did not use chemical fertilisers, only organic fertilisers made from human dung and some compost from water plants. Sometimes a dam was built without considering water flow and interfered with the natural water flow to create a problem. But where I worked some dams are still being used. I helped make small bunds to divide fields into one hectare each, but after liberation, when the Khmer Rouge were defeated, farmers came back and started to divide the land [into small fields] again."

Ms. Mak Solieng, the third of the counterparts originally assigned to CIAP, no longer worked at the Ministry of Agriculture when I talked with her. I was late for our early morning appointment because it took me some time to realise that the driver was mistakenly taking me out to CARDI instead of to the building where she worked in Phnom Penh. Solieng's first work with CIAP was a ten-day social economic study with Richard Lando on a 'baseline' assessment of local farmer practices. It was intended to identify what research would be most helpful for improving rice production. Her talent for working with the team was quickly recognised and she remained with the project for the next twelve years.

In relating her history Solieng said that she had learned to be very independent. She was thirteen years old when her family was forced out of Phnom Penh and sent north to Battambang province to work in the fields. After a year she was separated from her family and sent to a separate camp for children where she helped dig canals and make dams, though sometimes she carried rice seedlings or bundles of harvested rice.

'My five brothers, one sister and my father were killed,' said Solieng, 'but I had two sisters in the village with my Mum, where she looked after them. Shortly before the Vietnamese came to Cambodia some of the Khmer Rouge took me with other kids to a mountainous area, but we escaped from the forest and I got back to meet my family in the camp. Then we returned home, walking more than three hundred kilometres. Sometimes we walked ten kilometres a day, but if it was raining we could only travel about seven kilometres. Back in Phnom Penh we had to start life again.'

Mak Solieng said that when she was living with the other kids they were woken at 4 a.m. every day to go to work in the fields. Lunch was at 11 a.m. and after that they were sent to learn the 'ABC.' Though she had attended school in Phnom Penh Solieng pretended not to know much because it was not wise to be literate. At 2 p.m. they returned to the fields and in the evenings had self-evaluation meetings where they were supposed to admit their faults. Solieng said she had to behave as a very quiet kid, but was smart enough to arrange which jobs she did, such as surveying dams rather than doing heavy labour. Some children looked after pigs, some made the black clothing they had to wear, some collected firewood and some did the cooking. Near harvest time they occasionally had good rice, but the majority of the time they ate a meagre porridge of boiled rice with water. 'It was a bad experience, but good because I learnt to survive,' said Solieng

It is a tribute to the courage and persistence of Phaloeun, Men Sarom, Solieng and other Cambodians that after the horrors of the rice fields under Pol Pot that they still chose agriculture as a career. However, in some ways it was also a matter of chance. For Men Sarom an instinctive desire came from his childhood. 'When I was a child I found a plant and wondered why it was green. I put the plant in a hole in the ground and let it grow for a few days. Then I dug it up and looked at it, put it back, and covered it again. When it became pale it was something I did not understand. I did other experiments with plants and insects. Small things, but they seemed important to me. Although I had these interests when I was young I did not think that I would become an agriculturist or biologist. I thought that I would become a historian or an astronomer, but it did not happen. I became a plant breeder.'

After Men Sarom returned to Phnom Penh, he sold bread to earn enough money to study in high school. He was eventually awarded a scholarship to study agriculture in Bulgaria. Sarom told me that during his six years in Bulgaria there was a lot of pressure to learn the language, to communicate with people, to adjust to University life and to adapt to the cold weather. Despite the difficulties he considered it was a good country for him to study in because it was mainly agricultural and supplied food to Eastern Europe. When he returned to Cambodia in 1987 the Ministry of Agriculture assigned him to work on a rice seed production farm, and the following year he was seconded to work with CIAP as the Cambodian counterpart for Dr. Ram Chaudhary.

Agriculture was definitely not Mak Solieng's first choice. Though her family had a garden about ten kilometres from central Phnom Penh they were not involved in agriculture and she did not want to study it. Solieng started secondary school before 1975, but could not graduate until after liberation from the Khmer Rouge. From high school she was awarded a scholarship to Cuba and applied to study clinical medicine, but only one place was available and she was passed over for an orphan girl. Solieng claimed that though she had the best score in the examination the government policy was to give orphans the first choice and that she was not given another opportunity for a medical career.

'I had to wait and let the others select,' said Solieng. 'The careers that were left were only agriculture and sugar cane technology, and I did not like my career allocation. After I started to study I tried to change to economics, but I was not allowed to do so. But agriculture in Cuba was good because it was integrated, a study of people, culture, and general agriculture, not just the science of agriculture.'

Solieng was able to see how Cuban farmers collaborated with researchers to develop an economic business, and she enjoyed the living and working environment. 'The Cubans were very joyful people,' she said. 'They treated us very well and helped each other. The farmers and other people were very sincere and very nice. When I returned to Cambodia I was sent to the department of Agronomy where I got a chance to work for ten days with CIAP. According to Harry I was good so I became part of the team for the next twelve years.'

Men Sarom, Chan Phaloeun, Mak Solieng and other Cambodians who studied abroad soon after the Khmer Rouge period were willing to accept the challenge. They accepted opportunities and they showed greater confidence than those who had not been away. 'You could see that there was a real distinction among the people who had been overseas, whether it was to Poland or Cuba or wherever,' said Gary Jahn. 'Those who stayed in the country the whole time seemed far less motivated and to have less ambition. It appeared they couldn't really see how what they did would really make a difference.'

In all about forty Ministry staff members were seconded to CIAP because foreigners could not hire Kampuchean staff directly. They were involved in research, administration, field station support and postgraduate studies. Of the thirty-four research staff working with CIAP all achieved at least a Diploma or Bachelor degree, and twenty-three gained a Master's or Ph.D. degree. Most had worked in the Department of Agronomy before CIAP, but some were transferred from other sections of the Ministry.

Soon after the beginning of the project Harry realised that it was necessary to provide salary supplements to counterpart staff. Typical government workers were receiving less than three US dollars in cash plus a few kilograms of rice per month. Most aid agencies and other international groups provided salary supplements of $100 to $300 per month depending on qualifications. While there were other reasons for staff to work at CIAP, the salary supplements were essential to keep CIAP operational. Nonprofessional support staff members such as drivers, guards and maids, were given 'overtime' payments to ensure that they came to work instead of spending their time looking for outside income.

Cambodians working with CIAP were not the only ones trying to escape the limitations of subsistence farming or lowly urban jobs. After graduating from university Mr. Miech Phalla from Takeo province spent two years in Australia and the story of his life that follows is written in the way he told it to me. Its personal conflicts, disappointments, hopes and fears, challenges and achievements in many ways illustrate the past and the future of Cambodia. His father had been a primary school teacher in Takeo and his mother told him that when he was a baby 'bombs dropped down like the rain and she would hide him in a hole.' When Pol Pot's Khmer Rouge soldiers entered Takeo town his father told them that he pushed a water cart in the market, not that he was a teacher, and they let his family go free.

Miech Phalla's father died working in the fields and three months later his older sister also died. His mother was sent to work near the Vietnamese border and his two brothers went to a youth work camp. Miech Phalla and his younger sister were left in the care of villagers. 'She would take my hand and we could go anywhere because we were still very small. We went to the rice mill and scraped the powder off the floor to eat so that we could have a full stomach and survive,' he said.

After the Khmer Rouge retreated to the Thai border, Miech Phalla lived with his remaining family in a low wooden house with a thatched roof and dirt floor. They were poor because only his mother worked. His older brothers were too young to join the army and his mother had to borrow rice to pay a tax for someone else to go on army service in their place. They were continually hungry and one day while she was out they had only one egg to eat, so they sat down on the mat with crossed legs and divided the egg into four parts. They let him choose first because he was the youngest, but told him that he should take the smallest part. Sometimes they ate rice fried with fat and salt, and sometimes with 'Prahoc' (fermented fish sauce) or sugar.

Miech Phalla's motivation to go to the Phnom Penh and attend university was somewhat unusual. He finished high school in 1991 but had few opportunities for work and wanted to get married. His mother said he was too young, but finally she relented and he asked 'one wonderful girl in my hometown' to marry him. Her parents agreed and one month before the marriage date he paid her parents with one cow, some cash, and three trees to provide wood for cooking fires. But during New Year celebrations a young man who was studying in Phnom Penh to become a teacher came to visit relatives in the village. He looked more interesting than a poor farm boy did, and when he asked to marry the same girl her parents returned all Miech Phalla's gifts to him. They said their daughter did not want to get married right then, that she was too young and wanted to learn how to make clothes in the city.

Miech Phalla had a broken heart. He could not eat and he could not sleep. He went to fields far from the village and sat down in the sunset and asked himself why they had stopped the marriage. He was so ashamed. All the people of the village knew that they intended to be married and he had lost face. Then he concluded that she married the other guy because he was studying at the university. So even though he had no money he decided to attend university in Phnom Penh.

It was the start of the wet season when the academic year started and people were busy planting rice in the fields. His mother gave him a small sack of rice and he set out. With no shoes and only a few clothes and the rice to carry he walked for thirty kilometres to the train station. As was usual for the time four flat wagons were pushed in front of the engine to protect it from mines on the tracks, and poor people sat on those wagons because they were not charged much. Miech Phalla joined them but when the ticket collector came he had no money, only rice. The collector said that in the city you need money everywhere, and if he had no money why was he going to the city? Finally a man who sat next to Miech Phalla paid for his ticket.

The train arrived in Phnom Penh after the curfew when the only people moving around the city were soldiers and police. Miech Phalla walked to an army compound where they repaired equipment and asked to sleep there one night, but the guard at the gate accused him of being a spy and told him to go away. He waited until the guards changed, then asked again and was allowed in for the night.

Next morning he cooked rice for the twenty soldiers and they agreed to let him stay a few days more. He washed their clothes and blankets and cooked and cleaned for them. They trusted him and he ate with them. Later he told the young soldier who had first allowed him to stay there that he wanted to learn more. He was referred to a rich man in the city who allowed Miech Phalla to guard a big plot of land. He lived on that land, cut and cleared the tall grass and planted vegetables. One weekend when the rich man's family came to visit the plot of land they were impressed and provided Miech Phalla with food. Finally he was asked whether he wanted to study or to work. 'In my heart I wanted to learn,' said Miech Phalla, 'but I thought that if I said I wanted to study he would support me for only a short time, then my studies would have to stop. So I said I wanted to work.'

At that time foreign embassies were just being established in Cambodia and Miech Phalla obtained employment as a security guard at the Japanese Embassy. He saved money, and after three years had one thousand US dollars, 'a heap of money' as he called it. He thought that the money would be enough for four years and six months at university and applied for the entrance test. He was very surprised to pass the test because he had not studied for a long time. He stopped work at the Japanese Embassy and started studying at the university. He had no place to live, so he built a hut beside a teacher's house near the university. He also bought motor cycle for $650, thinking that he could operate a motor cycle taxi to extend his money to the end of his studies. However, he did not have enough free time and the remaining $350 was spent within one year. So he sold the motor cycle, built a bigger hut and bought ten pigs. But disease killed some of the pigs and the market value for the remaining pigs was very low and by the end of the second year of study his money was all gone.

Miech Phalla said it was very hard to face the remaining two years and six months left to gain his University degree. Then a month later a church charity started a food cannery and training project at the University. He helped them clean the classrooms and finally they gave him part-time work for forty dollars per month, enough money for the university course and some English and computer courses at a private school. He worked in the cannery and cleaned up after student experiments. He also had a second part time job as a volunteer at the University of Tropical Agriculture, which provided him with a place to stay and electricity and water.

The guy that married his former girl friend became a high school teacher in Miech Phalla's hometown. When they met again Miech Phalla was still a security guard in the Japanese Embassy, but when they compared salaries Miech Phalla earned a hundred and fifty dollars a month, while the teacher received only fifteen dollars per month, so he felt a little better. The parents of the girl were very sorry. 'They said that if they had another daughter they would give her to me,' he said. 'So that was the thing that pushed me out to university. Before that I never imagined that I would study at university, but when something pushed me I finally made a success. I think sometimes the bad times made us stronger, to become successful.'

When Miech Phalla graduated in 1998 he achieved

a high grade in his Bachelor of Science degree, but said that the students only gained theoretical knowledge, not the necessary practical skills. For example, there were no computers for university students studying computing. The teacher drew on the board and said 'This is called a monitor'; 'This is a keyboard' and 'Click this and show this on the screen'. The students were not interested because they did not understand. He studied veterinary surgery, but the teacher just talked.

Documents for research were only available in foreign languages and the teachers had to translate sections for their students. The salary for a university teacher was only about twenty US dollars per month and many of the best teachers left to work outside because they did not earn enough to support their families. 'It is very hard for them,' Miech Phalla said. 'Some teachers prepared well and worked hard to share what they knew with their students. They did their best. And some dedicated teachers that earned enough money outside returned to the university to teach.'

The same determination to succeed despite lack of previous education opportunities extended to the CIAP office where Margaret Jingco trained, with patience and perseverance, her Khmer administrative support staff. The first two were high school graduates with negligible office experience. Ms. Kim Rany had, despite limited English knowledge, served most of her time as translator to an aid organisation. Her co-worker, Ms. Theavy, had been a cook/helper at a research station before being given a minor desk job and had zero English knowledge. Margaret gave lessons on the rudiments of business letters and English grammar, on spelling and punctuation and on file management and library acquisitions. She helped the support staff to establish a specialised library. They learnt computer operations, even though they had never even seen a computer before, and were trained in proper handling of telephone calls and how to entertain visitors. They had no previous accounting experience but learnt nearly all aspects of money management, and when Margaret left in mid-1996 they were confidently operating an automated bookkeeping system.

Ms. Kim Rany told me that she was one of the lucky people during the Pol Pot period. She escaped to Vietnam with her family by walking day and night to get to the border. It was difficult and dangerous but they were fortunate to be accompanied by a Chinese man who could ask for directions because his brother had worked for Pol Pot. When they reached the border late one night Rany's small niece and nephew were crying because insects were biting them. The Vietnamese heard the children crying and called out to ask if the group were refugees. Rany and her family then shone light on their faces and the Vietnamese allowed them into Vietnam and found places for them to stay.

Rany said that when they eventually returned to Cambodia, it looked terrible. They were afraid to walk on the roads in Phnom Penh at night because there were so few people, only a few bicycles, and it was very quiet. 'Most of the people looked like farmers and there were no cars and no lights.'

Before starting in the CIAP office Rany had worked
in the international office of the Agronomy Department. She had learnt some English by going to a private school for one hour a day and was assigned to
work on an agricultural development project with
the World Council of Churches as a translator. However, Rany had no knowledge of agriculture so Vice-
Minister Chhea Song arranged for her to attend the
second IRRI training course. At IRRI she was taught
both theory and practical work, though she said she
learnt most from the field practical classes on methods of transplanting, how to maintain a field, when
to apply the fertiliser and other topics. She said her
time at IRRI was also a great opportunity to learn
more English as their English teacher, Ms. Jill Sulli-
van, not only gave English instruction but explained
terms or phases of the work that they did not understand.

Rany liked working in the office with Margaret
Jingco and interacting with people, but she and the
other Cambodian women were used to top-down
decisions. Margaret said that at first they relied on
her for direction and to do an attitude shift they role-
played. Margaret gave them different case studies
and they had to pretend that she was not there and
decide what they would do and how would they do
it. Margaret would suggest a more appropriate action
to take if it appeared necessary. 'It was like teaching
small kids,' said Margaret. 'I asked them to repeat my
instructions because my purpose was to make sure
that instructions were properly understood and carried out. That also encouraged them to improve their
English comprehension and expression.'

Rany's training course at IRRI was in session when Harry and Betty Nesbitt made their first visit to Kampuchea. When Glenn telephoned me at my apartment in Bangkok about locating Betty for the trip to Phnom Penh next day, his voice sounded as if the burdens of co-ordinating the Kampuchea program were almost too much to carry. So I asked if there was any other problem besides finding a missing wife. There was. It had taken a long time to get approval for Rany's group of trainees to leave Kampuchea and Glenn had not wanted anything to go wrong while they were at IRRI. But Rany and the other two women trainees were robbed in their shared IRRI dormitory room a few days before Glenn and Harry left for Bangkok.

Rany told me that they had just returned from shopping at the market when there was a knock at the door and two men came in. The first said that he was the electrician and that he had to check the lights, then the second man locked the door and pulled out a knife. The women were tied to chairs and ordered to give the men money and jewellery and warned that if they shouted out they would be killed. Nothing like that had previously happened at IRRI, so Glenn was quite distressed.

Rany was married soon after she joined CIAP and Margaret Jingco hosted a luncheon for her bridal shower, a practice unknown to the Cambodian girls. Margaret invited seven other women from the Department of Agronomy and they all walked together from the CIAP office to a restaurant about three hundred metres away. An all-women group walking on the street was an unusual sight that at-tracted stares from 'People on motorcycles, bicycles and 'cyclos' and diners at the restaurant,' said Mar-garet. 'Women eating by themselves at a restaurant without their husbands or male relatives to escort them was unheard of.'

Rany considered Margaret and the other IRRI ex-patriate staff her good friends. 'I loved them. I liked them very much; they were our friends. They did not think they were in a high position or something like that. If we had any problem or trouble that we could not solve, we just went to them and told them and they helped.'

Despite good support from the Ministry of Agricul-ture the obstacles to research in Cambodia empha-sised that to be effective expatriate research leaders needed previous experience in developing countries. There were some simple limitations that many peo-ple would not even think about. For example, how could a provincial research co-operator travel to a distant village if there were no roads, or if the roads were only accessible by motor bike and the motor bike did not have enough fuel? And if supplies could only be bought in the city, what would the co-opera-tor do when he or she arrived at that village? 'There are all kinds of logistic problems that you wouldn't think of unless you worked there,' said Gary Jahn. 'There are all kinds of things that can go wrong. You have to expect that, and you have to put a little less trust in information collected by your national co-operators than in something you do yourself. Previ-ous experience led to better understanding of how farmers in the country think and what is important to them.'

Gary said that no doubt things could have been done differently. 'Every person would approach a problem in his or her own way. A different mix of personalities makes for different chemistry and then things happen differently, it is not surprising. Everything is based on your own experience.' He said it was possible that they could have put more emphasis on learning the Cambodian language, on trying to fit into the Cambodian culture, to fit in and to be able to work with people much more closely, but there was a downside to that. For example, in the IRRI-Laos project communication was nearly all in the Lao or Thai languages. The result was that a great many of the Lao trainees did not have sufficient English language skills to get scholarships to study overseas and they had a hard time communicating when they went to international meetings. 'So in terms of opening them to the international community it was not a very good strategy,' said Gary. 'But in terms of working closely with the people, and giving them a feeling of autonomy, it was a very good strategy. So, there are pluses and minuses whichever way you do it.'

The cultural environment was an important factor for effective work and personal relationships. Margaret Jingco said that she could mix well with Cambodians because of her Filipino features and rapport was easily established. She felt they were comfortable with her because she looked like one of them. And at a time when travel permits were still needed for foreigners to go outside the city limits Margaret and other Filipinos could go out with the local staff for Sunday picnics without a permit as long as they did not speak English loudly. However, Margaret sometimes found being accepted as a local could be embarrassing. For example, one night she was subjected to intense questioning by police for going home after curfew in the company of a male Caucasian — no decent Cambodian lady should be doing that!

Cultural factors influenced integration into the research program. When Gary Jahn first arrived in Cambodia he expected more or less a repeat of his two-year Peace Corp experience in Thailand. There he had been the only foreigner in the area where he worked and everyone around him spoke Thai. In Cambodia it wasn't like that at all. Though he was working with Cambodians on a daily basis he was really a part of the expatriate community, and never really part of the Cambodian community or language. He said that if one is always thinking and using the local language then it is not difficult to become fluent, whereas if one's entire social life is in English, and only occasionally is it necessary to use some Khmer language [Cambodian], it is much harder to gain fluency.

Another cultural factor was that initially many Cambodian co-workers did not question the way things were done. They had ideas, but it took a long time before they felt comfortable in expressing their opinions. The first time Gary met with his team and asked them for their ideas on what to do there was just silence. There was no feed back or discussion and they would agree to whatever Gary proposed. He would say, what do you think? What should we do? His counterparts would say 'It is up to you' and he would reply that he had just arrived and had no experience in this country. 'It may have been a subconscious fear that they could not describe,' said Gary. He thought that it could be a fear that if you say or do anything you might get punished for it, so it is always best to agree with everything and not express an opinion. 'Part of it may be the culture, but a bigger part I think is what they went through with the Khmer Rouge,' said Gary. 'You just accepted what someone gave you and you didn't try to ask too much.'

Like the other expatriates Gary Jahn wanted his counterparts to really be co-workers — but it was very clear at first they had the attitude that he was the boss and was running the Integrated Pest Management (IPM) program. And because it was difficult to get his Cambodian counterparts to express their opinions and present their ideas he probably was really the boss for his first two years. He ran the program, he designed everything, and he laid out the work plans with details and instructions. 'A lot depended on your own attitude and your own expectations,' said Gary. 'When you said something like 'do you understand this,' nobody wanted to say, no I do not understand. So they tried to follow instructions even though they did not understand, but they did the best they could. There was a language barrier but I don't really think that language was the issue and I don't think that it was lack of interest.

I suspect that people were interested, but they are afraid of asking the wrong question. But slowly they moved towards taking on more responsibility. By the end of the five years they were pretty much running things for themselves and I was more or less an adviser, which is how it should be. But it took a long time to get there.'

Memories of the Khmer Rouge period were always close. Harry's first trip from Phnom Penh to Battambang in the northern provinces with counterparts had been very tense. There were government soldiers all along the road and at every culvert there was a soldier or someone else with a gun. On the return trip it was obvious that Chan Phaloeun and Men Sarom were feeling much less tense. They were laughing and joking and Harry asked them what they were laughing about. 'Well,' said Phaloeun, 'it was a beautiful day when we were walking around looking at the fields near Battambang. We were saying isn't this fantastic, we are being paid to do this. In the old days in the Pol Pot time we would never have felt like that. We would never take notice of the beauty of Cambodia, of the bird sounds in the background, reflections in the water, clean green grass growing. We were always shuffling around with eyes glued on the ground, looking for something to eat.'

It was sometimes hard for foreigners to understand the Cambodian culture and ways of doing things. Gary Jahn related an example from a meeting in the Department of Agronomy when an expatriate was invited to give a seminar. The meeting started late and the Secretary for Agriculture joined the meeting a half-hour after the start. The speaker was really annoyed that the Secretary showed up so late for his talk, but Gary told him that it was a compliment that the Secretary actually made the effort to come at all. Normally high officials did not show up for such meetings, or if they did it was only to make an appearance in the last five minutes.

Despite the history of war and famine, there was another side to Cambodia, one of innocence and honesty. Gary Jahn was buying some CD's from a woman in the market and she quoted the price in US dollars. The only American money Gary had was a $100 bill so it was too much. He had Thai Baht and asked if the woman would take Baht, but she did not know the exchange rate. Gary told her the exchange rate and what it should cost in Baht, so she said OK and accepted it. But of course she had no way of knowing whether he was giving her the right rate or not. Later he wanted to buy something else and now all he had was the $100 bill. She had no change, but said she would get some. So he gave her the $100 bill and she went away while he stood there talking to someone else. Twenty minutes later she came back with an assortment of change and Gary did not think anything of it until later, when it occurred to him that it was really quite remarkable that she had returned. 'She did not know me and I did not know her,' said Gary. 'In most instances where you go into a poor country as a stranger and give someone a hundred-dollar bill they run away with it. That $100 was probably three or four month's salary for her, yet she was honest enough to come back and give me the change. I think that in other places you wouldn't really expect that. So in spite of the crime and violence there is still a sort of innocence about Cambodia. At the personal level things are very open and honest.'

Gary Jahn's wife Sunee, a Thai, enjoyed her five years in Cambodia. 'I think I adapted to Cambodia very easily — it was small and nothing much to do, but there was a lot of culture there,' said Sunee. 'The people are very nice and very interested to talk to you when you start to learn their language. At first the 'Russian Market' in Phnom Penh was the only one we could enjoy. Later I also spent a lot of time in the mornings at the local fresh food market. It was very easy for me to go there and it was a good place to learn to speak their language. The farmers selling fruit and vegetables don't let you speak English. You have to start with little words and they really try to listen to you. For me it was very nice, and I am always looking for opportunities to return to Cambodia. I still have a lot of friends there, and people always remember one. I went back last month, after five years, and even the people who sell fruit and other things still remembered me and came and talked to me. Everybody was so happy to see me back. I had a nice feeling and I was surprised that my Khmer language was still OK.'

'Gary travelled a lot when we were in Cambodia, but we lived in the housing compound and we had two children and a lot of friends. Even when Gary was not around we could always get together with another family. A lot of things are different now, more buildings and more business. I was there for five years and there was only one small supermarket, but when I went back last month there were many supermarkets. You can get goods from Thailand, from Australia and from France. The airport was so nice and clean it was hard to believe. When we moved to the Philippines I was kind of sad. I liked Cambodia a lot.'

7

*'From the fourth to the ninth moon
there is rain every afternoon, and
the level of the Great Lake may rise
seven to eight fathoms. Large trees
go under water, with only
the tops showing.'*
(Chou Ta-Kuan, 1297)

In the rain-drenched field a barefoot farmer followed his pair of plodding oxen as they sloshed through the water, ropes dangling from the pole across their necks swaying in harmony as they pulled the single furrow plough. The sleek coats of the oxen shone in the sun as the farmer following them manoeuvred the curved handle of the plough to guide the blade in the furrow. Behind him a pair of black buffalo followed with a second plough and operator. Clods of earth jutted out above the brown water, the unploughed weedy area gradually diminishing. The wet season had begun and soon the soil in the field would be raked until it was churned to soft wet 'puddled' mud ready for transplanting.

Rice cultivation was introduced to Cambodia around 1,500 years ago and for centuries agriculture dominated the economy with most rural families engaged in rice cultivation. Family land holdings were small but the rural population was largely self-sufficient. A one-hectare field could provide enough rice for a family of five people while fishing, fruit, vegetables and livestock satisfied supplementary requirements. Famine is a relatively recent phenomenon.

A myth about Cambodia has been that it is a land well endowed by nature, but it is not so. Most of its soils are sandy and infertile and the majority of rice farmers depend on irregular rainfall for growth of their crops. Drought and floods damage significant proportions of the Cambodian rice crop each year. Floods cause large-scale destruction of crops, infra-structure, property and means of communication. One of the worst was in September 2000 when half a million people were driven from their homes and al-most four hundred people died. Floodwater depths commonly differ by two metres or more from year to year, thus imposing a tremendous challenge for farmers. Yet seasonal flooding has long been a gift of life to the region. Annual flooding of the Mekong River brings an abundance of fish and plant life, and the people of the Mekong have learned to live with its annual rhythms, creating their livelihoods from the great river's ebb and flow.

Rice grows best with bright sunshine and plentiful water, so if there is enough water the tropical condi-tions of Cambodia are suited to year round cultiva-tion. However, rain seldom falls in the 4-5 month 'dry season' from December to April. Farmers say that the dry season ends and the wet season begins when the 'mango washing rains' between March and May cleanse blossoming mango trees of dust. The ensuing wet season generally lasts from May to November with the highest rainfall in September-October. Average annual rainfall ranges from 1,250 to 1,750 mm over the main rainfed rice-growing areas of Cambodia, but even in the wet season there are periods without rain during which rainfed crops may suffer badly.

Most farmers in Cambodia still transplant their rice crops. They grow seedlings close together in 'nursery beds' then uproot them for transfer to the main fields. Nursery beds must be located close to a source of water that can be used for puddling and for watering the plants when there is no rain. Rice seeds for sowing in a nursery are first soaked in water for twenty-four to thirty-six hours then spread thickly and evenly over the surface of level puddled mud. The seedlings continue to grow in the nursery until conditions in the main fields are suitable and may be one to three months old when transplanted.

Farmers must wait until there is plenty of water in the field and cultivate only as much land as can be transplanted within the next few hours. At least half the lowland rice soils in Cambodia are sandy, and within a few hours of puddling they consolidate as sand and silt grains settle, making transplanting difficult. When the main field is ready the nursery is flooded with water to soften the soil. Then the seedlings are uprooted by pulling them out of the soil by hand, hard work that is usually done by women, tied into bundles and carried to the main field where clumps of two or three plants are pushed by hand into the puddled mud. These clumps of plants, usually called 'hills,' are spaced about twenty to twenty-five centimetres apart.

Continuous bending while ankle deep in the mud makes transplanting slow and tiring work. It takes several days of labour to pull seedlings and transplant them on one hectare field. As an example of the time involved, if it takes just one minute to transplant the seedlings into one square metre of puddled soil, about twenty 'hills', it takes about one hundred and sixty six hours of labour to transplant one hectare (ten thousand square metres). At the same rate of work it would take two million people about three weeks to transplant the entire Cambodian rice crop.[18]

As mentioned previously, when the grain is mature the stems bearing the finely branched 'panicles' of ripe grain are cut with a hand sickle and tied into bundles. The sickle blade is curved so that the stems are gathered together for grasping by one hand while the serrated edge of the blade cuts the stems. The traditional Cambodian practice was to dry the rice sheaves in the field and then cart or carry them to near the farmhouse where the grain is separated from the straw by beating or by trampling with animals on a smooth piece of ground. In recent years

---

18. Harry Nesbitt gave groups of expatriate children from the International School of Phnom Penh opportunities to experience transplanting and other rice farming activities. They were not allowed to harvest rice because the sickles are very sharp but they watched demonstrations and did most other tasks. They helped to prepare a field and sowed rice into a small area for a seedling nursery. They uprooted rice seedlings and transplanted them into a field that was about knee deep with water and mud. Third grade pupils were all sent into the mud. Some protested 'its all muddy, I am not going in there', but finally they jumped in happily, and were planting rice when one said 'I am tired' and sat down, waist deep in mud, with transplanted rice in circles around him. An observer said that it was one of the best things that he had ever seen. Not just the boy sitting down, but the whole scene of 20-30 international children learning to transplant rice, and all having a great time.

engine driven threshers owned by contractors who move from field to field have become common. In all methods the rice grain, still in its husk, is separated from chaff and other small impurities by pouring from a height so that the impurities are blown away by the wind. The rice straw left after threshing is heaped in a stack, usually over a post, for animal feed and is the major energy source for cattle and buffalo during the wet season and at other times when there is little pasture to graze. Cattle and buffalo graze the harvested fields, either tethered to a peg or roaming freely under the care of a herd boy who is often seen asleep on an animal's back.

Rice is the major source of food energy for Cambodian farming families and a lot is needed every day, particularly by nursing mothers and those doing hard physical work, so the harvest is vitally important. 'Paddy', the rough rice still covered with a husk after harvest and threshing, is relatively easily stored and protected from damage by weather or pests on the farm. Traditionally the husks were removed by pounding with a pestle in a mortar, but nowadays the paddy is usually taken to a village rice mill to be processed into white milled rice ready for cooking. Milling is usually a cash-free transaction in which the miller keeps the bran and broken grains for payment.

Surplus rice may be sold for cash and, as economists say, has an advantage over animals in that it is not a 'lumpy' asset. Different quantities of rice can be sold whereas for livestock the minimum sale is one animal, a 'lump.' Many Cambodian farmers, however, do not have a surplus to sell. They are poor and face constraints such as difficult and infertile soils, drought, flood, sickness, and lack of finance. They have little food security and tend to go hungry for 1-2 months each year. They own few assets and in emergencies may be forced to borrow from money lenders at high interest rates.

Rice farmers use different cropping systems to match the wide range of soil and water environments. Each system has a common name that indicates the main conditions. 'Rainfed lowland rice' depends on rainfall and runoff from nearby areas to water a field and so is grown only during the wet season from May to November. It covers around three-quarters of the rice area of Cambodia. 'Deepwater rice' is grown where floodwater is very deep during the growing season. 'Recession rice' is transplanted into the edges of the receding floodwater at the end of the wet season and usually receives supplementary watering as the fields dry out. 'Irrigated rice' is grown during the dry season using water from rivers, dams and wells to irrigate the fields. 'Early wet season rice' is a modification of rainfed lowland rice that is sown early and is given supplementary irrigation during water shortages at the beginning of the wet season. 'Upland rice' is grown in fields that have porous soil and water does not accumulate on the surface.

The rainfed lowland rice crop is primarily cultivated on flat land where it is easy to make 'bunds,' the small banks at the edges of fields. Bunds stop water running off the field and hold it for ploughing and puddling and for crop growth during rainless periods. Although the fields may be relatively level, the depth and duration of flooding of the soil varies greatly from week to week, from year-to-year, and over relatively short distances within a field. The heavy rains of September and October are critical. Too much rain causes deep flooding in lower fields and too little rain or too rapid drainage from the field results in the crop drying out before the grain is mature.

In the rainfed lowlands the topography is not really uniform and a 'high' field may adjoin a 'low' field. The difference may be only twenty or thirty centimetres, but it has a major effect on crop growth. In low fields the maximum depth of standing water usually exceeds thirty centimetres and is frequently deeper than fifty centimetres. High fields drain more quickly and plants often suffer from drought. In general, low fields are planted with tall 'late maturing' varieties that can tolerate the deeper water. Mid elevation fields have fewer drought or flooding problems than other fields, and are usually planted with 'medium-duration' varieties, particularly those with good eating quality. These classifications are based on the number of months the rice varieties need from seed germination to harvest. Early 'mid-season' rice varieties planted May-June mature in five to six months whereas 'very early' varieties mature in from three to four months.

For most rainfed lowland and deepwater rice varieties, the time from germination to maturity is controlled by the number of hours of daylight, which in Cambodia varies from around eleven and a half hours to just over thirteen hours. They are known as photoperiod-sensitive varieties. Late varieties that are planted in June-July and harvested in January cover the largest area of the country, approximately one million hectares.

The urgency of preparing the fields for transplanting rainfed lowland rice was spectacularly demonstrated by a scene that I saw in northern Vietnam after leaving Phnom Penh. I travelled north to Hanoi, the capital of Vietnam, hoping to get more information on the Vietnamese view of the conditions in Cambodia immediately after their army entered the country. It was not possible to contact any senior army personnel and instead two of my Vietnamese colleagues arranged a visit to a farmer who they knew had been a Vietnamese soldier in Cambodia in 1979. Before making that visit they took me to see some historic ruins in the mountainous area about 60 kilometres west of Hanoi.

As we descended from the hills on our return journey I looked over a fertile plain that stretched all the way to Hanoi. It was the afternoon of a beautiful last day of June and the rain of the previous few days had accumulated in the level rice fields. Clouds floated in the sky and the sun gave a mirror-like shine to the flooded fields. For as far as one could see there were hundreds, maybe thousands, of farmers working in their small plots. Women were working close together in seedbeds, pulling up the bright green seedlings and tying them into bundles. Small groups of men and women were working at different tasks in the numberless fields. A man was levelling mud with a rake-like implement drawn by an ox. A woman carried bundles of rice seedlings along a bank, her reflection keeping in step. A man with a hoe over his shoulder was duplicated by his image in the water. Groups of two or three people with mud over their ankles bent to push seedlings into the mud. Traditional conical hats and dots of colour from clothes adorned the landscape, with red and white standing out. A magnificent sight where the combination of weather and so many people working at once could only happen on one or two days in a year, if that. But we could not stop because we had an appointment with farmer Mr. Le Van Cong on the outskirts of Hanoi.

When we reached Mr. Cong's village we parked the vehicle by a rice field and walked on brick paving along a narrow lane bordered by high stone walls painted in shades of yellow. As we turned into his gateway we found a neat well-organised farmyard enclosed by two-metre high stone walls. The first enclosure of a low building against the farmyard wall on our left contained a few farm tools; the second was home to two large pigs peacefully sleeping on the clean floor. On the right was a two-storey house designed to take up as little ground area as possible. A stone balustrade at the edge of a cemented area about 5 m x 10 m in front of the house separated it from a stack of hay and the holding yard for two buffalo. The ground floor had two rooms, the first open-fronted and containing the inevitable low table with a teapot and miniature cups, chairs, stored items and a small portable saw bench. Mr. Cong used the saw bench in work as a carpenter to supplement his income from farming. He was now aged 42 with a wife and three grown children. His two sons were out working in the rice field.

Mr. Cong was a gracious host and with the assistance of translation by IRRI's Ms. Nguyen Thanh Huyen freely shared his memories as a Vietnamese soldier in Cambodia from 1977 to 1982. He was at first sent to protect the Vietnam side of the border with Cambodia, then in 1979 received orders to move into Cambodia with his unit. He said that most of the Pol Pot army ran away and hid in the forest. Only the Cambodian civilians stayed and they were frightened, though it was difficult to know who were soldiers and who were civilians because they all wore the same black clothing. But gradually the local Cambodians began to think the Vietnamese soldiers were not as bad as they had been led to believe.

Food for the Vietnamese soldiers was only rice, salt and dry vegetables, but the Cambodians were in worse circumstance and sometimes the Vietnamese soldiers were able to give them bowls of rice and they were very pleased. Mr Cong said that after liberation all the Cambodian people were miserable, with few clothes, no belongings, no homes and no food. Once he saw empty houses and a hamlet where no one lived, but buffalo, cows and chickens were left behind when the people were taken away with the retreating Pol Pot army. 'At that time the Vietnamese soldiers were miserable and without enough to eat and though they saw many cows roaming on the road, they were not allowed to take them for food,' said Mr. Cong.

In contrast to rainfed lowland rice of Cambodia and

other places, bunds are not necessary for deepwater rice fields since the crop is grown on large fields that are naturally flooded through most of the growing period. Its cultivation was almost completely stopped by the Pol Pot government and farmers were compelled to convert much of the deepwater rice area to transplanted rice. The transplanted varieties used were not adapted to deep floods, the rice harvest was poor and the government blamed sabotage by enemy agents.

Some Khmer Rouge leaders who had implemented a more lenient agricultural policy near the border with Vietnam were ruthlessly purged and replaced by stricter cadres determined to implement the national yield target of three tonnes of rice grain per hectare. Cultivation of deepwater rice was banned and the new leaders confiscated all of the deepwater rice seed and transported it out of the region. All of the deepwater and floating rice seed collections at the experiment stations also disappeared. Consequently many of the deepwater and floating rice varieties which had undergone thousands of years of conscious and unconscious selection were lost.

Some fortunate farmers near the Vietnamese border were able to recoup many of their traditional varieties after the Khmer Rouge left. When ethnic Vietnamese who had lived and farmed in the area for generations were expelled by the Khmer Rouge they took with them seed of commonly grown deepwater rice varieties. Years later they returned to trade salt with their former neighbours and the local farmers learned of the surviving varieties. A delegation of Cambodian farmers then went to Vietnam and traded other seed for the old deepwater and floating varieties and also acquired new varieties.

Older farmers in southeast Cambodia said they had cultivated nearly five hectares of deepwater rice before 1975, but complained that in recent years the average family allocation of deepwater rice land declined to less than one hectare. They said making a living from agriculture was increasingly difficult and that it was nearly impossible to acquire new agricultural land. Their only option was to increase production on their current land area, so they turned to other kinds of rice culture for family subsistence and to crops such as beans for cash income.

A relatively recent development has been sequential planting of 'recession rice' in shallow water at the edges of receding floodwater at the end of the wet season. Nursery beds sown at 5-10 day intervals provide seedlings of the correct age for serial transplanting into lower and lower fields as water recedes down the slope.

One example of recession rice culture that we saw before the technique became common was in the south-eastern province of Prey Veng late in the dry season. It was just a few hundred square metres of poor green rice, at the bottom of the slope near a shallow pool of water. A ditch led from the pool to the edge of the field where the farmer steadfastly trod a water wheel, endeavouring to transfer water to the crop faster than it was evaporating from the field.

The water wheel was nearly two metres in diameter and was supported in a triangular bamboo framework. It had wooden spokes and a bamboo axle and rotated as the farmer walked on bamboo steps attached to one side of wheel. An effective part of the design was that the bamboo footholds were offset as left and right sets so that the farmer, his upper body balanced on a crossbar, was always placing his feet in a straight line while he walked. As the wheel turned about 40 paddle blades fixed around the rim pushed water up a narrow wooden channel and splashed it onto the edge of the field. The whole structure was nearly three metres in height and from a distance appeared like a small Ferris wheel with a marionette attached at the top, its jointed legs moving endlessly with the rotation of the wheel.

At the base of the water wheel, a small basket contained the neatly cleaned carcasses of five frogs and four small rats, the day's catch of meat. We could identify the rats by their furry feet. Close by a woman squatted on the ground picking up individual grains of rice from where the previous crop had been harvested. Not an easy way to make a living, but the neighbouring children around looked healthy.

Such dry season rice production, virtually insignificant in the early 1980s, became much more productive as time went by. The rapid spread of recession rice crops to replace deepwater rice increased the demand for hired labour, particularly for traditional women's tasks such as watering, transplanting, weeding and harvesting. Water supplies were developed and water control became more efficient. Farmers used varieties that could be harvested within less than three months after transplanting, and applied more fertiliser than on rainfed crops. They relied on surface water catchments to hold water until needed and then moved it onto their fields by gravity and other means, such as the water wheel described above. An alternative manual watering method was where two people stood about two metres apart to scoop up water with a bucket suspended between them by a pair of ropes. Their rhythmic bending and straightening as they lower and lift the bucket can continue for hours and from a distance looks as effortless as a child on a swing. A third method is the use of a bucket-sized scoop suspended by ropes beneath a tripod and swung backwards and forwards to dip up water and tip it into a small canal.

Dry season crops that are fully irrigated, usually by pumping water, have also increased in area and have the highest grain yields of any type of rice production. They receive more sunshine, water control is better than in any other system and because production risks are reduced the farmers apply more fertiliser. The dominant rice varieties in dry season rice production are rapidly maturing modern varieties for which flowering time is not controlled by day length. A crop can be produced in about three months and the dry season national average yield is more than one tonne per hectare higher than the average wet season rice yield.

Despite the high yields of dry season irrigated crops, the best economic returns have been in the provinces southeast of Phnom Penh where much of the farmland is just above sea level and farmers grow recession rice. Irrigation requirements are less than for the fully irrigated dry season crops and after the floodwaters recede it is only necessary to pump water from the canals up one to two metres to the field level. Farmers also grow recession rice around the northern edge of the Tonle Sap near Siem Reap, but use a different system because it is too difficult to provide supplementary irrigation. The water level in the lake falls as much as ten metres during the dry season, so canals would need to be very deep as well as around 25-km long. Farmers in those areas have adapted to the situation by broadcasting rice seed directly into their fields while the floodwater is still fifty centimetres deep. The seeds germinate under water and since the water is very clear light can reach the submerged seedlings. There is enough oxygen in the water for the seedlings to survive until the water level falls sufficiently for their leaves to emerge above the water surface. Because of the early start the crop can mature before it runs out of water. It is a matter of experience where farmers match the time of broadcasting seed to their knowledge of the rate of fall of the water level.

The upland rice area in Cambodia uses different rice varieties to the other crop systems because it is cultivated on sloping land where the soils are usually too porous to retain water. The plants must be deep-rooted and drought resistant. The area is very small compared with other ecosystems but is a part of the identity and culture of many ethnic groups. Farmers in the north and north-eastern provinces often sow upland rice between rows of maize, cassava or beans on land that has been recently cleared of existing forest or shrub cover by slashing and burning. The seed is usually 'dibbled,' which means that it is dropped into holes made with a sharp stick, and germinates with the rain.

All of the rice systems were a challenge to the plant breeders and within two months of commencing his work Ram Chaudhary had designed a huge program for the plant-breeding group. In the first three years he travelled with Men Sarom in nearly all provinces, working with the local people and trying to identify the best rice varieties for the different conditions. Personal security was uncertain, working conditions on their field trips were difficult, they did not have good places to stay and food was not readily available. Nevertheless they managed to accomplish a great deal.

The extensive rice variety improvement program that grew out of their work began with the collection of hundreds of the local rice varieties grown by farmers and selecting from them those that were best adapted to the different soil and water conditions throughout Cambodia. With help from local agricultural officials and other groups CIAP staff collected nearly three thousand different genotypes of rice from thirteen provinces in their first two years. More were collected in subsequent years.[19] Through a series of tests the

---

[19] Conservation of these different varieties and strains is important for the future. All the recent Cambodian germplasm collections are conserved in freezers in Cambodia, with a duplicate set in the International Rice Germplasm Collection at IRRI, Philippines, which maintains over 85,000 rice accessions from throughout the world. Harry Nesbitt questioned Michael Jackson, then head of the genetic resources centre at IRRI, about access to the germplasm stored at IRRI. He wrote, 'Before I make any rash statements regarding the Gene Bank at Los Baños, I thought I had better check up on the facts. Who has access to the Cambodian germplasm at Los Baños, at what cost, and how does one go about obtaining it? Can farmers request a sample of particular rice for example?' A rapid reply from Mike Jackson stated that IRRI would continue to make seed held in trust freely available at no cost to the recipient for the normal sample of 10g of seed. IRRI does not charge for the rice seed itself, but for large amounts that require special work or high freight charges then there is a request for field costs or freight to be reimbursed.

best plants were selected and their seed multiplied for production of pure lines that were later released to farmers as 'Cambodian Rice' varieties, now commonly known as 'CAR' varieties.

An example of how this varietal improvement program worked is taken from the deepwater rice section of the program. In the two years before Harry and his team moved into Cambodia small quantities of seeds of different deepwater rice varieties were brought from Thailand and tested in research stations and farmers fields by local researchers and farmers. A more systematic operation was initiated after the location of Ram Chaudhary in Phnom Penh. In his first year a total of three hundred and seventy six plots of rice were tested at seven locations. The next year there were twenty-four locations, but floods rose very rapidly and destroyed much of the work. In the third year nearly five hundred varieties were tested in small plots at fifty-eight locations in all eight of the major deepwater provinces of Cambodia.

Volunteer farmers then grew the two or three best new varieties identified through those preliminary trials in 'on-farm trials' on their own fields, using their own labour and crop management and growing their own best variety for comparison with the new varieties. CIAP researchers and their provincial co-operators provided the seed and explained to farmers how to do the experiments. The on-farm trials were a very effective method of transferring knowledge and rice varieties to farmers and obtaining feedback on what they thought of the new varieties. A large number of sites could be handled at minimum expense and time, and since farmers themselves were involved in testing the technology any improvements got rapid acceptance by the farming community.

Deepwater rice, although only a small percentage of the total rice area, is ecologically complex and challenging to plant breeders. On one occasion, Ram Chaudhary visited a site about twenty kilometres north of the town of Svay Rieng to inspect a trial on the outskirts of a village where floodwater in the field was about one metre deep. From the roadway one of the four rice varieties being tested looked particularly green and impressive, its foliage well above the water. Armed with camera and diary, Ram set off from the roadside in a sugar-palm boat, a hollowed out sugar palm stem about ten feet long that can just carry one person in calm water. He reported:

'As I reached the rice plot, paddling with my hands in the water, I realised that it was a promising deepwater rice, which we later named as 'Don'. As I tried to stand to photograph the crop the boat tilted and water spilled in. It was only then that I realised that my moving hands had attracted many leeches and along with the water they entered the boat and quickly attached to my feet. I panicked, the boat overturned and I was tipped into the water. All around me in that clear water were hundreds of leeches, from very small to 20 cm long. While trying to remove them from my legs, many attached to my hand. I cried for help, but my team mates in their safe places on the roadway did not know the problem and only laughed. Finally I waded the 200 metres to the roadside. My companions could now see the reason for my distress signals, and there was no lack of sympathetic fingers pulling leeches from my body.'

On-farm trials for rainfed lowland rice, early wet season rice and irrigated dry season rice followed the same principles, though with fewer problems of leeches! Seeds were sent to provinces through officials of the Ministry of Agriculture and through NGOs. Frequent visits were made to monitor the trials and farmers' reaction, then before harvest a 'field day' was organised by provincial staff to show the crops to other farmers in the area. At the end of the season the co-operating farmers harvested the seed of the new varieties for use as their next crop or to share with friends and relatives.

Ram Chaudhary and Men Sarom worked with all types of rice and tested hundreds of varieties from other countries. One of these was the IRRI rice variety IR66, which became the main rice variety in irrigated areas. The first IRRI trainees were given one kilogram of IR66 seed to take back to Cambodia. They used it for demonstration plots and the farmers were quick to realise its advantages. Other people had also introduced it before CIAP started, but CIAP organised testing and seed production and was responsible for its successful spread. IR66 eventually covered about ninety percent of the dry season and early wet season rice area and had a major effect on increased rice production and food security in Cambodia.

The 'IR' before the number indicated that the variety was developed by IRRI. When translating to farmers Chan Phaloeun was usually careful to state that IR66 was a rice variety that came from IRRI. 'Most people had no idea,' said Harry. 'Even co-operators of CIAP did not know what IRRI meant. Not that we wanted any acknowledgement, but it was difficult to collect data in surveys if they did not know'. Harry remembered one farmer who knew that IR66 came from IRRI and that Harry was a representative of IRRI. The farm was then producing four times more rice than previously and the farmer told Harry 'I now own the farm and was able to buy more land. I owe this to you,' he said.

One farmer who obtained two kilograms of IR66 rice seed from a Church World Service project said that in a good season with enough rain he could grow two crops because IR66 took only a few months to mature. Before he grew IR66 his family of nine could not produce enough rice to eat and needed to buy rice each year. Now he had four hundred and eighty kilograms of surplus rice and planned to expand his IR66 crop by one more hectare to help improve his family's living standard. 'If I make enough money from this additional crop I will buy a water pump,' he said.

Another farmer, Mr. Ith Yat in Prey Veng province, bought IR66 seed from a relative. Its yield was much better than his traditional variety and two years later he was able to sell two tonnes of paddy rice, the first time he had ever produced a surplus. 'Last wet season, I saw my neighbour conduct an on-farm trial and I saw another variety that looked very good,' said Mr. Ith Yat. 'Next wet season I would like to try that variety in a field that is not suitable for early maturing varieties like IR66. But this dry season I also hired a field to conduct an on-farm trial of my own because I heard that there is a new variety being tested.' The success of IR66 under the partial watering practices found in many rice areas provided solid evidence of the benefits from agricultural research and development in Cambodia.

Such gains were not easily achieved in the rainfed lowland rice areas, but each year the varietal improvement program pushed on, its success measured by the release of improved rice varieties and the acceptance of those varieties by farmers.

Ram Chaudhary's successor, Edwin Javier, said that a plant breeder in Cambodia could make a lot of progress. 'Cambodia was where you could really try what you had learned from the textbook,' said Edwin. He said that selection of the best plants from traditional varieties was a very simple approach, very useful and with a rapid impact. 'The people will accept those varieties because they have been using similar varieties for a long time,' said Edwin. 'The traditional varieties of Cambodia have a lot of variation in height and in maturity in a farmer's field. So what we did, we tried to select plants with uniform characteristics and height. It was very successful, and during my stay we released twelve new varieties, which we called CAR varieties.'

'Would I do it differently if I started again? I don't think so,' said Edwin. 'Because of the help we had the number of trials conducted in Cambodia was many times what I could do in the Philippines. When new varieties were introduced to farmers in on-farm trials we got feedback from the farmers. They would say what was missing in a variety and its good points. They would plant their best local rice and we would grow our new varieties alongside. They had the same type of grains, but our yield of grain was better and the farmers would then ask where they could get this CAR variety.'

The spread of such new varieties in the rainfed lowlands was somewhat slower than IR66 in the irrigated areas. However, a study covering twelve provinces found that those who had adopted the new CAR varieties reported improved food security, higher income and a better life style. Some benefits of the higher income were the ability to purchase motor cycles, water pumps, cattle or fertiliser or to have a reserve of cash. The new varieties often benefited farmers without significant increases in fertiliser application and increased yield twenty to fifty percent over traditional rice varieties. For female-headed households lacking access to water control, labour and credit the use of the CAR varieties was a means for increasing production that was both feasible and affordable.

CIAP plant breeders could produce and test new varieties, but they did not have the resources to multiply and store the huge quantities of seed needed for distribution to farmers. Those activities became the main operations of the UN sponsored Cambodia Area Rehabilitation and Regeneration Project (CARERE). Their extension workers worked closely with farmers who produced rice seed and sold it to a seed association. The association then provided other poor farmers with enough seed to transplant a field. After harvest that amount of seed plus an additional three percent was returned to the association for passing on to other farmers in the next season. Seed of a good variety spread quickly if the first on-farm trials produced good yields.

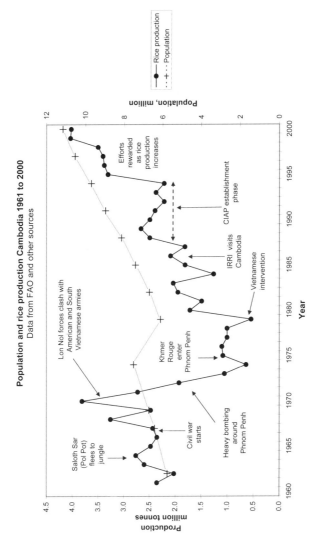

Population and rice production Cambodia 1961 to 2000
Data from FAO and other sources

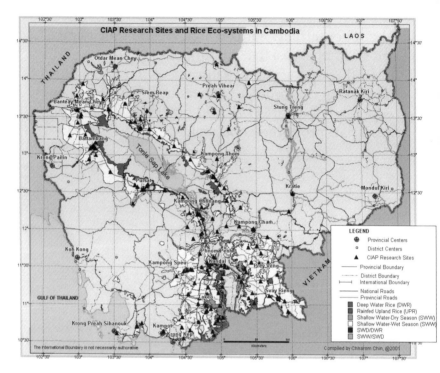

Samaki hotel and aid vehicles, Phnom Penh 1986

Cattle grazing by a bomb crater, Takeo 1986

Watering by bucket from bomb crater, Takeo 1986

Rush hour, central Phnom Penh 1986

Rush hour, central Phnom Penh 2001

Village market on the road to Takeo 1986

Ox carts by the road to Takeo 1986

Woman washing in roadside ditch, Takeo 1986

Thatched house and malnourished children, Takeo Province 1986

House moving by people power, 1986

Morning snack on way to Kampong Trabek, 1986

Piglets in a basket, Takeo 1986

Children at Prey Yutka 1987

Village water pump installed by UNICEF

Stream at Prek Ambil. The wet season flood level was two metres above the bridge

*Woman weighing fish at market on a country path,
Takeo province 1987*

Greg Wells and followers, Prey Yutka 1987

Bringing home the harvest, Kap Srau 1987

Pot Pol canal, Svey Rieng 1989

Community digging a small canal, KapSrau 1987

Phaloeun and Socheata, Prey Yutka 1988

Farmer treading water wheel to irrigate rice crop, Takeo 1988

Our boat on the Takeo river 1986

*The widowed transplanter shown on the cover
can smile about the future*

Tube-well hose watering a field, Prey Krabah 2001

Ram Chaudhary (hat) and Chhim Sarin with deepwater rice plots before flood, 1989

Harry Nesbitt, Kep Poch and farmers 2001 (photo courtesy of Brad Collis)

Harvesting rice near CARDI administration building, 2001

8

*'Men of the people own their houses,
but possess no tables, benches,
basins, or buckets. An earthenware
pot serves to cook the rice, and
sometimes an earthenware stove
for making sauce.'
(Chou Ta-Kuan, 1297)*

The dire condition of Cambodia in the 1980's and the paucity of international support encouraged close co-operation in pursuit of common goals. From the very beginning of IRRI involvement there was a sense of welcome and mutual assistance from other organisations. The dramatic improvement in rice production that ensued can be attributed in many ways to the spirit of partnership that developed. Without the partnership between government, researchers, NGOs and their Cambodian counterparts, and especially with farmers, very little would have been achieved.

The Red Cross provided vehicles until IRRI obtained its own. UNICEF provided logistic support. The Mennonite Central Committee in-country leaders were some of IRRI's first contacts. A good relationship with them continued in the ensuing years, as it did with World Vision International,

World Church Service, the Adventist Development and Relief Agency, Catholic Relief Services, Oxfam-Quebec, Food for the Hungry International and many others.

For CIAP, such early support was very encouraging, and each research area lent itself to different opportunities and forms of collaboration. Harry said the partnership approach was essential because the Ministry had a severe shortage of funds and qualified staff, and CIAP had neither the mandate nor the resources for direct work with farmers. This was even though the value of the project was to be measured by farmers' success in adopting improved practices.

Vice-Minister Chhea Song said that he wanted IRRI to work with the NGOs because at the time they provided the only means of transferring information to farmers. The NGOs substituted for the government in providing services to rural areas and most funding donated to Cambodia for farmer training and the transfer of technology was initially channelled through them. Many NGOs had relatively limited resources and could target only one or two districts, but although their individual impact on Cambodian rice production was small, overall it was very important. By the year 2000 some 150 international NGOs were operating in Cambodia and about thirty five of them implemented projects related to rice production. Eventually they had networks that together reached hundreds of thousands of farmers, enabling the rapid spread of acceptable technologies and management practices. [20]

Because NGOs had a commitment to improving farmers' lives and needed to show results to attract financial support they were motivated to help farmers quickly adopt promising new practices. They placed a strong emphasis on local knowledge as the guiding framework for problem solving, with NGO staff demonstrating a preference for being 'facilitators' rather than providing a top-down flow of information. But they did not all use the same approaches. Some provided a free service while others insisted on cost recovery. Such differences had the potential to undermine each other's work unless they were relatively isolated from each other.

Many NGOs used a 'participatory' approach, the method of working with farmers' ideas, to ensure that the outcome reflected the constraints within which farmers had to operate. Some were reluctant to participate in experiments, even those funded by CIAP, if the farmers could not afford to purchase the recommended inputs such as fertilisers on their own. Other larger NGOs subsequently organised farmer credit associations and seed banks in response to farmer demand to purchase fertiliser and other items.

The majority of NGOs gained farmers' trust and acceptance by being able to offer them something

---

20. Large multilateral projects of agencies such as the Food and Agriculture Organisation of the UN (FAO), the UNDP's Cambodia Area Rehabilitation and Regeneration Project (CARERE), the World Food Programme and other government to government aid programs also became operational in later years as the political situation was resolved.

tangible, such as seeds of a new variety or a method of pest control. So for many NGOs the improved rice varieties from CIAP made the most direct and immediate impact on their efforts to improve food security. Therefore making CIAP research knowledge, varieties and other outputs available to NGOs enhanced their effectiveness and credibility among farmers. The on-farm trials were particularly useful in demonstrating new technologies for NGOs and the extension workers who relayed information to farmers. NGOs conducted nearly one third of the over seven hundred CIAP on-farm trials conducted in 1999. Hundreds more trials and demonstrations using CIAP seed were independently funded and managed by NGOs and other international projects each year. In one year alone CIAP supplied over 10 tonnes of seed of improved rice varieties for those projects.

But, despite the importance of new rice varieties, CIAP's most important contribution to NGOs was building skills through training. CIAP staff and counterparts provided thousands of person hours of training for NGO staff in seed production, pest management, fertiliser use and farming systems. Other training courses were provided in English language, program management, proposal writing, and statistics and database management. Many experienced CIAP co-operators from provincial agriculture offices were also seconded to NGOs and other agencies to strengthen their capacity in agricultural research activities.

A few NGOs contended that IRRI was too far removed from the concerns of the local farmer. One NGO spokesman was quoted in a local newspaper as stating that 'National research personnel and NGOs are the ones working on the ground with the farmers, doing practical applied research, while an IRRI scientist is a 'distant enemy' to numerous small farmer groups working on sustainable agriculture.' Similarly, a book intended to influence public policy and donor agencies questioned IRRI's rice growing policy in Southeast Asia and stated that IRRI was drawing money away from national agriculture research systems of countries in the region. It suggested that NGOs resented the amount of money donors poured into IRRI. It said forty million dollars flowing into IRRI each year was 'an immense amount of money compared to what others engaged in sustainable agricultural research in the region would ever dream of.' However to put things into perspective, in the mid 1990s when the IRRI annual budget for all its international programs was around US$40 million, the national budget for agricultural research and extension in Thailand, Cambodia's neighbour, was four times that amount. Fortunately such negative attitudes applied to only a few individuals in Cambodia, and it really paid for all of them to work together.

The 'Cambodian Society of Agriculture' started from a meeting for NGOs in the CIAP office in 1989, but it was with some trepidation that Harry Nesbitt entered that first joint meeting. 'When the NGOs discovered how we were going about our project they appeared to be supportive,' he said, 'but I could physically feel tension in the air when I walked into the room, it was really uncomfortable.' The NGO personnel were very concerned about IRRI and its possible use of high technology and pesticides, but when they started talking about using the pesticides they were importing, Harry was the one that opposed the import. He told them, 'You guys can't import that stuff, you know what class one pesticides do.' CIAP's philosophy on pest management was to limit the use of pesticides in rice and in the early years they also worked extensively with locally available inputs such as organic manure, rock phosphate and other traditional ways to improve production. That research was published in the Khmer and English languages in CIAP's widely distributed '*TechNotes* and '*AgNotes*.'

Dr. Klaus Lampe, then Director General of IRRI, attended one of the meetings with NGOs and astounded Harry by asking the group to tell him what they thought about the IRRI-Cambodia Project, and specifically what they thought about '*HIM*, indicating Harry. Despite his embarrassment Harry was pleased to hear positive responses from the NGO representatives and later thanked them for their comments. But they told him they were just telling the truth, that at first they had been concerned about the approach CIAP was going to take, but now they were not and they had confidence in Harry. 'It was a mutually beneficial relationship,' said Harry. 'The NGOs were able to be included in training courses, to have the inputs to use in trials, to have the supervision of those trials, and to use the results.' [21]

---

21. Co-operation involved not only rice research. For example CIAP and the Asian Institute of Technology worked together on fish culture and published the 'Ricefield Fisheries Handbook,' a comprehensive reference guide on fisheries in rice fields and farm ponds. CIAP also published 'Livestock in Cambodian Rice Farming Systems.'

The formation of partnerships with NGOs appears to have been a natural solution to the lack of an effective national system for agricultural research and development. But it was a significant departure from the traditional *'research-extension-farmer'* model commonly promoted for developing countries by external agencies. The Cambodian experience suggests that formal research and development organisations may be able to leverage their impact and more effectively increase farmer participation by forming such partnerships with NGOs and related organisations. Unfortunately this partnership approach has not always received support from the scientific community or from donors.

'The NGO system is not a replacement of the national system; it's possible to work together,' said a member of Catholic Relief Services. 'The CIAP model was unique within the international system and could become a model for other countries.'

Undoubtedly many of CIAP's longest-standing relationships grew out of personal contact between expatriate advisors and staff of other organisations. But no matter how it was done, or by whom, the ultimate aim was to provide farmers with the knowledge and the methods that would enable them to improve production on their farms. To accomplish this Harry ensured that CIAP personnel worked more in farm fields than they did on research stations. Some use of the research facilities in glass houses or on research stations was necessary to resolve specific problems and refine methods, but as quickly as possible the work was moved to farmer fields.

Towards the end of the project more and more time was spent providing ways to help farmers analyse their own problems and find a solution for themselves. The farmers were organising trials themselves without being directed; the initiative was coming from them. Farmers who had not known the difference between common fertilisers being sold in the market now said that they had learnt what soil types they had and the type of fertiliser balance required for those soils. They had found that by using the right combination of fertilisers and by applying it at the right time they could reduce their fertiliser costs by thirty percent and still increase their yield.

When farmers were involved in trials they could assess what was best for them and their personal likes and dislikes could be evaluated. They adapted rapidly, sometimes too rapidly for CIAP researchers. An example was when CIAP researchers used about thirty farm sites to test deep ploughing. They knew from Peter White's experiments that deep ploughing of some soils would mix the sand and clay and make the soils more productive. The researchers used a tractor to plough about fifteen centimetres deep, then levelled the field, planted rice and added fertiliser. The plan was to compare their research crop with the farmer's crop on his untreated field and with a neighbour's farm. But often the farmer would watch what CIAP was doing and try to do the same. "It was unbelievable the number of times that happened,' said Harry. 'If we ploughed our half of the field the farmer would hire a tractor and plough the other half of the field. When we levelled ours the farmers would say, 'Oh, that's a good idea', and level their half. It became impossible for us to make a direct comparison of treatments. We would apply fertiliser, they would apply fertiliser, we would do something, and they would do the same. We would plant a particular rice variety; they would use a similar variety. It was amazing the number of times that a farmer copying our methods ruined the trials.'

On average the CIAP managed field produced about one third more than that of the co-operating farmer and twice as much as the neighbour's crop. Harry said it was not that the next-door neighbours were afraid to use the methods; they just did not know how to do so. Part of the problem was that they did not want to ask, to lose face by appearing ignorant.

Yet when farmers had access to training or other sources of knowledge they were quick to learn. CIAP was nominated for a 'Conrad Hilton Prize' and a representative of that organisation visited Cambodia to evaluate CIAP's achievements. His program included visits to farmers in Takeo province who had received training in improved crop management. Harry said that when the representative asked questions like 'What have you gained from working with the project?' it almost sounded as if the farmers had been briefed beforehand. The pattern of their answers went something like, 'Well we now have new varieties and we get the best seed. We know the difference between fertiliser types and we did not know the difference before. We now know the correct spacing for plants, and when to change spacing, and we now know the best timing of practices which we feel improves our production.' He said that both female and male farmers gave equivalent answers.

The on-farm trials where farmers could directly observe results were a key factor in helping them gain such knowledge. CIAP conducted nearly two thousand of those trials in eighteen provinces for rainfed lowland rice varieties alone, all arranged through provincial agricultural offices. The work could not have been accomplished without that help, but the co-operators needed assistance with their expenses. They were paid thirty-five dollars for each on-farm trial and CIAP also provided a motorbike if they established ten trials within a reasonable distance from their office. The provincial staff rode the motorbike to check the trials at one or two-week intervals and received money for fuel and expenses. Harry knew they made some profit, but he said they could not afford to do it without support.

Even though farmers were quick to learn' it was very difficult for many of them to improve their standard of living because their farms were often less than half a hectare in area. If such farmers have no irrigation water, few resources and limited access to credit they have very few options. If their rice crops fail they have little opportunity for supplementing food or income.

The most common reason that farmers are not able to use new methods of farming is that they lack money to purchase the necessary supplies. The majority of farmers lack cash. They need it to buy food not provided by the farm, for farm costs, for clothing and schooling, for medical expenses and to meet social responsibilities like weddings, funerals and religious festivals. Surplus rice can be sold, breeding animals generate cash through sale of offspring, and draft cattle can be hired out for ploughing. Cattle and buffalo can graze fields and so convert feed into energy and potential cash for the farmer, and since it is primarily children's work to care for cattle there is little effect on other farm operations when there are children in the family. However, unless a farmer can produce and sell surplus rice or animals these assets remain only a potential benefit.

The lack of reliable financial services is a major concern in rural Cambodia. Nearly half of the rural population have no commercial bank branches in their provinces, and according to one estimate, only about one in ten of the population had access to credit schemes. Without cash or credit farmers cannot purchase the items needed to improve their farm production or to purchase land or equipment. Those NGOs that provided credit as part of their development projects were convinced that attempts to introduce new agricultural technologies would fail if they did not consider credit needs of farmers, and farmers cannot get credit unless they have assets.

For centuries Cambodian farmers had nominal ownership of the land they ploughed and when the old land ceased to be fertile they could move on to another field. Those rights disappeared under the Khmer Rouge and were in abeyance during the later *Krom Samaki* collective system. When traditional rights of land tenure and inheritance were restored in rural areas the *Krom Samaki* system began to break down and changes were made to give more incentive to the farmers. When families became owners of their own farms they began growing their own crops and receiving the benefits. They planted fruit trees, grew non-rice crops and dug farm ponds. There was still poverty throughout the country, but there were also more contractors operating threshers and four-wheel tractors, as well as development of retail outlets for farm supplies and the construction of commercial rice mills.

In June 2001 the 'Cambodian Daily' reported that further changes to land laws were on the way. It stated that the proposed new laws would completely restructure the way property was divided, given away, traded and registered — attempting to bring order to a system that had brought chaos and corruption, benefiting wealth and power at the cost of fairness and the national good. Even to tackle the issue was revolutionary. It remains to be seen if new land laws will be effective, but the location of the very poor people in Cambodia is important to public planning.

Poor rural families, as in much of the world, spend over three-quarters of their income on food, leaving little for housing, health, education or the management of natural resources. In 1997 an estimated eleven percent of the population of Phnom Penh was below the poverty line, whereas in rural areas over forty percent of the people were in that category. Prime Minister Hun Sen noted that if the poor were mainly in the cities it would be logical to concentrate on the limited areas of highly productive irrigated rice to feed the population. He said, however, that the main agricultural programs should concentrate on isolated rural regions because the majority of the poor are in those areas.

Poor farmers, particularly subsistence farmers whose production is mostly consumed by the family, live under a constant threat that a seasonal food shortage or increased food prices or medical emergencies will topple them from privation to starvation. Medicam, an organisation representing over one hundred health care NGOs in Cambodia, reported that the high cost of health care is a primary cause of poverty. Nearly half of those who lost their land and became landless labourers were those who sold land to settle debts related to health costs.

While great progress has been made in recent years, there is still not much money to be gained from growing rice in Cambodia, especially for small farms in rainfed lowland rice systems. In the rainfed rice areas of Takeo province, south of Phnom Penh, the majority of farms ranged from only 800 square metres to 1.6 hectares (16,000 square metres) in area. Farmers with water for irrigation can produce two rice crops in the wet season and other crops such as corn, mustard, sesame, bitter gourd, cucumber, cabbage, yard-long bean and yam beans in the dry season. But most farmers do not have irrigation.

Working with such poor farmers is a learning experience that gives a realistic idea of what national programs can do, and a realistic idea of what farmers really want and need and can use, said Gary Jahn. He explained that sometimes a scientist thinks of problems in a theoretical sense, about how and why do things work, and how to solve the problems. So in the end the technology that comes out of it may not be suitable for a poor illiterate farmer who has very few resources. For example a lot of research was done to develop economic thresholds for all of the different rice pests. An economic threshold is supposed to be the number of pests that can be present in a field before it is necessary to control them. Gary said that he had not met a single farmer in any country who used those economic thresholds. 'An economic threshold will depend on how much it costs to control the pests and on the price of rice, and they both fluctuate all the time. Farmers know that very well and in the end it does not make sense for the farmer to have a threshold number of insects per plant. It may well be that the cost of controlling those insects is more than the value of the entire rice crop. So even if the farmer saves the crop he or she has spent too much money. On the other hand, if farmers do not have access to food elsewhere they must save their crops. A scientist can develop models to predict with fairly good accuracy whether insect populations will increase or decrease, but the farmers don't have those models and don't know how to use them,' said Gary. 'So I think developing tools that the farmers can really use is something you learn when you live in a place like Cambodia. There were things that never would have occurred to us if we hadn't done the work with farmers.'

The first step in working with farmers was to assess their existing practices, but it was not always easy to collect information or find people. One of the things found by a foreigner in Cambodia was that people were almost anonymous, like the widow whose photo is on the cover of this book. Once Gary was looking for his driver's house and knew the neighbourhood, but didn't know exactly which house it was. Gary asked a group of people where his driver lived, but they all said they didn't know him. Soon afterwards he was standing on the street talking to a woman who also said she did not know him, when right above her head his driver put his head out of the window and said 'Hey, I'm here.' Gary was so surprised that he asked his driver why no one in the neighbourhood knew him. The driver said that people generally didn't go out of their way to become acquainted, but added that under the Khmer Rouge there were spies living in the community and people needed to be very careful. When people were asked about somebody else they just said, 'I don't know them'. That way it was safer for both parties.

Such behaviour became entrenched and it made survey work for CIAP rather difficult. If researchers interviewing a farmer started asking about names and background information like how many children were in the family the farmer would become suspicious and not want to talk. So interviews with farmers were much better if they were just asked questions about their crops. In contrast to Cambodia, Gary said that in a village in Thailand he could ask, 'Do you know Lek, he raises pigs?' and everybody would say 'Yes'. But in Cambodia they could go into a village with the full name of the person and details about them, and everyone would insist that they did not know him or her. Whereas it may be that he or she was the next door neighbour of the person they were talking to.

Greg Wells, the part time IRRI representative in

Kampuchea before Harry Nesbitt and his team arrived, emphasised the dependence on interpreters
to collect such information. Meetings Greg attended
ranged from large regional gatherings organised by
government officials to village gatherings of just a
few farmers. He said that the problem analysis approach he used with small groups was a new experience for the farmers and a chance for him to
spend meaningful time with them out of the glare
of the internal security police, 'except of course, my
translator and 'minder' Sokchea!' At the regional
meetings there were usually two or three technical
talks followed by the mandatory political harangue.
Greg once asked Sokchea to translate the political
speech and he just replied 'You know better than to
ask that!' Many of the farmers just settled back and
closed their eyes.

The whole CIAP program was directed at providing
farmers with information, rice varieties and other
materials, and farmers missed out on benefits if they
did not receive enough quality information to make
their own decisions. Harry gave an example of Tim,
a young adviser with high ideals about sustainable
agriculture who worked in irrigated areas of Siem
Reap province. Tim would only promote the use
of green manure, cow manure and local rice varieties. He would not use any of the introduced varieties, even though he knew that Takeo province in
the south had become wealthy with a huge export of
rice by growing those varieties. Finally Tim realised
his lack of progress, and said to Harry, 'I am going to
try your IR66.' He started promoting high yielding

varieties, the farmers rapidly increased their rice production, and Tim became a hero in the area.

Continued provision of information to farmers will have an important role in Cambodia, but some people are concerned about an unrealistically short time span for projects and their aims of recovering costs from farmers. On a trip with Phaloeun and her co-workers I met Jeff Milne, an Australian working on his third project in Cambodia. While Phaloeun was meeting with a group of farmers, Jeff and I sat on the steps of an elegant Pagoda close by and discussed his project and government extension services. He told me that his project was planning to achieve in five years results that had taken extension services in Australia maybe fifty or sixty years. In Australia agricultural extension had been a public funded service that was only recently partly privatised and to Jeff it seemed inappropriate to apply the same philosophy to subsistence farmers with a very low level of education.

'To think that over a five-year program cycle you can build up agricultural specialists to such a level that these really poor farmers are going to be falling over themselves to pay for information from people at the district level is not realistic,' he said. 'There needs to be more recognition that in a country where eighty five percent of the people are poor farmers that agricultural extension is a public good.'

Jeff had just come from a district were the district leader had four agricultural support staff. He said that those staff members had probably received only a primary school education and though their local knowledge was good, their training in agricultural development or community-based education was very limited. 'It probably means that when the government wants to collect information they give them some money and send them out to collect statistics or measure crop yield or something like that,' said Jeff.

'I see a first step is getting them some really good training, so that they are able to work with farmers more meaningfully. They need to set up a district office that is relevant to the farming community so the farmers can say 'If I go and ask that person in the district office they will find out for me.' At present farmers don't do that and I see that a first step is to try and build capacity at the district level, so that it actually becomes a district agricultural office where farmers go as a point of contact.'

'Rats are to be seen as large as cats,
and also a sort of rat with a head
exactly like that of a young puppy.'
(Chou Ta-Kuan, 1297)

New rice varieties alone, without other changes, were not the answers to low rice production in Cambodia. The soils are some of the least fertile in Asia and fertiliser was in short supply. Low rice production meant less feed for animals and less manure to apply to the fields. Rats and other pests were a constant menace and water was unevenly distributed in most farm fields. Farmers were struggling to find the means to diversify their production; much of their rice grain was lost during milling; and so on. There were many limitations that farmers needed to overcome. Fortunately CIAP's efforts were supported long enough to effectively address many of the problems and for progress to be made.

Most Cambodian soils are low in phosphorus and nitrogen, the major plant nutrients commonly applied in fertiliser, and many are also low in potassium. A survey soon after CIAP started work found that farmers applied on average around thirteen small cart loads of farmyard manure to nursery beds and seven cart loads to the much larger transplanted fields. Some farmers applied small amounts of chemical fertiliser in good seasons but avoided using expensive fertiliser or limited supplies of manure in times of drought or flood. The government could not provide fertiliser at subsidised prices, especially after fertiliser imports from eastern bloc countries ended in 1990, and most farmers could not afford unsubsidised fertiliser.

CIAP's initial research on soil fertility focused on identifying problems associated with different soil types and then on developing appropriate fertiliser strategies. Various NGOs also promoted more efficient organic fertiliser use and CIAP provided them with technical advice.

The nutrient management program started in earnest with the arrival of Peter White. He worked with several Cambodian counterparts and said that they made a tremendous contribution to the progress of his work, particularly because he was a relatively young scientist still learning a lot about Cambodia and farming systems. 'They were educating me on everything and we worked as a team,' said Peter. 'I think they realised that I was learning and they helped a lot. They had a lot of patience.'

The prime objective of Peter White's group was to develop the simplified soil classification system for Cambodia mentioned earlier. If that could be accomplished researchers would have a useful tool for their work and provincial agricultural staff would have access to the latest information on the soils in their region. The ultimate aim was to develop sensible ways to match fertiliser application to soil type and crop needs so farmers could increase and stabilise crop yields without adverse environmental or social consequences.

To that end Peter's soil nutrient team put much of their initial effort into the 'Cambodian Agronomic Soil Classification' and a soil manual that enabled field workers to classify soils without using specialised equipment. The manual was gradually completed but it was not easy. Peter sent an advanced draft to an IRRI colleague with the following comments. 'As you will see when the manual arrives, some work is still needed but I think we can polish this off pretty quickly if we can get together. I have reached a bit of a mental block with it at the moment, and feel that working with it by myself further won't be productive. The manual will never be as good as I had hoped. It still has a lot of shortcomings. I suppose, however, this is only to be expected. We just never get time to do as thorough and as good a job as we would like.'

The resulting manual was simple and easily used. Persons classifying the soil worked through a series of steps and questions. They decided whether or not the soil was flooded by water, whether there were cracks or gravel in the soil, the colour of the soil and so on. Part of the analysis required them to dig a hole about fifty centimetres deep to see how the soil texture changed over that depth. They then re-checked the questions until they were confident that they had identified the soil correctly.

Jeff Milne, the Australian I talked to on the steps of a pagoda in Kampong Cham Province, gave an example of how well the soil manual was accepted by provincial officials. He had prepared a draft soil map of his area based on previously published data, and then showed it to the director of the provincial department of agriculture. The director looked at it and said 'No, no, no. That is not how we classify soils in Cambodia.' He went out and got the new CIAP manual, showed it to Jeff and said, 'This is how we now classify soils.'

Many farmers significantly changed their fertiliser practices after receiving training from extension workers on crop requirements at different development stages. However, other farmers were reluctant to adopt new methods because they lacked money and the cost of credit from lenders was prohibitive at around twenty percent per month. So in some projects, fertiliser recommendations were linked to a credit scheme. For example, one German aid project that trained farmers from over fifty villages on the use of appropriate fertilisers also provided them with credit to purchase fertiliser

The best results from fertiliser application to rice are normally in irrigated fields where the water supply and depth can be controlled. Rivers and dams are obvious choices as a source of water for irrigation, but use of underground water was a new development in Cambodia. In some areas close to rivers the water is close enough to the surface for lifting with relatively simple pumping equipment. Farmers in Prey Krabas district of Takeo province had invested in tube-wells for this purpose and I had an opportunity to see them during my visit in 2001 when Mr. Kep Poch of Chan Phaloeun's farming systems group at CARDI took me to visit some of his co-operators

We left early in the morning and stopped for breakfast at a crowded open roadside restaurant on the outskirts of Phnom Penh. There were twenty tables with plastic chairs, a dozen staff bustling around, paper tissues in plastic boxes on the tables. Milk was in sealed cans and chopsticks in paper sleeves. The food counter was a tiled bench in an open shed and the main fare noodles with boiled meat and blood cubes. We ate quickly then moved on, noting the frequent changes of the countryside as we passed by.

At a road junction we saw ten women quietly competing in the sale of the traditional long bread rolls. Further from the city cars were replaced by motor cycles pulling trailers carrying twelve or more people seated on planks of wood. The clatter-clatter of a steel bridge heralded an open-air market with clothes and fruit displayed on mats on the ground. Next were open fields of the countryside, then a brick kiln with flames rising fiercely above the roof and new red bricks stacked by the roadside. Lush green rice fields near a stream were in the minority as bare fields waited patiently for rain. A lone cyclist followed a line of trucks slowed by holes in the road. Fuel stations consisted of a single petrol drum with a hand pump mounted on its top, and then incongruously we came to a modern petrol station with electric pumps and bright colours situated on an almost deserted stretch of the road.

Further on a wooden house was framed by bright pink bougainvillaea. A concrete manufacturing yard offered pipes for irrigation and cement rings for

animal feed troughs. A graceful pagoda provided a
focal point on the edge of woods. A market thronged
with people and motor cycles denoted a 'town', while
a green cross on the front of a wooden house identified
a one-room medical clinic. We turned left into a side
road, the corner marked by four schoolgirls standing in a conversational huddle. Domed hills rose out
of the plain to the south and an extended village of
spreading trees and houses stretched along the road
for two kilometres or more. The dirt floors under the
substantial wooden houses were swept clear and ox-
carts parked under a house were the background for
oxen sleeping in the yard. A group of women and
children squatted under the shade of trees at the side
of the road, cracking stones with hammers. A school
with closed shutters had no children in sight. Then
we saw the tube-well irrigated rice fields of Takeo
province that we had come to see.

A tube-well consists of a hole about 10 cm in diameter that is drilled down into the underground
water and lined with plastic water pipe. When water is required a centrifugal pump driven by a small
portable engine is connected to the top of the pipe to
deliver a continuous stream of water onto the field
through a long hose. We inspected a field being wa-
tered by that method then spoke with CIAP co-operator Mr. Touch Ly, who met us at a pleasant open
community shelter next to a village pond. The pond
provided an opportunity to evaluate the traditional
village water supply. The pond was square, about
twenty metres across and all sides of the excavation
sloped evenly downwards. A flight of concrete steps

led down to about three metres below ground level, to where the surface of the visually clean water was adorned with colourful water lilies. Before tube-wells and pumps it was the only source of water and the villagers regularly carried water up those stairs, then through the trees to their houses.

Mr. Touch Ly had been a resident of Prey Krabas for over twenty years, so I was surprised when I asked him where he had been during Pol Pot times. He gave a hesitant smile and his translated answer was, 'I was a Khmer Rouge soldier.' He had been pressed to serve in the mountains of Pursat province and was later stationed near Prey Krabas, which influenced him to settle there. Neighbours listening to the conversation did not seem at all concerned about his past association with the Khmer Rouge.

Mr. Touch Ly was relatively well off. He had saved for nearly three years to buy the pump for his tube well and did not have to borrow money. As a co-operator with the CIAP project he had almost tripled his rice production. He now grew three crops a year and produced enough for the family and a surplus to sell to the market. With that money he was able to buy more land and so grow more rice for sale. He now owned six hectares, a large farm in Cambodia, and in the past four dry seasons had irrigated two hectares of the IR66 rice variety. Before that he grew only one crop on a small area and for two to three months of the year the family did not have enough to eat. 'There are ten members in my family — seven children, one grandmother, one mother-in law, and one wife,' he said. He has provided his neighbour with IR66 seed in exchange for equal quantities of other rice. For his wet season rainfed lowland crop Touch Ly changed from a local variety that he had used for seventeen years to a CAR variety which gave almost twice the amount of rice. The increased yield was not due to the CAR variety alone, but also better use of fertiliser and supplementary irrigation from his tube well.

Other farmers who joined in the conversation agreed that their lives have improved by the adoption of the new farming methods. One woman said that the amount of rice produced from one crop on her field had doubled and she was able to get two crops per year, thereby increasing her total rice production fourfold.

We continued on to Dong Kea village a few kilometres away and met its village chief, Mr. Ouk Chor. His tidy wooden house was separated from others in the village by trees and a small plot of cassava plants. The village had over eight hundred people in one hundred and seventy six households set randomly among the tall shady trees and palms and linked by winding tracks. Ouk Chor and his wife sat cross-legged on a traditional slatted-bed under the main floor of their house as we talked. Two sleek oxen contentedly munched green leaves from a manger under the far corner of the house, quite unconcerned by our presence.

Ouk Chor had lived in the area all his life except during the Pol Pot regime, when he was sent to dig canals, build dikes and grow rice. His wife-to-be was in a separate Khmer Rouge work group, but, unusual for the time, they were permitted to marry.

This is surprising because under the Khmer Rouge leadership family relationships were secondary to work.

When I asked Chan Phaloeun about this she said that married couples were sometimes allowed to stay together, but it depended on the work. If the wife was assigned to one group and the husband was under a different leader they could not live together even if they worked nearby, but if they worked together they could live together. During the wet season the Khmer Rouge allowed married people to stay in a village, but single people continued to work on dikes or dams or canals because they were the 'first manpower.' The married group were the 'second manpower' and the children and old people the 'third manpower'. The single group usually lived far from their parent's village and had no time to stay with them. But Phaloeun told her group leaders that she was a widow. She knew that they did not have any education and had not understood when she had originally said that she was single. Consequently she was able to stay in the village with her parents, which may have saved her life.

Phaloeun's younger sister moved from camp to camp for nearly four years. 'It depended on the policy,' said Phaloeun. 'If one dam was finished they dissolved the group, organised a new group, collected the people back again and built another dam or dug another canal. The people had no choice, it depended on the leaders.'

Ouk Chor owned a half-hectare field on one side of the village, his 'upper field' where he grew transplanted rice, and another three and a half hectares of broadcast deepwater rice land closer to the river, some five kilometres away on the opposite side of the village. He had installed a tube well to irrigate his upper field and regularly transported his engine and pump by ox-cart along a winding three-km track through the trees and palms. His crop of IR66 rice was a healthy green, a marked contrast to the surrounding hard dry fields. Total rice production from his half-hectare upper field was about four and a half tonnes per year, whereas his deepwater rice field with seven times the area produced only about six tonnes of poor quality rice that he used for animal feed. When asked why he did not grow recession rice in the DWR area he gave no clear answer.

The Ouk Chor family also appeared relatively well off, but I gained the impression that in the future his children might not be so fortunate. Four of his six children attended the local school, which provided education to eighth grade. One son was working as a builder's labourer in Phnom Penh and the others hoped to continue with farming and related work. But for what future if farms are continually divided as population pressures increase?

Alternative occupations for uneducated farmers' sons and daughters, such as labouring or working in garment factories appeared limited. In early 2001 Cambodia's garment industry employed around 150,000 workers, mostly women, but the worldwide economic slowdown combined with turmoil in the garment sector had caused many factories to close. Of 225 factories registered with the Commerce Ministry after the beginning of 1999, thirty-nine had temporarily or permanently closed by mid 2001. The industry had experienced continual unrest because of long working hours and factories not complying with existing labour codes. Strikes the previous year had brought a $5 pay rise to workers, bringing the minimum wage to $45 a month, but between three and four thousand workers were without jobs as purchase orders from the USA, Europe and other countries continued to decline.

Ouk Chor's wife made no comments during our visit, though she looked comfortable with our discussion. Many Cambodian males assume that women have a much lesser understanding of technical issues than do men, an assumption that sociologist Ms. Chou Meng Tarr stated may not be grounded in the realities of village life. She wrote that there are many examples of the determination and effectiveness of Cambodian women. To illustrate her point she gave the example of a young woman in a poor village who defied her father's order to stop attending high school and spend her time on household work. That young woman became far better than the males in her village at making networking contacts. First, she managed to convince the World Food Programme to support a food-for-work project, and then she was able to convince CIAP researchers to spend time in the village developing a range of livelihood projects.

Joe Rickman, CIAP's agricultural engineer, first became involved with farmers using tube-wells in the districts we visited near Prey Krabas. The first farmer to install a tube well had owned only one hectare of land and had considered selling it because he could produce only one tonne of rice a year, not enough for his family. However, in the first year after installing the tube-well he grew three crops and produced over eight tons of rice. He then asked to buy his neighbour's land. The neighbour replied something like, 'Don't be stupid, I have to put in one of those wells.'

'As soon as those guys in Prey Krabas got water, they started working on fertiliser use and different varieties.' said Joe. 'The man who started it became a rice trader as well and is now rich. He saw an opportunity and did a good job. We think that there are people like that all over Cambodia, but they are probably not used enough.'

At the beginning of this new development CIAP engineers asked surrounding farmers what help they needed. Most wanted finance to install wells but CIAP could not provide credit. Official lenders were not interested. They considered farmers a bad risk, especially poor farmers, saying that they would never pay the money back, even though in other developing countries poor farmers have been very diligent in repaying debts.

The engineers went back to the farmers and instead of money offered to train them on how to install their own tube-wells. About twenty farmers participated and installed twenty tube-wells in less than two weeks. Some became contractors and within eighteen months there were nearly five hundred tube-wells in the area, most about forty metres deep.

The engineers were concerned that the farmers might use too much water, but through testing the aquifer they found that during the flood period the Mekong was fully recharging the underground water to about thirty kilometres from its banks. The original contact farmer often visited CARDI, even though he no longer needed help. He photocopied any information he obtained and distributed it to other farmers in his district, acting as the local extension officer. The area really blossomed, showing that farmers were not always slow to share knowledge.

Another farmer we visited was Ms. Mon Khum Tee in the neat village of Tabong Damrai, close to the highway from Phnom Penh to Takeo and much further from the river than Mr. Touch Ly and Mr. Ouk Chor. Our stop at her village was an opportunity to meet farmers who were not CIAP co-operators and Mr. Kep Poch picked her house at random. She was sitting on the customary slatted-bamboo bed-type bench in a lean-to shelter at the side of her house talking with women neighbours when we arrived. Her husband was present for a few minutes, but once she was identified as the farmer he soon left.

We learnt that the underground water in their area was too far from the soil surface for centrifugal pumps to lift water for irrigation, though Church World Service had installed three tube-wells with hand operated pumps that supplied the village with clean drinking water. The organisation also provided about thirty dollars a year for maintenance of the pumps.

Ms. Mon Khum Tee had been a farmer for twenty-two years. She owned a half-hectare of land and her one crop of rainfed lowland rice produced just over one tonne of rice each year. For two to three months of the year there was not enough rice for her family so they borrowed rice from other farmers. Her crop was transplanted using the same methods and rice varieties of twenty years earlier. I asked, through Mr. Kep Poch who was translating, if they knew anything about the new rice varieties, or if any organisation helped them.

The group had heard something about rice on television but did not know about CIAP and CARDI. Mon Khum Tee said she had not taken much notice of the information. Some villages have a community television which people pay to watch so I asked whose television they watched. 'My television,' was the answer. What do you watch? 'We like to watch the movies?' I mentioned a shiny new motor cycle close by but they said it belonged to one of the rich people of the village.

Even though short of food for three months of the year they appeared to enjoy sitting in the shade while they waited for rain to start the crop season. One of them asked Poch to provide some seed of the new varieties. We presented them with a tin of biscuits and some sweets for the children, whereupon we were jokingly told that we should have brought another bag. Mon Khum Tee, who was feeding her baby, then made some comment that Poch was too embarrassed to translate. We left them chatting in the shade.

Next we visited Mr. Srey Sambol in Prey Malup village a few kilometres away. He had been a CIAP co-operator from 1997-99, the three-year limit for co-operators. We sat in the open area under his wooden house on yet another slatted bed. This one shared the floor space with a large sow that grunted vigorously while feeding her ten piglets. The piglets finished and two of them came and nibbled at my shoelaces before all ten retired to sleep in the dust at the base of the far wall. The sow was tied up outside for a while, then brought back, which meant that the hammock being used on and off by the two girls watching our discussion had to be moved to make way for the pig.

Mr. Srey Sambol courteously provided fresh coconuts for drinking before telling us about his farming. The groundwater in his area was also too deep for irrigation so it was only possible to grow one rice crop per year. However, he said that when he changed from his traditional rice variety to an improved CAR variety his yields nearly doubled. Many factors were involved in his improved production and in order of importance they were land levelling, new varieties, and water management and fertiliser application. About twenty families in his commune of eighty families now used the new rice variety CAR11. It had spread to at least twenty kilometres from his farm, though some superstitious farmers considered they must wait three years before making a change. Mr. Srey Sambol used the money he made from selling the extra rice to buy a rice mill and more land.

While we talked Srey Sambol brought out neatly written records of all the operations on his farm, did the conversions from local measurements to international units on a calculator and kept his radiophone handy.

When we mentioned our previous visit to Ms. Mon Khum Tee's village Srey Sambol said that the soil in her village was better than in his area and that Mon Khum Tee should have good production if she changed to a new variety. I took a photo of his family and promised to send a copy through Kep Poch, who also agreed to introduce Mon Khum Tee to the local agricultural extension agents.

It was significant that Mr. Srey Sambol considered levelling of his fields was very important for improved rice production. CIAP engineer Joe Rickman explained that the water in one section of unlevelled fields could be over thirty cm deep before the highest parts received any water, so plants suffered from drought in the high spots and were often flooded in the low spots.

Joe's work on land levelling started late in the CIAP project. An item in 'The Nation' newspaper of March 1997 reported the start. 'A new land levelling method was introduced on Wednesday at the new Cambodian Agronomic Research and Development Institute [CARDI]. The system is based on laser technology, with a transmitter emitting a thin 360-degree light. A receiving system mounted on earth-moving equipment detects the laser signal and guides the implement's cutting edge.'

Joe recounted how that came about. 'One midnight a guy called me from the USA, and said, 'I believe you are doing a lot of land levelling work in Cambodia.' I said yes, but how did you find out? He answered that I did not really need to know, but said 'I'm from Spectra-Physics and we sell laser equipment. Would you be interested in us doing some work together?'

Joe said he was interested and that if the company brought the equipment to Cambodia he would try it. The work was to be started during the dry season, but six months passed by and there was no further contact from the USA. So Joe telephoned the company one Friday and said that his CIAP engineers were building a bucket scraper for the back of a tractor and it would be ready to start levelling fields in forty-eight hours. The company representative said that he would reach Cambodia on Sunday.

He arrived at the IRRI Villa the following morning with a laser-levelling unit that Spectra had never tried before and said he would have to fly out next day. He was a salesman, not a technician, and they had assembled the system in Singapore just two nights earlier. Originally he had said to mount the scraper bucket on the three-point linkage at the back of the tractor, but when he arrived he said it had to be dragged, not mounted on the tractor. Joe told him that would be no problem, 'You sort out the electronics, and we will make a hitch.'

'We did that on the spot — in one day,' said Joe. 'It was unreal! At six o'clock that night he was short of one electrical wire, so we had to go down to the market, then open the electronic control box to make the connection. We did not know what was going to happen and this guy was going to leave next morning. We hooked it all up, we fiddled with it here and we fiddled with it there, and all of a sudden the bucket went up and down as it was supposed to do. He was very happy. Eventually we got it to work in the front yard with the remote control module, and he said, 'See you later.'

'We then had to work out a plan of action. Our tractor driver had only just learnt to drive a tractor – before that he had only driven oxen. So all of a sudden 'Sam', as we called him, went from being a village farmer using two oxen to driving an eighty-horsepower tractor with a laser operated levelling bucket on the back. It was fantastic how quickly he learned. I went out with him for two or three days and he was great. Six months later I could go into a field with a farmer and say, where does the water flow in and where do you want it to run out? The farmer would say, 'Here and here'. Sam would say to the farmer, 'How many fields do you want on your farm?' then he levelled and squared the area and there was much better water control.'

In the first year the engineers travelled to many locations and levelled forty or fifty farmers' fields. 'Then everyone wanted to be part of the action,' said Joe. 'We worked in nine or ten provinces, levelling fields and doing comparative work and used basic inputs such as new varieties and fertiliser to improve the whole farm system.'

At the end of the season they organised 'farm walks' where farmers went to different sites to see what had been accomplished. 'We always went with some piece of technology, fertiliser input or whatever and would have a bit of a yarn about the theory behind what was being done,' said Joe. 'We found the local extension guys knew less than the farmers did, so they were also on a steep learning curve. What was really great was that the farmers would tell us their success stories. But I guess the best satisfaction I got was in seeing our engineers develop their skills.

'That was all done with the laser and one reason we did it with the laser was that we could get a result fast,' said Joe. 'And then I thought, OK, we will not be here forever, lasers are probably a contractor's piece of gear, what can a farmer do? So we went right back to basics and started training on animal based systems. We were involved with an extension group in the north that selected one or two farmers from each district and we put them on contract. If they came to the training course they had to agree to level at least one field when they went home. We had to work out things like 'what was the most effective weight of the man on the board when we were using a levelling board pulled behind an ox or a buffalo?' If a farmer weighed only 40 kg he could not pull much soil around with a two-meter long board. He needed at least forty kilograms for each one metre length of the board.'

'We taught them how to measure levels in their fields by buying a length of clear plastic hose from the market, filling it with water and making two marker sticks. Then the fields were ploughed and pumped full of water and flattened out. And it worked really well. My counterpart engineer, Mr. Meas Pyseth, found that around ninety percent of the farmers complied with their contract. What was really nice was that they told us that they had modified our technique to make it better. The water control was improved and they could get on their fields earlier. When we asked them what were the differences they saw, they always said that they had fewer weeds and that they were getting around five hundred kilograms more grain. But that may not be accurate because they did not have good means of measuring the area. They believed they had higher yields, they believed that they had better control over their weeds and their diseases and pests, and they could also plough their whole field when it rained. I guess it was self-sustaining, the farmers had taken ownership.'

'What we didn't realise was that the neighbours had watched all the way through to harvest and they said, 'Will you come and do our fields.' It was not just levelling; it was a combination of factors,' said Joe. 'We levelled the soil; we put banks around the field, checked the water source and improved the drainage. Where the topsoil had been moved we told farmers what fertiliser to add. Of course everybody wants to know how much did land levelling contribute to production, what did the new rice varieties contribute, what did fertiliser? If everyone added their bits together we should have been doubling crop yields, but over time it came out that the increase was about thirty percent when using the same variety. The objective is, in working with farmers, to try and maximise the use of what they've got. We have run into criticism that land levelling increases the cost of the operation. Yes it does, we don't deny that, but you don't get anything for nothing. We said to the farmers, if you do this right the first time, you will get a benefit for eight to ten years, and we are sure that over that time period the returns will be much more than what it cost.'

One socio-economics researcher commented that land levelling was either unsuitable for female farmers with less than one hectare of crop or that it was not understood by them. Many women were reluctant to level their fields, mostly due to the cost of hiring tractors, but some did not realise the benefits. They did not realise that levelling fields to improve water control could dramatically reduce weeding by as much as fifteen person days per hectare. One woman farmer recouped the cost of land levelling in the first year. She reduced her seed and water costs by thirty percent and her crop yield was higher. But she said she had to work harder or hire labour to assist her.

Gender issues were, however, not necessarily foremost in the minds of poor farmers. Gary Jahn told me that an interviewer once asked him what he thought were the biggest pest management problems facing Cambodian farmers. So Gary talked about subsistence farming and described how a farmer who has one very bad pest outbreak could lose fifty percent or more of his crop and plunge into debt for five to ten years. 'That one loss has terrible repercussions because the farmer does not have seed and he can't afford fertiliser and so on,' said Gary. 'So even though an outbreak is rare, the farmer ends up with very bad problems, whereas on a large-scale commercial farm if one hectare is affected it doesn't matter. But if that half-hectare happens to be the whole farm, the farmer is sunk.' He said that the questioners were vaguely interested in his replies, but then asked 'What about democracy? What about government issues and gender issues, don't you think that is what is really important to the farmers?' And Gary told them frankly that he didn't believe that farmers without enough to eat are thinking about democracy and gender issues.

It was clearly not the answer they wanted to hear and they looked at him as if he was from another planet. They continued with 'What would you do to address gender inequity in Cambodia?' So he suggested that if you compare Cambodia to a western country you will see some gender inequity, but if you are a Cambodian comparing Cambodia today to the way it was twenty years ago, you would say things are not so bad. And whether you were a man or a woman, you would probably say that. 'If you spoke to a widowed farmer with five kids — and asked her what problems she is facing, gender equity is never going to come up in that conversation,' said Gary. 'She is going to talk about not having enough food, not having enough money, not having medicine, not being able to send her kids to school. She is not going to say 'Because I am a woman I cannot get a job or I am discriminated against.'

Chou Meng Tarr, the researcher who commented on levelling, stated that Cambodia has been fortunate because IRRI, with Australian support, decided to invest in generating local research capability. She stated that CIAP had set in motion the processes whereby more-relevant agricultural research and development could be carried out, but she also implied that more consideration of the role of women in agriculture was still needed.

At the village level it may be relatively easy to break down social and cultural barriers, particularly with so many households headed by women. On the other hand at the professional level, despite the success and leadership of women like Phaloeun and Mak Solieng, the educational and cultural barriers to Cambodian women participating in agricultural research and development are quite formidable. Rural Cambodian women are often not literate enough to study agriculture as a profession, and it is very clear that in urban societies agricultural science is not a preferred profession for women. It is considered neither prestigious nor lucrative and it requires unmarried women to spend time in the countryside, something most urban-based Cambodian women and their families reject.

In rural Cambodia girls are usually responsible for household chores and for the care of younger siblings as well as assisting with rice production, fetching firewood and water and looking after animals. So even when girls are not directly contributing to farm labour they are freeing up their mother's time. As a result girls have a lower rate of school enrolment after the age of ten than boys. About forty percent of rural women above the age of fifteen have never attended school, compared to twenty percent of men. In the lower secondary level, enrolment of girls is less than half of that for boys. The implications are wide reaching. Illiterate women may be perceived as inappropriate targets for information and training activities. This excludes them from learning about new farming techniques or equipment even though in many households both men and women jointly decide what kind of crops to plant. Females have a greater say in marketing, but men are more involved in farm management and pesticide use.

CIAP researchers discovered that most pesticides on sale in the markets in 1994 were extremely dangerous and had been banned or severely restricted in other countries and farmers were being cheated with diluted or fake products. They emphasised the need to curb pesticide use and called for a pesticide legislation to be enforced. Four years later the Cambodian government passed a law to regulate pesticides and the Agriculture Ministry directed that all pest management efforts should aim to reduce the use of pesticides.

Mr. Khiev Bunnarith, now head of pest management at CARDI, said that when CIAP started its pest management research most farmers thought that all insects in the field were pests. Now at least half of them know that spiders and some insects are natural enemies that help to control pests. Currently Cambodia's rice fields are relatively pesticide free and the natural enemies of insect pests are more diverse and in relatively greater numbers than in Thailand or Vietnam. Consequently Cambodia is considered a good place to develop some ecologically friendly pest management techniques. Unfortunately more intense agriculture will probably bring with it the risk of greater pesticide use regardless of research recommendations. This could lead to the accumulation of chemicals in the food chain, particularly in fish and other aquatic organisms.

Unfortunately it is difficult to convince some farmers about the dangers. 'If you tell poor farmers

"You are risking your health and you are risking the environment, you are going to kill birds and you are going to kill natural enemies, and you are destroying the environment by using this pesticide," it does not concern them much,' said Gary Jahn. 'Farmers risk their health and the environment every day in order to survive. And if it is a choice between risking cancer in twenty years and feeding their children today, they feed their children today and hope that twenty years on will take care of itself.'

The first step in the pest management program was to ask farmers what pests caused the most damage. Researchers interviewed over one thousand lowland rice farmers, in one hundred and fifty four villages, in ten provinces. They found farmers' names for different pests varied greatly from village to village, so it was difficult to know which pests the farmers were talking about. However, once a list was compiled the researchers were able to focus on the pests most likely to reduce yields and that farmers would probably be able to manage. They developed pest activity calendars and pest distribution maps to show when and where particular pests were most likely to be a problem, and then planned a pest management system.

Many farmers throughout Cambodia already used natural methods of pest control. For example farmers controlled crabs by spreading a local plant in the rice fields. They had to be careful because sap of the plants could cause blindness, and trapping crabs is undoubtedly safer and probably more sustainable. Some villages had community hunts to collect grasshoppers and crickets. The collected insects could be fried for eating, fed to farm animals or used in compost.

The researchers built on what farmers were already doing and assumed that what farmers were doing was correct. Introduction of outside technology without understanding the farmer context was a recipe for disaster.

Much of the credit for improved methods of pest management is due to the 'Farmer Field School' program run by the UN's Food and Agriculture Organisation (FAO) for the Ministry of Agriculture. The program conducted training courses for 'Master Trainers' who then went on to train ten to fifty other 'Trainers,' who in turn conducted the farmer field schools. The schools trained over ten thousand farmers directly, but the model was expanded by other organisations to teach more than ten times that number. CIAP staff acted as technical advisers to the program and ensured that during the courses the farmers also learnt other skills. The eventual effect was to both reduce pesticides and improve rice yields.

CIAP staff constantly received requests for advice on insect and disease outbreaks from all over the country. They provided information on how a problem could be tackled, and in many cases suggested alternatives to pesticides. One example was where farmers had been incorrectly applying a pesticide to control an outbreak of armyworms that had destroyed nearly a thousand rice seedbeds. In this case field tests by CIAP staff soon demonstrated that flooding the seedbeds with water was more effective than using pesticides.

On the other hand, emergency measures are sometimes needed to prevent more serious problems. The appearance in Phnom Penh markets of the 'Golden apple snail' and its sale to farmers in the provinces as a food source illustrated the ease with which a pest can enter a country. People did not know that the 'golden apple' snail was a danger to crops, but radio broadcasts and press releases soon after the discovery calling it the 'rice-eating snail' had good effect. One farmer in Pursat heard the broadcast and destroyed the golden snails he had just purchased. He in turn told his neighbours and word spread.

The snails were already a major rice pest in Nhge An Province of Vietnam where, despite a government ban, a fishing company had distributed them to farmers to use as a food source. I was told that beer drinkers tried the snails, but the eating quality was so poor that they soon lost interest. The snails spread, destroying rice fields and other crops almost overnight. Three years later the Vietnamese farmers of the area organised a community drive to destroy the snails in that province. They collected 23 tons of snails and 1.3 tons of eggs in just one day, yet the red egg masses soon re-appeared everywhere.

Insects, crabs and snails are not the only pest problems facing farmers. Rats attack all stages of the rice crop and farmers often regarded rat infestations as being, like the weather, a force that cannot be controlled. When rat populations build up farmers may lose their entire crop, sending them into a cycle of poverty from which they cannot escape.

A collaborative project between a Catholic Relief Service team and CIAP researchers in Svay Rieng Province illustrated how farmers and professional researchers can learn from each other in the search for a solution to a problem. The researchers suggested poison baiting would be more effective if farmers used coconut shells to keep the baits dry. Soon farmers improved on that by making bait stations of beer cans fixed on bamboo sticks. The cans were better at keeping bait dry than the coconut shells promoted by the researchers. They were also lighter, easily removed during the day to prevent pigs and dogs from eating the baits and then replaced at night. Researchers told farmers that baits must be placed over a wide area, that baiting single fields was not effective because most rats can move up to a kilometre a night and some 'tourist rats,' a Cambodian term for rats without a home range, move up to 5 km a week.

Farmers complained that some rat poisons were ineffective. Researchers analysed rat poisons sold in the markets and found that a purple powder on sale was a fake and others were diluted. Adding to the confusion, the rat poisons sold in the markets were without labels or with only Thai, Vietnamese or Chinese labels.

Farmers preferred hunting and digging out rat burrows to using bait stations. Hunting the rats at the beginning of the season was effective when groups of people took sticks and shovels to dig out rat burrows and kill all the rats. Rat hunts were relatively easy and low cost and for some farmers the rats were a source of meat for their families. Researchers advised that rat hunting, like baiting, had to involve the whole community if it was to be effective. Farmers often hunted rats in trees in recently flooded areas up to several kilometres away from their rice fields because they believed that such hunts would control rats before they migrated to their fields. Researchers told them that though rats in trees and those in rice fields look the same they are a different species, so farmers were probably killing the wrong rats, and the timing was also wrong. Killing fifty rats at the right time early in the season can prevent their multiplication to over twenty thousand later in the season. Thus although a well-timed rat hunt doesn't make headline scientific news, it is a very effective and appropriate technology for farmers, as well as being fun.

Researchers thought that if farmers used plastic fences and traps around early wet season crops it would help protect later rice crops, but that system failed to catch enough rats to justify the cost. On the other hand farmers successfully used the same type of plastic fence around their irrigated crops during the dry season. Some visiting professional rat researchers explained that the success might have been expected because during the dry season the irrigated rice crops were the only green crops and thus attracted rats.

Protection of crops from pests fitted into CIAP's major objective of increasing the amount of rice harvested from farmers' fields, but reducing other losses during threshing, storage and milling of harvested rice is also important.

Threshing produces 'rough rice' in which the grains are still covered by the protective 'hulls' or 'husks' which must be removed to give clean rice grains. The traditional method of removing husks was by pounding the rough rice with a pestle in a mortar. In recent years, however, Cambodia has seen increased mechanisation of the process in large commercial mills and small village mills. First the husks are removed to separate the 'brown' rice grains. Further milling then removes the outer coats of the grain, the bran, to produce white rice.

The CIAP engineering group helped a group of commercial millers in northern Cambodia to improve milling efficiency. Much of the white rice produced by the mills was cracked or broken and the Cambodians wanted to compete with Thai millers who were buying Cambodian rough rice at low prices and then selling it as top quality rice.

An expatriate adviser working with the Cambodian millers told Joe Rickman that the millers needed new equipment, but Joe said that before they spent a lot of money the CIAP engineers would test their milling machines. 'Basically all that we did was put a bag over every outlet of the mill and monitor it over time,' said Joe.

The variability between mills was phenomenal. Some mills had been producing only fifty-five percent white rice, with a high percentage of cracked and broken rice, while others obtained as much as sixty-eight percent. So the engineers checked when the millers were changing the rubber rollers and when they were re-facing the grinding stones. 'Generally the equipment was not the problem; it was just not properly maintained,' said Joe. 'We were lucky. The boys in engineering had never done any of this before, but by showing the millers what was happening they were able to fix their own problems.'

Sometime after that the millers formed an association of around two hundred members whose aim was to help each other maintain quality standards. Their mill capacities ranged from five thousand to ten thousand tons of milled rice per year.

The engineers also decided to check the small village mills that processed a basket of rice at a time. 'And that was another story,' said Joe. 'A farmer could take two baskets of rough rice to the mill and take only one home. They were losing fifteen percent of the good white rice and the question was why? The answer was simple — the miller kept the broken grains and the bran and the husks as payment for milling, so there was no incentive for him to improve the mill.'

Joe is a firm believer that if advisers actually measure things and show farmers or engineers the measurements, then they will make changes or adaptations very quickly. One of the problems he noted was the lack of equipment for weighing products, for measuring distance, and for recording moisture content of grain. All of these are critical to good management. By actually showing people the results of what they are doing they can then judge for themselves the benefit of making changes. 'If they don't change there is usually some other social or risk factor that we have not considered,' said Joe.

The full effect of increased mechanisation is yet to be determined. Two-wheel tractor units with attachments cost about the same as eight medium-sized working cattle and should be able to plough one hectare a day. That is equivalent to the work of about six pairs of oxen, and need only one operator instead of six — a driver for each pair of oxen. Tractors can also be used for small road vehicles that travel more quickly than cattle and buffalo, for driving water-pumps and for other mechanical tasks and they are not as easy to steal as cattle or buffalo. On the other hand, cattle and buffalo can convert weeds and rice straw to useful products like calves, draft power and fertiliser.

There are different risk factors. Cattle can get sick and die, or be stolen: tractors may break down. Cattle may increase in value as time progresses; tractors usually depreciate with time. Tractors are more powerful and the fields need less water for ploughing than when cattle and buffalo are used, but the contract cost per hectare is about the same whether a farmer hires a tractor or animals. On the other hand, labour could soon be a constraint in the northwest provinces where there is the greatest potential for crop expansion. Cambodia may eventually follow the same path as Thailand where rural labour shortages left no option other than to increase mechanisation.

Although machinery does have potential to change the farming system, it is as yet a small part of the rural scene. Livestock are closely interwoven with rice production and family life. The livestock industry has increased in parallel with rice production and neither can be properly studied or understood in isolation. Increased rice production provides more rice straw that in turn supports greater numbers of cattle and buffalo, while more cattle enable an increase in the area of rice cultivated. Animals that are stronger and healthier can plough fields more effectively and more quickly. By-products such as broken rice and rice bran are used for animal feeds and the increased availability of rice bran has increased pig numbers. Farmers that profit from rice and associated animal and fish production invest in more land and agricultural machinery, such as threshers, motorcycles and trailers, 2-wheel tractors, and portable pumps that in turn generate more income.

Livestock and fish contribute in different ways to the farming systems. Fish are most efficient at turning grain into protein — they are cold-blooded so do not use calories to keep warm, and their movement in water to search for food uses very little energy. Cattle if fed in an enclosure require around seven kilograms of grain to produce one kilogram of weight; pigs need about four kilograms of grain and chickens just over two kilograms, while catfish may use less than two kilograms of grain per kilogram of weight gain.

Cattle and buffalo, though raised mainly for ploughing and transport, are eventually slaughtered for food. Most Cambodian farmers are Khmer Buddhists whose religion prohibits killing animals, but they eat meat and commonly raise pigs and poultry. Cattle are generally slaughtered by Muslims of the Cham minority; and pigs by Chinese businesses. Ethnic minorities in northeast Cambodia believe in spirits that inhabit the environment and determine the fortunes of the people. They sacrifice animals but do not use cattle or buffalo for ploughing.

All these factors are interwoven into the farming system and the introduction of more profitable crop production and labour saving methods must take them into account. Sometimes the introduction of new technology has quite unexpected results. A local adviser told how he introduced a high yielding rice variety and fertiliser improvements to a village and how the farmers had doubled their rice yields. It seemed a great success story, but the adviser said it was not so great. He had gone back to the village to check on how the variety was performing and thought everyone would be growing twice the amount of rice. But instead a farmer told him 'Its great, now we only have to plant half as much.' In this case the farmer found it useful, but not in the way the adviser anticipated. It meant that the farmer had more time to do something else, or perhaps more land to plant other crops.

Some parts of the country, such as the northeastern Kratie province are yet to benefit. Most things are transported to Kratie by boat because roads can be impassable in the wet season, but at times it is dangerous to go by boat. CIAP had neglected the province because it was too expensive, the return on investment did not appear to be worthwhile and it was too difficult to supervise research. For example, on one occasion while Harry was away some of the CIAP Cambodian staff decided to organise experiments in Kratie Province. They gave money for the experiments to a man who simply kept it for himself and moved to Phnom Penh.

Despite these factors Harry thought the agricultural potential for the province was huge. He travelled to Kratie with CARDI staff in June 2001 and said that the province mainly needed infrastructure, particularly roads, and some technical support. Some provincial officers he met knew about CIAP because they had been to training courses, yet many local agricultural personnel had no idea of how to go about conducting field trials and extending technology to farmers. 'Too few had been educated to that level and though they have a fair bit of ability, they had no resources at all, no motorcycles and no money for supplies.' said Harry.

During the visit his group were introduced to a commune in Kratie province that was home to six hundred farm families. Most of them had grown just one crop of traditional rice each year and about one third of the families had been short of food for several months of the year. But in the previous year a farmer in the commune had purchased IR66 rice seed from another province, over fifty kilometres away. The seed was distributed to twenty-six families and they grew two crops of IR66 in that year and produced four to five times the rice they had been harvesting previously. The commune chief believed that if all farmers grew IR66 on part of their area the food shortage would be solved within two years.

10

*'Points of dispute between citizens,
however trifling, are taken to the
ruler.' (Chou Ta-Kuan, 1297)*

In parallel with CIAP's research and training program was the continuing saga of establishing a national institute for rice research and development. The national institute was expected to bring together a 'critical mass' of researchers to work on specific problems and to act as a focal point through which other organisations could interact. The original proposal for a 'Kampuchean Rice Research and Development Institute', designated 'KRRDI', was strongly endorsed by the government in IRRI's second year of co-operation with Kampuchea, well before Harry and his team took residence in the country.

It took another thirteen years of negotiations, planning, threats, promises, thumb prints, protests, gunshots, burnt buildings, disappointments, acceptances and name changes before the proposal became reality. Eventually in November 2000, as CIAP was drawing to a close, the 'Cambodian Agricultural Research and Development Institute', or 'CARDI' as it is commonly known, held its inauguration ceremony at its site at Prateah Lang, about sixteen kilometres southwest of Phnom Penh.

In December 1987 Dr. Swaminathan, the current IRRI Director General, wrote to Kampuchean Prime Minister Hun Sen to suggest setting up a project design team to prepare a plan for the speedy establishment of the institute. He also informed the Prime Minister that he had sought support and participation from the Government of India. Six months later Vice-Minister Chhea Song, four other Cambodians and IRRI's Glenn Denning and Greg Wells inspected four possible sites. Their decision to select a site at Prateah Lang, sixteen kilometres south of Phnom Penh was unanimous.

Besides being easily reached from Phnom Penh, an electricity supply was available from a glass factory nine kilometres away and, most importantly, the site was representative the rice-growing environment over large areas of the country. Enough water was also available from the Prek Thnot River only 2.3 kilometres away for thirty hectares of irrigation. So far so good!

It seemed that the only possible constraint to establishing KARRDI — the 'A' was added at this stage to include agriculture and make the name easier to pronounce — at Prateah Lang was relocation of farmers occupying the area or finding work for them at the new institute. The Ministry of Agriculture did not regard that as a major problem but indicated it was sensitive to the aspirations of the rural population and was approaching the whole matter with due care and consideration. It was a positive sentiment that was unfortunately not reciprocated by the farmers!

Analysis of the soil samples from the site indicated that it was indeed suitable, and Glenn Denning recommended to Vice Minister Chhea Song that the Cambodian authorities proceed to acquire the land. He also informed the Vice-Minister that a research station specialist, Dr. Ernie Nunn, would be engaged to help plan the institute.

Ernie Nunn, with the assistance of Ms. Chan Phaloeun, proceeded to develop a master plan for the institute soon after he arrived in Phnom Penh in October 1988. His plan included the layout of roads, fields, and irrigation systems, and the locations of buildings and other structures. The site was almost flat with less than one metre difference in elevation across the station. A month later he reported that the Department of Hydrology had started a topographical survey of the site and that he had paid $150 as an advance towards the cost; another $150 was due upon completion of the work. A well drilled to find a water supply for the laboratories reached hard rock at twenty-eight metres depth and produced water with good smell and taste.

The detailed site plan was completed at IRRI headquarters in February 1989, a month after Harry settled in Phnom Penh. The summary read:

'From the front gate the approach to the building complex is via a straight road approximately 800 m in length. The road will be built up 75 cm above the rice fields and should provide a good view of experiments that may be conducted on either side of the approach road. As one enters KARRDI the administration building will be on the right with the tory building on the left. The farm and the service buildings are located on the south side in order to facilitate easy movement of farm equipment and staff to and from the service centre. The dormitory and cafeteria building is centrally located in order to provide convenient access from other buildings. The houses are located to the northwest and some distance from the main buildings in order to provide privacy and a quiet atmosphere. All buildings are to be of a single storey design and constructed of locally available materials with the exception of imported items of plumbing, cement, and reinforcement steel. The design will be similar to buildings found in the area for which local contractors and craftsman have the required skills to construct.'

A good plan, but it would not be built in the near future.

Harry met with the Phnom Penh Municipal Agricultural Officer soon after he arrived in Kampuchea and subsequently expressed his concerns for the future of the two hundred families on the KARRDI site. No provision had been made to relocate the families because the government considered it 'owned' the land and should be able to 'resume' it at will. However, the operation would not be that simple.

It was quite clear that no funding agency would be willing finance KARRDI until the area was officially designated for its development and the farmers had fully agreed to the take-over. Harry considered that the farmers should be compensated, but the Kampuchean Government had not budgeted for doing so, so he wrote to Glenn Denning suggesting that $200,000 should be reserved in the IRRI budget for that purpose. He concluded, 'I have not mentioned this to any other person in fear of raising false hopes. However, I strongly feel that this would be a prudent move.'

Harry was also concerned with the lack of provision for maintenance and administration of KARRDI after construction was completed. If KARRDI were to be successful outside sources would need to provide one hundred percent of the funding of the institute for at least ten years. At that time Soviet countries were still providing the government with all its official fuel and subsidizing general government administration expenses. It was expected that the government budget would be severely cut after a peace settlement, particularly if the Soviets withdrew their support. One possibility was to extend the project, and Harry was certain that it would be needed for at least five to ten years more.

Glenn Denning reported these matters in a memo to the new IRRI Director General, Dr. Klaus Lampe.

'You will note Dr. Nesbitt's concern regarding sustained support for the (proposed) Kampuchean Rice Research and Development Institute (KARRDI). Kampuchea is an unusual case in that the Government is almost entirely financed from outside sources —currently the Soviet Union. This situation is unlikely to improve for another decade, even though the source of support may shift. As a result, we cannot readily apply the old principle of 'counterpart' contributions for such items as maintenance of facilities, or even for land compensation and local staffing. I suggested to Dr. Nesbitt that we explore the possibility of an endowment for operating and maintenance costs of KARRDI — perhaps US$2.0 million that would 'run down' over a 10 to 15 year period. By then, hopefully, Kampuchea would be in a better financial position and could run KARRDI independently.'

While these negotiations were taking place a more detailed soil survey of the area was completed and the soil samples from the survey were packed ready to be sent to the Philippines for chemical analysis. It had taken all of April to prepare export papers, but the customs personnel said they were not correct and refused exit permits.

By May the next year the only progress was a change of name. Kampuchea had reverted back to the old name of Cambodia and KARRDI became 'CARRDI', the 'Cambodian Rice Research and Development Institute. The extra 'R' was removed later. There was still no confirmed funding for such an institute but IRRI scientists in both Cambodia and the Philippines were expected to play a major role in its development.

Harry emphasised that any request to the Australian government for money to establish the institute should include full details on the purpose of each unit and its management. He wanted special emphasis placed on CARRDI's co-ordinating role in the national research process and its training potential. Copies of the proposal were given to the Ministry of Agriculture leaders, but they had 'too many other things (drought included) on their minds to make any quick decisions.'

Meanwhile the Department of Agronomy commenced negotiations with the farmers occupying the land at Prateah Lang, and early in January 1990 the farmers agreed to sell their land for the Cambodian currency equivalent of US$230 per hectare. In addition to the money, the farmers were promised the use of unused land and first preference for work as labourers at the institute. They all agreed to this proposal and endorsed their consent with a thumb-print. However, Cambodia's agricultural policy had changed in the previous year and the farmers soon learned that they could now apply for titles to the land that they still farmed.

The next problem faced was the inability of the Cambodian Government to pay the farmers. It could not even buy fuel for the city electricity supply. Harry again proposed that project funds be used as a grant to the Government to compensate displaced farmers. This time he estimated that only US$40,000 would be needed if the transaction could be made soon and wrote to Glenn, stating: 'We realise that land compensation is usually regarded as a recipient country expense. However, the miserable state of the Cambodian economy leaves us with no real alternative but to make an exception in this case.'

In 1990 Denning received advice from the Australian government that though it supported the concept of developing CARRDI it could not commit a large amount for establishing the institute in the current unstable political climate of Cambodia. Nor could AusAID agree to use project funds for land compensation. IRRI was requested to strongly encourage the Cambodian government to meet the expense.

Cambodia's severe financial difficulties continued and the farmers were not paid until September. By then the value of the purchase contracts, paid in the local currency, had fallen from US$230 to around US$100 per hectare. Since US dollars were almost solely used in the markets this currency depreciation reduced the real value farmers would receive to less than half of that originally expected. They reluctantly accepted the contracts but were obviously not happy with the price.

In early 1991 Harry again offered to arrange for farmers to be paid the full amount. He considered that since the farmers would be the Institute's neighbours an investment of CIAP funds would be well worthwhile to ensure that they were happy. However, he was told by the Ministry of Agriculture not to worry and was later informed that the farmers were satisfied. Land prices were beginning to rise in Phnom Penh but the effect had not yet reached the countryside.

However, over the next few months the arrival of personnel of the United Nations Transitional Authority in Cambodia (UNTAC) dramatically increased all land prices in and near Phnom Penh as UN money flowed into Cambodia. More dissatisfaction was caused when speculators offered some farmers near CARRDI ten times the real price. No money was forthcoming, but the farmers' expectations had been raised.

Harry continued to search for financial support and was pleased when the local United Nations Development Program (UNDP) officials offered to provide up to US$700,000 for the establishment of

CARRDI, the maximum that their Phnom Penh Office had authority to approve. Harry expected that the UNDP money plus an allocation of $400,000 from the Australian budget would be more than adequate for CARRDI development for at least the next ten years.

By June the following year, 1992, some work on roads and canals had commenced at the CARRDI site and the Prateah Lang farmers were showing increasing animosity towards the project activities. There was little or no support from government agencies and one district official was actually co-ordinating the unrest. Another senior local official virtually told the villagers that they could do as they wished. CIAP contractors and staff members were threatened with knives, axes and gunshots. The Government responded to CIAP's concerns with the announcement that other possible sites would be examined.

By September prospects for establishing CARDI at Prateah Lang were dim. In October the 'Cambodia Times' reported, 'An International Research Institute (IRRI) proposal for the construction of the Cambodian Rice Research and Development Institute (CARRDI) is in danger of being forever grounded after some 200 farmers residing in the chosen site refused to vacate the area.'

'The price of land had started to escalate,' said Harry. 'All the farmers had accepted the original offer, by thumb print and signature, and some bought more land closer to their home. But UNTAC was here, elections were approaching, and immediately the price of land skyrocketed — from $100 to $200 to $400 to $1600 per hectare and more. The farmers felt cheated and saw that if they protested they could get more money, and they apparently had support from one of the political groups.' Agents who expected to receive a share of the money also worked to involve the farmers.

All of these forces combined to stir up the farmers in the neighbouring Kork Ksarch Village. Some villagers cut the access road to the CARDI site by digging a big trench across it and threatened to burn the vehicles, excavators, bulldozers and dump trucks if they operated any further. Other villagers working as labourers at the site were threatened and pressured in their home village to stop work. 'And this occurred despite our continued efforts to try to come to some arrangement with them,' said Harry.

There was nothing much that Harry and other CIAP personnel could do. It was a government matter and they were not really involved. Pressure was mounting all the time and Chhea Song, who was by then the First Secretary of State, kept asking whether CARDI should really be established at Prateah Lang or not. Harry said it was up to the Ministry of Agriculture and gave a list of reasons why they should either continue with Prateah Lang or move to another site. Prateah Lang was the obvious choice because it was so representative of farmland in much of Cambodia. It was an ideal site on a good road with a nice area for constructing buildings.

A bullet fired through the gate of the IRRI Villa the

day Harry returned from Australia in May 1993 demonstrated an even more militant attitude by disgruntled landowners from the Prateah Lang site. The gate was just below his apartment and Harry considered the bullet definitely a warning. 'One guy had threatened to cut out my liver and eat it while I was still alive, and they put a bounty on my head,' said Harry. 'I was only worth $1,500, but in the local community $1,500 was a lot of money. Things got worse and they threatened that a big mob would destroy our little house on the site. Our guys removed their personal belongings then the villagers burnt the building down. They just set fire to the building and watched it burn.'

By January 1994 it appeared that the Prateah Lang site was lost and a new site was sought for CARRDI. One block of sixty hectares of land about sixteen kilometres from Phnom Penh appeared a possibility. It was surrounded by a wall and designated as industrial land, but the owners had already received offers of US$100,000 per hectare. 'Affordable' land was more than an hour from Phnom Penh and an institute that far away would have trouble keeping its staff. Land was available at a price, but 'agents' were charging US$400 per hectare to negotiate the transfer, so purchase of any large parcel of land from small landholders would not be cheap. Furthermore, probably no amount was 'affordable' to Cambodia's bankrupt government. The alternative was to use other government owned land.

The main possibility was the Kap Srau site developed and then abandoned by the failed Russian mechanised farming project. Unfortunately the site was inferior to Prateah Lang. The soils were different from most rice growing areas and had been ploughed deeply by the big Russian machines, and therefore not representative of typical farmland. It was closer to Phnom Penh so there would also be more problems with bird and rat damage. However, after another visit to the site and further discussions with the Ministry Glenn and Harry decided they could not afford any further delay in establishing CARDI and reluctantly agreed to accept Kap Srau. Adding to the urgency, the UNDP advised that it would withdraw the $700,000 committed over a year earlier if work was not soon started. It seemed that it was necessary to accept the Kap Srau site or to discard CARRDI as a project objective altogether.

By that time almost $200,000 had already been spent in short-term consultancies and infrastructure development at the Prateah Lang site and though they had already spent years attempting to resolve the dispute without success, Harry and the Ministry representatives considered that Prateah Lang was still worth another try.

By March 1994 another round of meetings had taken place with no progress in sight. Harry thought the Agriculture Ministry wanted to take the easy way out and go to Kap Srau but he was reluctant to admit defeat just yet. The Ministry had not relinquished its right to the one hundred and seventy hectares at Prateah Lang, but neither had the farmers shown any interest in giving up the land without more money.

They would not leave for less than US$2,500/ha, and nobody could be certain that they or other claimants would not cause trouble again.

After more long discussions with Secretary of State for Agriculture Chhea Song and others Glenn and Harry concluded, with great regret, that the Prateah Lang site was not retrievable. The Director of the Agronomy Department then decided on Kap Srau for CARRDI and advised Chhea Song of his conclusion. Just one day later, Chhea Song told Harry that he would continue negotiations for Prateah Lang. 'The waiting game would be a lot easier if we had even a small inkling of what each player was thinking,' wrote Harry to Glenn Denning. 'Meanwhile I'm avoiding UNDP personnel in an attempt to delay an adverse decision regarding their funding.'

Four years later, in September 1998, a letter was sent to HE Chhea Song, Secretary of State, on behalf of AusAID asking if a final decision on the establishment of the proposed Cambodian Agricultural Research and Development Institute could soon be made. The letter stated that AusAID's assumption that CARDI would have been created much earlier as an organisation with a clear management structure at Prateah Lang had 'not proved to be a correct assumption.'

Eventually, however, CARDI was established at Prateah Lang. One hundred hectares of the original one hundred and seventy were sold off and the funds distributed to the farmers. The new 'Royal

Government of Cambodia' received title to the remaining seventy hectares and 'The Cambodian Agricultural Research and Development Institute' was
officially established by government sub-decree
Number 74 of August 1999. The development plan
was completed and construction of CARDI commenced on the original site, more than ten years after the land was originally selected. CARDI became
operational at the beginning of 2000 with over forty
professional staff, of whom most had been trained
through CIAP. Some were still completing post-
graduate training abroad.

The culmination of the negotiations and hard work
was an International Conference held at CARDI in
October 2000 on 'The Impact of Agricultural Research for Development in Southeast Asia'. The conference was a great success despite floodwater washing out the entrance road. The first bus got bogged
and a group of Japanese participants in beautiful
suits walked all the way from the front gate. 'They
were covered in perspiration and with mud on their
shoes and the legs of their trousers, but as happy as
could be,' said Harry. 'They felt that was just part of
being at CARDI, part of the atmosphere. CARDI was
looking beautiful, the lawns were neatly trimmed,
banners were fluttering in the breeze and colourful
posters were displayed all around the verandas.'

A lot of time and effort had gone into organising
the conference and it impressed many international visitors. Harry had invited the new Australian
Ambassador to Cambodia, Ms. Louise Hand, to the

opening ceremony. He recalled that on the way to coffee after the opening a man came over, pushed in between them and said to Harry, 'I have to tell you, that this is the best conference that I have ever been to, you must be proud of all that you have done here, CIAP is a fantastic project.' The Ambassador started laughing and said it was a set up, but the man turned to her and said that he had never met Harry before.

They then walked out to the reception area where Joe Rickman was talking. Harry started to introduce her to Joe, but then said 'Oh I am sorry, first I would like to introduce you to David Catling who is working on a World Bank Project.' David immediately said something like 'I know you want to talk with Joe, but I must say before I go that you should be commended for getting this all together. It is really an amazing institute, an achievement of which you should be proud.' Outside at coffee another person said the same thing, and as the Ambassador walked away she said she would not believe any more of those words. A few minutes later she came back to tell Harry that each person she talked with had said exactly the same thing and that he must have done a great job in going around and convincing everybody.

Harry said that it was pleasing to receive such comments and acknowledgement from farmers and others of the project's contribution to increasing agricultural production and developing CARDI. He also said that it was nice working in the new facilities but that he derived the most satisfaction from seeing his Cambodian colleagues develop as confident scientists. 'Our dreams of CIAP living on lie firmly in the hands of the CARDI staff and Ministry and provincial staff,' said Harry. 'The capacity is there. So long as the will remains, continued production improvements for farmers are a real possibility.'

At the Institute's official inauguration ceremony the next month, on 21 November 2000, Prime Minister Hun Sen stated in his address:

> *'I am confident that CARDI will be instrumental in rais-ing public awareness on the benefits of research. More importantly the institute will play a crucial role in link-ing up researchers, extension workers and farmers, an important factor in agricultural modernisation in Cam-bodia.'*[22]

During my month in Phnom Penh I used a desk in one of the offices of the CARDI 'Training and Con-ference Centre.' It was next door to Harry's spacious corner office that looked out across the fields to the neighbouring Kork Ksarch village, the village at the centre of the controversy over establishment of CARDI. I shared the room with Lingling Domingo, Harry's Filipino administrative assistant, and Simon Moore, an Australian journalist who was working as a volunteer to prepare a history of CARDI and help Harry to complete his final reports. Outside a windmill pumping water for the laboratories gave an Australian look to the surroundings, as did the wide verandas encircling the main buildings. The verandas were functional in keeping the heat of the tropical sun off the walls and providing a sheltered place to walk during rain. Some of the Cambodians,

22. From the Address by Prime Minister of the Royal Government of Cambodia Samdech Hun Sen. (November 21, 2000).

however, lamented that the buildings were not in Khmer style, even though they appreciated the protection of the verandas.

CARDI is now considered to be a world-class research and development centre, fully equipped with modern and useful facilities and equipment. Fourteen years earlier most of the present staff had never seen a computer, now most have one on their desks. A well known rice research leader from the Philippines stated that 'CARDI is a legacy of CIAP to Cambodian agriculture, an excellent product of the financial and technical support of Australia and IRRI to Cambodia. The project has spent $24 million, but if spent elsewhere it would not have made such an impact. CARDI is a legacy of co-operation that must be sustained for the benefit of Cambodian farmers.'

It is only a short walk from the buildings to the CARDI boundary adjoining Kork Ksarch village. After all the animosity there is now an improving relationship between CARDI and the two hundred and forty seven families in the village.

'You can understand why they stirred things up so long,' said Harry. 'The original agreement was that the farmers could use the land until it was required. CARDI was to use five hectares the first year, ten the next year and so on. In the meantime the farmers could use the land. But the farmers considered, without it being known to us, that land was land and trees were trees and they were not the same. People were renting the trees, so every time a tree was knocked down they wanted us to compensate them for that tree. They also felt the same way about the canals and everything else. When we dug a trench to get soil for the main access road a woman claimed ownership for the trench and rented it out as a fishpond. She made more money from that trench than she would have made by using the same piece of land to grow rice.'

'After the second round of negotiations we made it very clear that the land included the trees and everything else on it and the farmers were not allowed to go back onto the land. But they are CARDI's neighbours and even during the conflict we constructed a school and a meeting area in the village.' Harry stopped for a moment. 'I hope the farmers are happy now', he said. 'They received an average of five thousand dollars per hectare, a lot of money. It would have been very difficult for them to get that much money otherwise.'

Mr. Kep Poch of Chan Phaloeun's farming systems group took me to visit Ms. Pol Sran, one of his contacts in Kork Ksarch. She was a woman of about fifty years of age with betel nut stained teeth living in a small house on stilts that almost touched the CARDI boundary. The earthen-floored area beneath her house where we talked was enclosed on three sides for storage and sitting. Six children from nearby houses, her relatives, watched our interpreted conversation with serious eyes. Puppies and chickens moved in and out and I felt the beat of a fowl's wings as it flew off a cupboard near my head.

Pol Sran told us that she had lived there for over twenty years. Her husband had moved away with a second wife, so she was head of the household. She owned a rice field of 800 square metres on the far side of the village and grew one rice crop each year. She said she could not afford to buy fertiliser and in good years harvested only one tonne of rough rice that gave 600 kilograms of milled rice. In years of low rainfall it was only about half that amount.

Pol Sran had recently changed her rice variety, but obtained the seed from a neighbouring village, not from CARDI. To augment her income she distils alcohol from broken rice grain bought in the market and sells the alcohol in the village. The rice mash remaining after distilling is fed to her four pigs and she makes a small profit from the operation. Two large sacks of rice hulls standing against the wall contained fuel for distilling. She also cultivates mangoes, bananas, jack fruit, longan and custard apple in the small area around her house.

Although Pol Sran did not work at CARDI she was glad that she could collaborate with the Farming Systems group. Mr. Kep Poch had supplied her with her fruit trees and vegetable seeds and by growing those she saved the money that she would otherwise need to spend in the market.

Nevertheless she had some complaints — she said that even though she could see the buildings from her house she knew next to nothing about CARDI. She also said that even when she had permission to go in to the institute it was very hard to get past the security guard. On one occasion she had waited an hour near an office for the people she wanted to see. 'I stood in one spot because I was afraid that if I moved the security guard would send me out.' she said forcefully. She does not talk much to her neighbours but says that they now accept that CARDI is there and that she herself would like to know more about what CARDI is doing. As we left she jokingly suggested that I should pay her ten dollars for the interview.

Employment at CARDI provides regular income for twenty of the villagers. Others work in Phnom Penh's garments factories. Kep Poch arranged for two of the CARDI workers to come into the CARDI training centre after finishing their morning work. There he translated their stories for me. Both were farmers from the Kork Ksarch village and their smiles and sparkling eyes suggested that they enjoyed talking about their situation.

They were born in the district and had been working five or six years with CARDI. Ms. Sheing Maiy owned 0.2 hectares of rice (two thousand square metres) and Ms. Khean Sokkim owned 0.4 hectares. Both said that their rice crops depended on the rain and that the land was not productive because it was not level. They considered that if it was in better condition they could use improved technology. One of them had a water pump, but she said the soil is so porous that the water soon drains away. They also said that before CARDI was finally established there was a lot of antagonism in the village, but those working at the institute are now happy because of the work it provides. Others still have some reservations.

More consistent interaction with Kork Ksarch village farmers is something that Gary Jahn thought was an opportunity for a mutual partnership that CARDI had so far missed. He was sure the previous resentment was nothing that could not be overcome. 'After we moved our office up to CARDI in 2000, the first thing that I would do each morning was to walk into that village next door,' said Gary. 'I would hand out information about crops in leaflets printed in English on one side and Khmer on the other. At first people were curious about what I was doing, but after I kept on doing it they were quite happy to see me and to get that information. They started asking questions and telling me about the kind of pest problems they had and things like that. It was very good; it helped me to ground our research in reality. I think that is still something that CARDI could capitalise on, that very close proximity to rice farmers.'

The Buddhist temple in the village can also be seen from CARDI and occasionally Gary would walk there, not to distribute literature, but just to talk to people and see what they were doing. 'The temple is a community centre and if you occasionally show up there I think it shows that you are part of the community.' he said.

Mr. Ty Channa, head of the Training and Information Centre where I interviewed the two farm workers, said that his group has been very successful in the past two years. Each year his group conducted fifteen to eighteen training courses for aid groups, government institutions and international organisations. Most were conducted in the CARDI training centre, but some group training for NGOs was provided in the provinces.

Ty Channa was only eight years old at the beginning of the Khmer Rouge period and eleven when it finished. Children were forced to work very hard in the fields and received no education at all. They were never told the purpose of the work and were too young to understand what it was all about. Later he learnt the value of education and as he sat behind his desk in front of book filled shelves he told me how he reached his present position.

Eight years after release from the Khmer Rouge Channa travelled to Bulgaria and studied for seven years to complete his Masters degree in general agriculture and plant breeding. Back in Cambodia he worked at a government experiment station, but after attending several CIAP training courses became the CIAP training co-ordinator. IRRI training staff from the Philippines helped him to develop training programs with different methods of teaching, schedules and curricula, the use of overhead projectors, making charts and so forth. Channa extended his experience with two trips to Australia to learn more about managing training programs and the use of assessments to determine what trainees needed. He said that the trainees make good use of the library next door where Ms. Socheata, who joined Phaloeun on our trip to Prey Yutka many years earlier, is the librarian.

CARDI is still a small institute and the government must treat it as a valuable resource in which to invest. Researchers who trained overseas are offered attractive opportunities outside of CARDI, so a continuing problem will be to keep qualified staff. Payment of adequate salaries by the government; good working conditions; promotion on the basis of competence; opportunities to attend conferences and training courses and effective delegation of responsibility in work programs may help retain present staff. Staff numbers will also need to increase as the institute assumes responsibility for new enterprises and complex farming systems.

'All of the people who worked with CIAP and now at CARDI could have left CIAP ten years ago with twice the salary,' said Harry. 'Phaloeun was offered three times her salary for one position and later it would have sky rocketed. But out of loyalty she did not go.' He said that unfortunately CARDI had developed a management system of specific teams consisting of a team leader, a senior researcher and a research assistant. If there were originally three highly qualified persons in a team, one position was demoted and the related salary was reduced. It was not widely discussed beforehand and the reaction was negative. Those that had their salary cut without being told the reason felt that they had been devalued, and that it was time for them to leave.

Most of those who left CIAP or CARDI continued work in agriculture; some in senior positions with development projects, others as consultants to national and international development organisations. Dr. Mak Solieng is an example of the ambitions and conflicting loyalties that tugged at those individuals.

Mak Solieng was head of farming systems socio-economics at CARDI until she took extended leave to do consulting work and voluntary work for other organisations. Her original training was in agricultural science, but her study in Australia and Cambodia for her Ph.D. was an outstanding socio-economic study of a rural community. It was considered to be better than some professional non-Cambodian social scientists could accomplish, partly because she had a better grasp of the language, but perhaps more importantly because she understood more about village level agriculture. Almost every week she went to the country, often staying in a farmer's house for three or four days.

Solieng told me that people often asked if she intended to return to CARDI, but said she had worked for ten years with CIAP and wanted to gain new experience and to benefit financially. She also said that she had built her career on what she had learnt from CIAP and would have liked to train someone else to take over her responsibilities at CARDI. But she had felt the CARDI management system was too strict and too time consuming — it might take a week to get permission to go on a field trip or to obtain a cash advance. 'I didn't like that,' said Solieng. 'Harry always allowed me to be independent. All I needed to do was to be well organised and to say what we needed. Then we could move very fast. We had to get approval, but the process was faster. Now at CARDI people have to write a permission letter for everything.'

'CARDI is new, so we face many challenges,' said its Director, Dr. Men Sarom, when I talked with him in his office in the main administration building. 'With CIAP we were working with everything provided for us, and we were accustomed to that pattern of work for more than ten years. The government working culture is not what we should be doing in this institute, so we encounter many problems, management problems, planning problems, accounting problems, regulation problems. CARDI is a semi-autonomous institute and we will need to work as independently as possible.'

'In support of Men Sarom, the CARDI problem is typical of top down Cambodian management style.' said Harry. 'CIAP provided an environment where responsibility was delegated to the team. They had to take control of their own lives to generate the technology and this was helped along for twelve or thirteen years by the expatriates telling them it is your life, your program and your decision. It was a great environment in the CIAP office in Phnom Penh, it was vibrant, and regularly people would walk in and say that they could feel it.'

'CIAP has been our primary source of new ideas and technologies.' remarked one provincial officer. 'Without such a source of information our efforts to improve Cambodian agriculture would have been far less effective. We know that in the future we will be looking to CARDI for this same assistance. We respect CARDI's scientists, but the institute is like a young bird. It is now healthy and has strong feathers, but it has never flown by itself. What will happen when it leaves the nest?'

11

'Two days of the week are feast days,
three are undistinguished, and two
days are of evil omen. On some days
it is auspicious to travel to the east;
on others one must go westward.'
(Chou Ta-Kuan, 1297)

The conflict between government and farmers over the establishment of CARDI was not surprising considering what was happening in the rest of the country. One UN advisor was quoted as saying 'Continuing strife is the biggest thing that affects sustainability of anything in Cambodia. Nothing is sustainable without some hope that you can plan for the future, which is what sustainability is all about.'

The IRRI project was warmly welcomed to war-torn Cambodia in 1986 — yet it was another fifteen years before a fragile peace came to Cambodia. For those fifteen years the CIAP team sustained their efforts in an environment of continued fighting and manoeuvring between different factions in the country.

A meeting between Kampuchean resistance leader Prince Sihanouk and Kampuchea's Premier Hun Sen in Paris in 1987, the year after IRRI commenced working with Kampuchea, was expected to pave the way for a political settlement. Vietnam had reaffirmed its intention to withdraw its soldiers as soon as foreign support for the resistance on the Thai border ended and appeared ready to talk about changes, largely as a result of increased Soviet pressure. The Chinese were believed to have told their Soviet counterpart at the UN that China would not seek to impose a Khmer Rouge regime on a post-war Kampuchea. Hun Sen and Sihanouk agreed that the Kampuchean people themselves must resolve the conflict in order to end the war and the bloodshed and to rebuild a peaceful, independent, democratic, sovereign, neutral, and non-aligned Kampuchea.

The Vietnamese withdrawal in 1989 led to the creation of a coalition government of all four factions including representatives of the Khmer Rouge. The country was still deeply scarred. Schools, pagodas, hospitals and other public buildings were crumbling. The University looked derelict with its broken windows and unkempt campus. Nearly eighty percent of the population in Phnom Penh had no piped water and poor people had to buy water by the drum at a cost equivalent to the daily wage of a civil servant. Repatriation of refugees from camps in Thailand had begun, but only ten percent of the young people born and raised in the camps aspired to be farmers in the new Cambodia. Even if they wished to farm they did not know how. Adding to the uncertainty was the continual conflict between factions.

Two years later a United Nations Transitional Authority in Cambodia (UNTAC) was set up to implement the Paris Peace Accords and to restore peace and civil government. It was to supervise 'free and fair' elections leading to a new constitution and to 'kick-start' the rehabilitation of the country. UNTAC involved 15,900 military personnel, 3,600 civilian police, 2,000 civilians and 450 UN Volunteers, as well as locally recruited staff and interpreters. The well-paid UN personnel poured money into Cambodia and boosted the local economy. 'All those people spent money,' said Betty Nesbitt. 'They bought things; they rented houses, employed maids and other help, purchased food in the market and brought in a lot of vehicles. It seemed everybody got some money. And they left the country with a lot of English speaking drivers and office staff.'[23]

The UNTAC operation was difficult to implement, notably because of the lack of co-operation from the Khmer Rouge. In the period leading up to the elections scheduled for May 1993 the Khmer Rouge leadership took advantage of any agreements that strengthened its hand while ignoring those that did not. It gained access to the entire territory of Cambodia without opening the zones it controlled near the borders to the scrutiny of international observers; it watched others disarm while refusing to demobilise its own forces; it benefited from participating in the legitimate political structure without submitting its own actions to UNTAC surveillance. And when the Khmer Rouge again declared war and started killing ethnic Vietnamese

23. Peter White said that nightlife was much livelier during UNTAC times and bars and restaurants lamented its passing. A year or two later a big bar with lots of staff and girls would have maybe only two or three foreign patrons. 'The few agricultural scientists were not big spenders or wild people who were going to spend a lot of money and keep all these people employed.' said Peter.

many of those still living in Cambodia decided that it would be safer to flee to Vietnam.

The elections succeeded despite not taking place in the proposed neutral, peaceful, free environment. Nearly ninety percent of the population voted in what were the first real elections ever held in Cambodia. Prince Ranariddh's FUNCINPEC party won most seats in the new assembly, and when Hun Sen's Cambodian People's Party failed to gain its expected electoral victory, it rejected the results. Prince Sihanouk feared a coup and compromised by organising a coalition 'provisional national Government' with Prince Ranariddh and Hun Sen as co-premiers. He then returned to the throne as King and the provisional government was renamed the Royal Government of Cambodia.

The Khmer Rouge still refused to disarm and ended co-operation with UNTAC. They boycotted the elections and later launched an unsuccessful military campaign. Its army, isolated in the remote western provinces of the country and increasingly dependent on gem smuggling for money, suffered a series of military defeats and grew weaker year by year.

The coalition in Phnom Penh maintained the peace for three years during which time the two major parties remained independent factions. Virtually every state body — from police commissariats to ministerial departments — had a dual-command structure, though Hun Sen's Cambodian People's Party retained a crucial advantage over the courts, subprovincial authorities, police and the army. The two

parties appeared to co-operate surprisingly well until July 1997 when Hun Sen staged a coup. After two
days of fighting his soldiers took control of Phnom
Penh and its outskirts and rampaged through the
city, looting televisions, washing machines and air
traffic control equipment. This coup was despite an
announcement two years earlier that

'The two parties agree to refrain from attacking
each other from this day on … and to form a coalition government based on the supreme interests of
the nation.'

The period leading up to the coup had been one
of ever-increasing tension. Both major parties had
used the label of 'national reconciliation' to cover
their alliance building. For one party it meant returning to the anti-Vietnamese rhetoric of pre-1993
and re-embracing former allies. For the other, it
meant using wealth and power to exploit internal
differences within the opposing party. Both had initiated contacts with segments of the Khmer Rouge
and their competition for its allegiance contributed
to its demise as various segments within the Khmer
Rouge defected to the coalition.

Despite the tragic excesses of Pol Pot's Khmer Rouge
and its eventual defeat, a lingering regard for Pol
Pot persisted among some sections of the population. An article in 'The Cambodia Daily' in June 2001
by Seth Mydans of 'The New York Times' illustrated
that regard.

'Only the buzz of cicadas and the croaking of frogs
break the silence in the remote Dangrek Mountains
where under a makeshift tin roof, lies the grave of

Pol Pot, one of the 20th century's worst mass killers, who left behind him a country stunned and ruined. He died on April 18, 1998, at the age of 73, still professing his innocence and complaining about his confinement. His name has become a code word for horror in Cambodia: 'the Pol Pot time.' Yet many Cambodians say they do not know whether to blame him for what happened. Few understood what was happening or why, only that they were sick, starving, exhausted and in fear for their lives. What is most unsettling to an outsider is not that the grave has been forgotten, but that it has been remembered. People go there for lottery numbers, others say they pray to him for health and good luck. Some say his spirit can cure disease. Until peace came to Cambodia the two friends who tend the grave saw nothing but fighting and privation. Recruited successively by the various armies that passed through the jungles they were at times enemies, at times allies. On occasion, they said, they shot at each other. 'It didn't matter to me who won,' said one. 'If they ordered me to fight, I fought. I wasn't trying to make anybody win.'

In contrast, another article in the same newspaper reported a former Khmer Rouge intellectual's contrition for the part that he played. Mey Mann, then 80, said he never should have become involved with Saloth Sar, later known by his revolutionary name of Pol Pot, and that he should never have joined the movement that became the Khmer Rouge. He said that he joined the movement because he thought something good would come out of it. On many later occasions he tried to understand why the Khmer Rouge had turned to the killing fields, but nobody knew.

'I don't know why it happened like that, why they tried the extreme way,' Mey Mann said.

The removal of Pol Pot and the path toward democracy did not alter Cambodian attitudes to Vietnam. Coloured by centuries of bitter history, Cambodians remain suspicious. My friend and interpreter Hieng Sokchea said that the reason it took only four or five months to get rid of the Khmer Rouge was that almost everyone hated them. It was a very cruel and barbarous regime enforced by young uneducated farmers pressed into service as soldiers. 'Some say the movement of Vietnam into Cambodia in 1979 was liberation and others say occupation,' said Sokchea. 'But most Cambodians were about to die of starvation, with nothing to eat, so the Vietnamese could take the opportunity to stay in Cambodia.' He added that the dislike of the Vietnamese stemmed in part from the ten-year occupation by the Vietnamese army, but a bigger part was the anti-Vietnamese propaganda that they were fed under the Khmer Rouge.

Gary Jahn said that many of the Cambodians that he worked with saw the Vietnamese occupation as somehow a continuation of the Khmer Rouge. It was like — we still have a military state and they blamed the Vietnamese, whereas outsiders would reason that the Vietnamese overthrew the Khmer Rouge. Most Cambodians only knew that their life was bad and they were suffering, and it was not clear whom to blame. Under the Khmer Rouge all their suffering was blamed on the Vietnamese and then the Vietnamese really came, so it seemed as if what Pol Pot said was true. Gary said that he had heard co-workers say that Pol Pot was the only one who stood up to the Vietnamese. 'But Pol Pot antagonised the Vietnamese to the point that they had to occupy the country to stop him from going to war. But most don't see it that way,' said Gary.

Once when Gary had his hair cut in Phnom Penh he noticed that a Cambodian barber spoke Vietnamese with the other barbers. Gary asked him how he learnt Vietnamese, and the Cambodian barber said it was because his wife was Vietnamese. When Gary recounted this story at work his listeners would not believe him. They said that no Cambodians marry Vietnamese. Gary said that this one did, but they said it is not true, the barber must have been lying. Gary's co-workers simply could not accept the story of the marriage even though Gary related how the barber met his wife and related circumstances. The prejudices of generations, even centuries, could not be set aside.

New elections were scheduled for 26 July 1998 and as the date approached the ruling Cambodian People's Party (CPP) appeared determined to control them. One human rights worker in Battambang was quoted as saying:

> 'The dog barks and the ox cart plods along. The leaders may make strong noises promising that the elections will be free and fair, and the ox cart -- the international community -- proceeds as usual, providing aid without looking carefully at what's really going on.'

The political manoeuvrings and associated violence throughout the country continued for nearly
the whole life of the project and at times it was not
easy for Harry and his CIAP team to keep operating.

In the first few years the IRRI Villa was robbed 10-
12 times and an exasperated Harry finally told the
guards that enough was enough; any more thefts and
they would have to pay. Losses still occurred and one
night a guard woke up to find the lights of the vehicles
gone. Some time later, after the city electricity supply
improved and it was no longer necessary to generate their own electricity, Harry asked the guards to
run the generator for two hours each Friday to keep
the batteries charged. One Friday he noticed that
the generator was not running and asked why. 'It's
not working, the battery is flat,' answered the guard.
'That's the reason we need to run it,' said Harry.

The mechanic called to fix the battery discovered,
however, that thieves had opened the generator's
locked door, unfolded a panel, taken out the automatic voltage regulator, replaced the panel and shut
the door, an operation that would have taken even
really good mechanics as long as twenty minutes to
accomplish. The guards were really worried because
a replacement automatic voltage regulator would
cost one thousand dollars.

CIAP also had three vehicles stolen. The first was
Peter White's Land Cruiser. He took his son to the
doctor in the centre of town, not far from the IRRI
Villa, and left his driver sitting in the vehicle. The
driver was just getting out to sit in the shade when

a man pushed him over to the passenger side of the car, got in, started driving away, opened the door and kicked Peter's driver out onto the street. The man staggered into the doctor's surgery and in poor English tried to describe to Peter how he had been shoved out.

A second vehicle was stolen only a couple of months later. A CIAP group was driving along a country road when a white car drove past and stopped in front of them. Men got out with AK47 rifles, ordered the CIAP group out of the Land Cruiser, and drove it away. One member of the CIAP group was so traumatised that he did not want to go to the provinces again. Harry offered a reward of one thousand dollars and some time later the police said they could get the vehicle back, but wanted ten thousand dollars. Harry had heard of vehicles being worth only half that amount after being returned and so he decided not to follow up. The robbers were apparently bandits with influential connections.

The third vehicle was stolen when Joe Rickman visited an office in the city and parked his vehicle around the corner. A street urchin offered to look after the car for a small fee, so Joe paid him the fee asked, but when he walked out of the office about two hours later his car was gone. A couple of foreigners sitting at a sidewalk restaurant told Joe that they had seen a man open the door with a key, get in, look at them, smile, pull out his mobile phone, make a telephone call, and then drive off.

On another occasion, early one Saturday evening, Joe and his family were held up at gunpoint. Three men approached as they reached the vehicle and as Joe was opening the driver's door, with his daughter beside him and his wife and son on the other side of the vehicle, one of the men drew a gun and demanded the keys to the car. Despite knowing that he should have just handed over the keys, Joe instinctively perceived danger for his daughter and grabbed the gun as it was being drawn up from pointing at the ground. The gun went off as Joe punched the robber in the face two or three times. The three men then made a quick exit leaving Joe with powder burns to one hand and bruises to the other.

Intermittent civil unrest and guerrilla warfare growing out of the political manoeuvrings made travelling in the country even more hazardous than living in Phnom Penh. A group led by Ram Chaudhary and including Mak Solieng, Men Sarom and Richard Lando and his wife became involved in one clash when they visited Kampong Thom in response to several requests from the provincial Governor.

Considerable importance was attached to their visit, probably the first visit by an international organisation since the Pol Pot years. The town was half-empty, the shops closed by 3 p.m. and there was a curfew at 7.00 p.m. After a tour of the area the Governor entertained them at a civic reception and told Ram that the curfew did not apply to them. However, while they were talking after dinner a tremendous noise reverberated through the room as a rocket flew overhead and exploded about one hundred metres from where they sat. Neighbouring houses, mostly thatched, caught fire. Fire tenders rolled in, the city lights were switched off and the army moved out towards the hillocks east of the city from whence the rockets had come.

Ram was advised that they should quickly return to the guesthouse but as they neared it another rocket thundered through the air to explode in a pond about twenty metres short of the guesthouse, fortunately only spreading mud everywhere. By then the government forces had taken up positions and the jet-black sky was lit by flying bullets and brilliant red flares. The shooting eventually stopped and at dawn word came from the Governor's Mansion that they should quickly eat their morning noodles and return to Phnom Penh. On the return trip they were escorted by dozens of troopers with AK47's and six mounted field guns.

During the build up to the 1993 elections a passenger in a CIAP vehicle was killed when it was fired on as researchers travelled up-country with research materials for the coming wet season experiments. One of their co-operators from Kampong Cham had asked if he could get a lift and was told that he could ride in the rear seat of the pickup, a dark blue vehicle clearly marked with CIAP stickers and flying an IRRI flag, white with 'IRRI' letters printed in green.

When they reached the ferry to cross the river it started to rain so they took the bags of fertiliser and seeds for the experiments out of the back of the vehicle and put them on the rear seat. The small plastic bags were enclosed in large sacks and may have looked like bundles of money. While they were moving the sacks another man asked for a lift, but the CIAP driver, Mr. Neang Sarath, was suspicious of his intentions and said that they did not have any spare room in their vehicle.

They continued onwards, and as they drove around a bend of the narrow road five kilometres beyond the ferry crossing a man standing close to the road opened fire at the pickup with a sub-machine gun. The first bullets blew out the left front tire, others went through the window and the side mirror and showered driver Sarath with shrapnel and glass. However, Sarath was such a good driver that he was able to duck down and accelerate past the gunman, who then fired a burst along the side of the vehicle. One bullet killed the co-operator who had asked for a ride and another grazed the waist of CIAP pest management specialist Mr Khiev Bunnarith.

As the gunman kept on firing from behind the vehicle a bullet went through the fertiliser and lodged in the back of the driver's headrest. Then an explosion from a grenade or rocket erupted just behind the pickup. If it had landed in the pickup's back tray it would have blown the vehicle to pieces. Luckily Sarath was able to keep driving with the blown out tire for about three or four kilometres. He then changed the wheel and drove up to Kampong Cham where they left the co-operator's body with his family before returning to Phnom Penh.

The dead co-operator left a wife and five children and Harry offered to pay compensation for his death, even though it was not a CIAP responsibility. He had been a really nice, hard working man and they all felt an obligation to the family. Harry decided to pay a total of one thousand dollars in instalments, though without telling the family the total amount because he knew how quickly such large sums of money could be dissipated.

Sarath, the same driver that drove us to Prey Yutka on the first trip with Phaloeun seven years earlier, was according to Harry 'a very clever guy who read amazing books.' He said that most people with limited English pick something simple to read, but Sarath would labour through a difficult hard cover book while waiting for a driving assignment.

Harry wanted to promote Sarath, because although very quiet he was a real leader. In English classes even the qualified graduates deferred to him. Harry tried to give him more responsibility and made him manager of the Department of Agronomy garage because he was so dependable and thorough, but Sarath did not want to manage the garage. He was happy to be a driver. Then one day he left to take a job with the Ministry of Interior. He would not say what sort of a job and Harry never really knew. He thought that Sarath was probably an investigator of some sort, working on tourist crimes and thefts of artefacts — but was not sure. Sarath later returned to driving.

The Hun Sen military coup of 1997 was a complete surprise to Harry, even though the city had been tense for a few days. That week he had been interviewing candidates for the socio-economics position and Betty had left on her scheduled July vacation the previous day. They were expecting that the tense situation would settle down as fast as it flared up and as Harry accompanied one candidate to the airport he assured him that there was no security problem in Cambodia. Harry had no idea that rockets would land near the runway as the candidate's international flight left Phnom Penh.

As a security warden registered with the Australian Embassy Harry was expected to report to the embassy if he saw three or more trucks with troops or any sign of tanks. On the return trip from the airport to Phnom Penh he saw two troop carriers, but the level of army activity did not appear to be excessive. He thought no more about it and continued on to the International School where he had an appointment to teach the guards how to regulate the water and chlorine intake of the swimming pool. After that he intended to pack for a Sunday morning flight to Australia and a long awaited fishing trip with his father.

Soon after Harry commenced explaining the complexity of water management at the swimming pool there was a loud noise that he thought was thunder. 'The guards suddenly lost interest in my lecture,' said Harry, 'and the thump of a second and third explosion had all the swimmers out of the pool and heading for home.'

He stopped the pool management lesson and offered the swimming teacher, Jo Craig from Western Australia, a lift to her home. As they started back it was apparent that something was seriously amiss. The only people on the street were heading purposely out of town and it was obvious Phnom Penh was experiencing an evacuation of almost the same magnitude as when the Khmer Rouge drove the residents from their homes to the countryside.

The tide of people was moving away from Jo's home district so Harry advised her to accompany him to the IRRI Villa. There they learned that three rockets had missed the Cambodian People's Party owned television tower and landed near the IRRI Villa. The explosions severely damaged nearby houses, blasted a mango tree from its roots and killed a Japanese man.

At the IRRI Villa Harry's warden's radio was making an enormous racket trying to encourage somebody to respond and IRRI residents were outside his front door wondering what had happened. 'I switched off the alarm and radioed the Australian embassy,' said Harry. 'We were warned not to leave home while the coup was in process. Some of us climbed to the top of the house and looked out over Phnom Penh. We saw two or three plumes of black smoke rising into the still air and it appeared that the fighting was concentrated near the airport.'

When Harry felt it safe enough they walked down the street to a nearby apartment to rescue Christine, a German student sponsored by CIAP. Later they visited the Australian defence attaché's wife, two hundred metres away. Almost all of the windows of her house had been blasted out and broken glass was strewn all over the floor. Luckily she was not hurt and several of her husband's team were helping to clean up.

Later that evening Christine was concerned about the fan that she had left running in her apartment and Jo joked that she didn't have a suitable dress or shoes to wear for a coup. They were hungry and finally somebody suggested ordering a pizza. Harry telephoned the pizza restaurant and was surprised to learn that they would still deliver, so tried to explain the IRRI Villa address. He was not successful and thought it prudent to allow Jo to use her superior Khmer. Jo's Khmer language skills were not what they were hoping for, so she then used a 'Cambodianised' version of English which went something like- 'You know my 'how', you know my 'how', it 'ILLI Villa' near bombed Mango tree'. The pizza was delivered at the normal price and was excellent.

After watching satellite television news on Sunday morning Harry sent an email to CNN. He explained that fighting was not 'being waged systematically from street to street,' the central market was not 'on fire' and 'all communications from Cambodia' were not down, 'otherwise it would not be possible for him to send them an email.'

By Monday morning their area had almost returned to normal, though elsewhere soldiers were completely out of control and there was still considerable looting and isolated burning buildings. A quick visit to the office found that the CIAP Cambodian staff that had gone there were feeling totally demoralised. They dreaded the prospect of the country plunging back into the conditions of yesteryear. 'When I visited the office on the Monday I stayed only long enough, as I found out later, to deter looters from coming in,' said Harry. 'But by Thursday, life at CIAP was getting back to normal.'

Peter White watched the coup on TV in Bangkok where his wife was waiting to give birth to their youngest daughter. She ended up having a caesarean section, so she was very lucky not to have been in Phnom Penh.

A few days later CIAP was ninety-nine percent operational. The Khmer team members recovered quickly from their generally demoralised malaise and had their programs well under control. Project personnel made trips to six provinces that week and Harry informed IRRI that travel was safe in nineteen of the twenty-one provinces. He would not permit the team members to travel to any part of the country where he would not travel himself. The bank was operating as normal and they could draw money for work. Surface mail had not resumed, but they expected delivery later in the week. International travel was improving and Ministry of Agriculture personnel were encouraged by the quick recovery of CIAP. In summary, it was work as usual.

It was also politics as usual as elections approached in early 2002. The international press reported: 'With colourful rallies and door-to-door visits, Cambodian parties yesterday began official campaigning for the country's first local elections, a pioneering effort to establish democracy at the grassroots level. But confidence in the process has already been shaken by the killing of nine opposition candidates and activists since November ... intimidation of voters and contestants is becoming rampant. At stake in the February 3 elections is control of the nation's 1621 communes.'

Extreme politics, prejudices, competition and strife had long been intertwined in Cambodian culture. It was in that environment that Harry and his team of expatriates and Cambodians made their contribution to the extraordinary recovery in rice production and farming efficiency in the country. Some of their experiences had been life threatening, others added a new dimension to their personal development.

12

*'Certain it is that in so short a time
the customs and peculiarities of this
country could not have been revealed
to us in all their details; however, we
were at least in a position to outline
its principal characteristics.'*
(Chou Ta-Kuan, 1297)

Although it generally takes many years between
the introduction of a new technology and detect-
able differences in farmer practice, there is no doubt
that CIAP was a key factor in Cambodia's recovery
in rice production. The outcome was also a culmination of the long-standing co-operation between
institutions, projects and individuals supporting
agricultural development. It was achieved in an efficient manner and had a substantial impact on farm
incomes and economic development. Thousands of
training opportunities were provided to Cambodian
researchers, research extended to all the provinces
and farm households were much better off.

The training component was very significant, providing over seven thousand training opportunities between 1987 and 2001 to nearly two thousand
Cambodians, many of them from the provinces.
Forty bright graduates received close nurturing

as scientific leaders. These highly trained personnel were assigned to work at CARDI in 2000 and accepted responsibility for continuing the work of CIAP programs. Nearly two thousand participants attended national workshops and conferences.

Around two hundred and fifty Cambodians attended short-term training courses abroad and nearly one hundred took part in study tours and conferences. Those trips allowed many individuals to evaluate research and management options in different environments and to exchange ideas and information with scientists in other countries. CIAP scholarships for post-graduate study in Australia and elsewhere maintained a Cambodian focus by requiring that thesis research be conducted in Cambodia or on problems of direct relevance to Cambodia.

More than a quarter of the places for 'in-country training', were devoted to English language study. Harry and his colleagues saw that a continued emphasis on English was essential for interaction of Cambodians with expatriate advisors and as preparation for training abroad, as well as access to the major sources of scientific information. Early technical training concentrated primarily on general crop production, plant breeding, plant protection and training methods. It soon quickly diversified into more specialised areas such as soil science and fertiliser management, seed production to meet a growing demand for seed, and management training to prepare future research leaders. These courses also provided staff of various institutions spread across the country with opportunities to interact and learn from others involved in similar activities.

The lack of ability to speak English was, however, not the only barrier to participation in a training course in CIAP's first years. Politics played a role. In her first year Phaloeun was recommended for a training course to IRRI but approval was denied. 'The Agronomy department refused,' said Phaloeun. 'They said that I did not understand English, but they just said that because they wanted to send other people who worked closely with the director. They thought that because I worked with a foreigner I might adopt Western culture. I told them that I was still a Cambodian woman and that I was not adopting Western culture; I had to work with foreigners and I needed to work effectively with them. The following year was different and I was permitted to go to the Philippines for on-the-job training in soil science. I went alone and once out of the country I felt very excited because I could speak English with them and practice easily. The two months I spent in the Philippines were very good. By then I had been working with IRRI for a year.'

Cambodians throughout the country are almost unanimous in their positive assessments of the benefits of their CIAP training. They say that it gave them new knowledge and skills, helped them to develop links with others and increased their confidence in dealing with colleagues and farmers. They in turn modified and used different versions of those courses throughout the country, thus extending the benefits of training to over 35,000 Cambodians.

Many NGOs stated that their work throughout the country could not have been carried out if CIAP had not spent so much effort in ensuring that provincial staff had adequate training in the basics of agricultural science and scientific research. They particularly highlighted the value of CIAP's English training. Communications between national scientists and the NGOs own foreign experts were greatly facilitated and outside knowledge could be understood and used constructively.

Training courses, although very effective, could not reach a large number of people as easily as the mass media in transferring knowledge and understanding of improved farming methods to farmers. CIAP produced and distributed some 300,000 copies of information and training materials in both Khmer and English. These included the CIAP annual reports, surveys, rice catalogues and booklets on soils, rice production, fisheries and livestock. In just three years NGOs were given over 900 copies of CIAP's annual research reports; 675 copies of surveys; 62,500 books; 620 maps; and 195 videotapes. The NGOs regularly used the '*CIAP Bulletin*' and '*AgNotes*', which contained detailed information on recent research findings and many '*how to*' articles. One thousand copies of each publication were printed every month.

Fifteen video titles produced in the Khmer language provide information on transplanting rice, fertiliser application, seed production, insect management, rat control and other crop practices. When the first CIAP videos were produced there were so few Khmer language tapes available in the markets that the CIAP videos were played almost continuously in restaurants, video parlours and provincial centres, and were on the television stations much of the time. Once when Harry was standing talking with his co-workers outside a restaurant in Takeo he heard a collective groan from the customers inside. A member of the CIAP group laughed and said, 'They are playing our video again'.

Unfortunately the first set of videos failed to acknowledge the contribution of Ministry of Agriculture personnel and the Minister was annoyed. When the second set also lacked the acknowledgements the Minister was furious and Harry had to send an urgent request to the tape production unit at IRRI to rectify the problem immediately. Fortunately Phaloeun was visiting IRRI headquarters at the time and translated the acknowledgements for inclusion in the next batch of videos.

The videos had positive results. After a year or so, low plastic fences to keep out rats appeared around the countryside and Harry saw examples where crops outside the plastic fence were badly damaged by rats whereas the crop inside the fence was healthy and good. The difference was outstanding and many kilometres of those plastic fences were soon seen around the countryside. Farmers often said they got the idea from a neighbour, but Harry considered it must have been the videos because the adoption of the technology was so close to when the videos were released.

AusAID funding enabled CIAP to provide research buildings in ten provincial centres, a complete new research station in another province and a glass-house complex for research in Phnom Penh. It provided seventeen four-wheel-drive vehicles, seven pickups, one truck, two buses, ninety-eight motorcycles, six four-wheel drive tractors, forty-one two-wheeled tractors, five threshers, and seventy-five water pumps. Essential research materials and fences were provided to more than forty agriculture centres. CIAP renovated offices, the training room, and the library at the Department of Agronomy in Phnom Penh. AusAID also funded the construction of roads, irrigation canals, and buildings at CARDI.

In parallel with the above operations, and undoubtedly the most effective mechanism for developing leadership capabilities of national research staff as distinct from technical skills, was on-the-job training within CIAP. The forty Cambodians assigned full-time to CIAP worked closely with expatriate and senior national scientists for several years and received close nurturing as scientific leaders. Staff turnover was low and the average length of service of the eight senior team leaders was over nine years. These highly trained personnel were eventually transferred to work at CARDI.

Study tours to Australian universities and research centres were arranged for counterparts and Ministry staff. An additional one hundred and twenty research co-operators from throughout the country were given an opportunity each year to work in close association with CIAP scientists in on-farm and on-station experiments.

Phaloeun had made the first of her two visits to Australia in 1991. She almost missed the plane when they transited in Bangkok because she was reading a cooking book at a duty free shop. She liked the pictures and forgot the time and that she was a passenger waiting for a plane until she heard the final call. In Australia she visited research stations, rice areas and universities. She was impressed by the clean environment, advanced technology and the general level of education, and astounded by family farms more than a thousand times larger than those in Cambodia.

Phaloeun said that she learned more on her second study trip to Australia because she was building on knowledge already gained. On the first trip her group had studied technology and the possibility of its transfer from Australia to Cambodia. The second trip she learned more about management at universities and research centres. 'On the first trip I was young, my knowledge was limited and I absorbed less than I saw,' said Phaloeun. 'On the second trip I already understood a lot and when I visited places I had ideas of my own so I learnt more. I could understand what was said about each university or research centre, what they could provide, their courses, how they organised their research centres and their research management. We learnt more about how to run an organisation, its structure and things like that. But we also increased our knowledge of technology because we attended research workshops.'

Participating in such different forms of training gave Cambodian researchers confidence in themselves. When the IRRI team first arrived in Cambodia people were in survival mode, thinking only in terms of food, clothes and shelter and not of career paths. There seemed to be an attitude of 'We can't do this or that.' The CIAP program helped instil a more positive attitude in people and expatriates saw a marked change in many of their Cambodian colleagues. In the beginning they were afraid to speak in public or to apply for a university positions or prepare research projects, though it was not necessarily that they did not know how. There was a sort of reticence about them — they did not want to take any sort of risk. But later most of the Cambodians in the project were applying for scholarships, taking language courses and writing research proposals. It was said that CIAP's biggest contribution may have been that people gained a more positive attitude.

Phaloeun and other Cambodian scientists were encouraged by Harry and his colleagues to present reports of their research at international conferences. The recognition gained and the opportunities for travel and interaction with other scientists were powerful motivational factors, but it required courage. Phaloeun's first experience was at a workshop in Ho Chi Minh City where she presented a paper on cropping system testing in Cambodia. 'I was really scared,' she said. 'My English was still very poor and I thought that the other participants would not understand me. The night before I presented the paper I could not sleep because I was thinking about my poor English. When I went to bed I could not close my eyes. I did not have any problem with the technical information, but I was scared about my English.' In the morning Phaloeun felt exhausted and since she was scheduled to present the first report she could not see what others did. 'I did not even know where to stand,' said Phaloeun. 'But when I started talking I felt OK. I just talked to them and when I finished I felt really happy because I had finished and could relax.'

Phaloeun's first independent work with IRRI had been as the co-ordinator of the research network. 'I learned a lot from that work,' said Phaloeun. 'We met many difficulties, but as we gained experience we could handle the difficulties ourselves. One of my friends had no chance to work with any NGO or any other international agency and has forgotten nearly all of the science and technology she learnt from the university. Now when I talk with her I realise that I had better opportunities and when I attend a workshop or a meeting somewhere I can understand the issues. I work very hard and I gain more than the people who have little to do. My friend feels that her training was useless and that she does not know much.'

Harry had great respect for his Cambodian counterparts and to watch their personal development over the years, particularly through advanced studies, was a great joy. On the other hand, one of his greatest sorrows was seeing Phaloeun suffer because she was not sponsored for post-graduate study in Australia. Some felt she would have found the pressure of Ph.D. studies in Australia too much. Nevertheless, seeing younger colleagues return from abroad with advanced qualifications ate away at her self-esteem. 'I sometimes regret not pushing her a little more to apply,' said Harry. 'Hopefully her position as Deputy Director for CARDI compensates somewhat. Phaloeun is, and will remain, one of the most respected persons at CARDI and is always admired for her efforts.'

Despite her disappointment at missing out on advanced studies, Phaloeun continued with dedication and loyalty through all the years of the project. 'For my work with IRRI, I feel that, as we say in Cambodian culture, it was my fate or destiny to have a chance to work with the project,' said Phaloeun. 'And I feel that I had a good fate in being involved with CIAP.'

Men Sarom and Mak Solieng both completed a Ph.D. degree with an Australian University. Harry encouraged Solieng to upgrade her qualifications even though she already had a Masters degree from Cuba. She studied at the University of Western Sydney and was impressed by the way that her advisers looked at agriculture as the interface between the natural and social environment where many factors interact. She was in a system of independent learning assisted by supervisors where the emphasis was on learning by doing. Solieng said she could cope with it, that she had learnt to be independent during the Pol Pot regime, and she had coped with that.

As the Director of CARDI Men Sarom now has a major role in the task of building on to previous gains and sustaining progress for the future. He was responsible for the CIAP plant-breeding program after Edwin Javier returned to the Philipines, and Ram Chaudhary told me that there were many of examples of Sarom's hard work, ingenuity and dedication. On one occasion they had just finished planting a number of rare and valuable rice plants when floodwater came so fast that they could only collect their belongings, field supplies and notebooks and run out of the area. Men Sarom spent the next morning diving from a boat to rescue the young rice plants.

Men Sarom's supervisor for his Ph.D. program in the University of Western Australia said that Men Sarom read widely, knew the literature and where he was heading, but would seldom seem to discuss or argue technical matters, or appear to think laterally. 'This worried me,' he said, 'and I tried during country trips to get Sarom to 'open up'. We would have a discussion and two or three weeks later he would come in to ask a few questions. It would slowly transpire that he had been doing a lot of thinking and was effectively challenging aspects of our discussion in a very diplomatic way. He would often raise an issue in a very casual manner — as if some thought had suddenly come to him. If I responded positively he would invite me to come out to the field. There alongside an experiment would be all sorts of 'ideas' he was testing. He was always thinking and worrying about things and doing something about it in a quiet way. I tried to figure out why it was that he was presenting himself in such a manner when, in fact, he was thinking deeply and laterally but seemingly lacking the conviction to express himself more strongly. Then one day when we were on a country trip and discussed the political upheavals in Cambodia, and how educated people like him survived those traumatic years his answer was to 'lie low' and keep his own counsel. I have no doubt he has ambitions and ideas for the future, but these he will pursue quietly and over time.'

According to Men Sarom, Cambodia is indeed rising above its history of wars and famine. It has maintained a national grain surplus since 1995, cattle numbers have been restored, pig and poultry numbers have more than doubled and Agriculture is destined to remain the backbone of the Cambodian economy for many years to come. 'We want to meet the challenge, the challenge for this tough environment,' he said. 'We have support from some people, from others discouragement. I feel bad about that, but I think that now we are better because when we started we did not have anything. I think we should develop ourselves; we should have more human resources, but to do so we need more money. I think money is around as long as we are good enough to get that money.'

'Cambodia suffered incalculable losses in human resources and physical facilities.' said Santiago Obien, Director of the Philippines Rice Research Institute. 'But there is enthusiasm to work and there is hope in the faces of people in the cities and in the countryside for a prosperous Cambodia. They are a people of noble culture whose past civilisation is embodied in the beauty and grandeur of Angkor Wat. But their immediate future is in the modernisation and productivity of their farms.'

'In retrospect you can always see things that could have been done better, but of course you did not know that at the time.' said Gary Jahn. 'At the time everyone is doing the best that they can, so just like when you look at your own life, if I had done this or that it might have been better, but perhaps not, because you would not end up where you are now.'

'I greatly regret not learning more Khmer language.' said Harry. 'Having more than a rudimentary understanding of the language, would have been an invaluable bridge building tool for breaking down barriers within the Ministry of Agriculture. If I had my time over again, knowing that my family and I would remain in Cambodia for thirteen years, the first six months of our contract would have been spent learning the language.'

Harry's colleagues in and out of CIAP admired his leadership and support. Margaret Jingco said, 'Harry was patient and persevered in teaching local researchers in conducting field experiments and in coaching them in their technical reports. He let the expatriate staff work independently on their areas of expertise, but would give suggestions as appropriate. He fully trusted me in money matters, both officially by authorising me to sign cheques in his absence, and personally by helping me if I needed it. Harry and his family served as my family in Cambodia, alleviating my homesickness.'

'Given where Harry started this project, I think CIAP has been fantastic,' said Joe Rickman.. 'Harry did not do it by himself, but he had the determination and foresight to make it succeed. The other expatriates also contributed in their own way, in big ways, to the development of unique individuals. If all of us have left anything worthwhile behind it is the enhanced capacity of Cambodian workers. And I think that is where we really can have satisfaction.'

'I think one of the nice things about Cambodia are the Cambodians.' said Betty Nesbitt not long before they left the country. 'They are a wonderful warm people. I find it really easy to live here now, a lot of English is spoken in the market and there are a lot of goods available. Though traffic is denser and it takes three times as long to get places now because the Khmers have vehicles, Cambodia is a still a lovely place to live.'

The Cambodians demonstrated their appreciation of CIAP achievements in the recovery of their country when Prime Minister Hun Sen honoured Harry Nesbitt and Glenn Denning with gold medals for their outstanding service. At the time Harry and Betty were the third-longest-serving expatriates in Cambodia.

Australia also honoured Dr. Harold John Nesbitt by appointing him a Member of the Order of Australia (AM) in the Queen's Birthday Honours List for 2003. The citation was for "Service to agriculture as project manager and agronomist for the Cambodia — International Rice Research Institute — Australia Project and, through this project, to the community of Cambodia." The award was recognition of the Australian nation's gratitude for that service.

Harry's award was thoroughly deserved and it was a privilege to follow developments from the first IRRI staff visit in 1986 to the final stages of CIAP and its transition in 2001 to an independent Cambodian Agricultural Research and Development Institute. Before Harry and his team arrived in Cambodia very little could be accomplished other than laying a foundation of goodwill and administration for a larger project. When they arrived the change was almost immediate. I visited Phnom Penh two months after Harry arrived and watched him conducting a training course for about fifty Cambodians under the reflected heat of the roof on the top floor of the Agronomy building of the Ministry of Agriculture. Three months later the CIAP office downstairs was in operation and from then on was always a hive of activity. And as time went by it was surprising how rapidly research and training expanded and how the Cambodian counterparts of the expatriates were developing in confidence and efficiency.

The team in Cambodia did not accomplish all this in isolation. Glenn Denning provided continuous support from IRRI headquarters and very little could have been accomplished without the understanding and long-term financial backing of the Australian Government through AusAID and its predecessors. Aid that was provided even when international support for the beleaguered country was limited by political differences and Australia was pressured against providing that aid. These inputs and the rapidly increasing capacity of the locals to rise above adversity and really contribute to the program are a testimony to the overall efforts. The net outcome was self-sufficiency in rice production over most of the country and the progress from famine to substantial rice exports.

It is a tribute to Harry's focus and co-ordination that so many people worked so well together. And when it is seen how much was accomplished under difficult conditions it is not surprising that he is rather sensitive to comments from newcomers on how things might be done differently.

Since the winding up of CIAP and transfer of activities to CARDI, a new four-year CARDI Assistance Project funded through AusAID commenced in August 2002. Its focus is on achieving the financial and management sustainability of CARDI and recognises that Cambodia remains one of the world's least developed countries with an estimated GDP of only US$300 per capita per year, barely one-tenth that of Thailand. Real poverty reduction depends on Cambodia's own success in mobilising and effectively managing non-aid resources for domestic investment, including that for agriculture as initiated through CIAP. The AusAID Internet web site of 2003 stated that the net financial benefit to Cambodian farmers since the CIAP project commenced in 1987 has been around US$40 million per year.

Cambodia is progressing, but it remains a land of fascinating contrasts, old and modern. On the return journey from Prey Kabas with Mr. Kep Poch we stopped for lunch at a traditional open-fronted restaurant with more plastic chairs, but not the same air of order as the restaurant closer to Phnom Penh where we had eaten breakfast. Busy women in slacks or colourful skirts were bustling back and forth from the dark kitchen to the tables. Shelves against the wall were stacked with contemporary supplies of bottled water, herbal wines, brandy, Angkor beer and Nestle's 'Bear Brand' condensed milk. Large chunks of ice, chopped off a huge block, were being put into glasses for the patrons, but we were careful of our health and asked for straws for our cans of soft drink. The meal was delicious spicy soup with thin sliced beef and a green vegetable of morning glory type, followed by crisply fried chicken and ginger — tasting as good as ever. Flies were waiting to pounce but avoided the chicken. Maybe the ginger helped. At 12:59 p.m. most customers stood up and left the tables and a lean dog joined the cats under the tables, hoping to find tasty morsels.

In contrast, the next Saturday evening I sat with Hieng Sokchea and John Wilson at a table in a multi-million dollar restaurant with a magnificent view across the mighty Mekong River and reminisced about the past. The restaurant could seat over 500 people and the live music was far enough away to be pleasant. The setting was great, the food delicious and the table was decorated with a spotless red cloth and a vase of flowers. There were several of these huge restaurants along the river — far different from the 'Number One' restaurant around the corner from the Monorom Hotel where years earlier I had seen girls maintaining the 'clean' image of the restaurant by opening paper sleeves for chopsticks by blowing into them. Phnom Penh was rapidly becoming a modern Asian city, though there are still some hiccups. A slum with 500 families was razed by fire, luckily with no loss of life. A few days later the area was bulldozed ready for a road and new development: a coincidence maybe, but not an unusual one.

Before I left Phnom Penh I went with Harry to visit Ngak Chhay Heng, our guide and interpreter on the first IRRI visit to Cambodia fifteen years earlier. Then Heng had owned little more than the clothes he wore and I had been glad to bring medicines for his family. Now his home is a three-storey shophouse in Phnom Penh. Heng was elsewhere, but 'no problem' as they commonly say, and his nephew sent a motor cycle to fetch him. As we renewed acquaintance after many years Heng happily showed us his home, including the spare room at the top of the stairs that he keeps 'free for guests'. His nephew runs a computer school on the first two floors and I counted forty computers with thirty-two students working on the latest computer programs. Heng was retired and planned to visit Sydney in 2002 to see his son become an Australian citizen, and to see his grandchild — William Heng.

Many years have passed since Heng, Phaloeun, Men Sarom, Sokchea, Mak Solieng and two million others were forced to leave Phnom Penh and disappear under the dark shadow of the Khmer rouge for three years, eight months and 20 days. Their story is one of determination and persistence in building knowledge and skills and playing a crucial role in

establishing a solid foundation for food security in
their country. Hunger has receded, people are beginning to feel secure, some have become prosperous and they are free to travel. As they look forward
to the future, for many people of Cambodia the dark
shadows of the past have faded.

'Time runs so quick,' said Ms. LingLing Domingo, Harry's last administrative assistant, a Filipino who came
to keep her father company while he was working on a
project and remained in Cambodia after he left. 'Cambodia is changing its face in terms of both culture and
infrastructure. Now you can see traffic lights, classy
restaurants, big buildings and grocery stores. Modern
gasoline stations with mini-markets are everywhere.
The number of Khmers speaking English is increasing,
they now wear jeans and security is far safer. I feel
privileged to have come to Cambodia and witnessed
the changes that have shaped the country to what it is
today. It is more than a learning experience and helps
me to appreciate life even more.'

Ms. Chan Phaloeun, a once confused young woman
endeavouring to learn Russian and then English as
she studied agriculture and agricultural research is
now the confident head of the Farming Systems section of the Cambodian Agricultural Research and
Development Institute (CARDI). Phaloeun led us on
an excursion up country to make arrangements with
co-operators and farmers for new crop experiments
and community development programs. We drove
over the Tonle Sap on the recently repaired bridge
— a bridge destroyed by war thirty years earlier. The

smooth bitumen road passed flood-prone flats where houses are built on stilts as high as five metres above the ground, then continued for over a hundred kilometres past parched rice fields waiting for rain.

Near Kampong Cham we turned off the main road and reality struck — this track had the sights and feel of the Cambodia I had first encountered. Holes in the road were as deep as fifty centimetres and we held tight as the Land Cruiser rocked from side to side, otherwise our heads would bang on the windows. Small boys knelt on the road to bow to passing vehicles in the hope of payment for putting soil in the holes — a very temporary measure.

I glimpsed a little black piglet tethered to a tree, nibbling grass, as we drove on to an area with better soil and higher rainfall, big timber, fruit trees and banana palms. The wooden houses were on stilts just above head height with thatched, tile or corrugated iron roofs, some houses very plain, some ornate, most well maintained with neat and tidy yards. We passed an occasional food stall by the roadside, then incongruously two photo shops with bold blue and white advertising panels in an area where a private camera was a rarity. A woman was pulling on a rope to draw water from a well. Rubber trees past their prime had been cut for fuel; their wood perhaps more value than the land they grew on.

Near the village of Chamcar Leu we reached a research station with huge 50 year-old avocado trees, coffee bushes under shade trees and chilli and pineapples in the fields. The research co-operator was nowhere to be seen and it was an hour before he came from the village. Phaloeun had a long talk with him in the Khmer language then guided us back to his substantial home in the village to collect soybean seed. Heavy rain started beating on the roof of his house and when we returned to the road the holes were filled with water and shirtless children stood watching in the rain.

It took a rough forty-five minutes to cover the sixteen kilometres to the main road where the smooth bitumen seemed even better than on our outward journey. After lunch in a neat restaurant offering good food and many types of canned drinks we moved on to the next road junction and waited five minutes for our local contacts to arrive. Vendor women at the junction offered snacks to passers by; pomelo fruit, boiled half-hatched eggs, rice cooked in bamboo stems and trays heaped with shiny fried black spiders with a leg span as big as a hand. No thanks! We travelled onwards beside a dry canal to another village where farmers, thirty men and eight women, waited for Chan Phaloeun and her two colleagues. They met in an open building that housed a large Buddha statue and a huge antique wooden drum hanging from the rafters.

After fifteen years of progress had the time arrived for drums to call the people to a modern celebration of *'the burning of the rice?'*

Phaloeun and her two colleagues greeted the farmers, then settled bare-foot and cross-legged on the matting floor to continue their work.

ACKNOWLEDGEMENTS

The contributions of many people and organisations involved with the Cambodian – IRRI – Australia – Project (CIAP) are gratefully acknowledged. Particular thanks go to Don Mentz for promoting publication of this book and for providing travel support through *The Crawford Fund* to enable updating of information in Cambodia, the Philippines and elsewhere. From the principal players there was a generous sharing of time, information and of thoughts, some of which were of a highly personal nature. Chan Phaloeun and her compatriots and Harry and Betty Nesbitt were particularly generous with their time, hospitality and provision of information about life in Cambodia and the project. Gary Jahn, Joe Rickman and others provided thoughtful insights into the operation of research projects, and Margaret Jingco patiently searched through files for historical records.

Special thanks are due to Claire Allan-Kamil for encouragement and her guidance on how to transform a mountain of material into readable form. Without her help the project may have been abandoned.

Thanks are also made on behalf of the Cambodian people to IRRI, AusAID and numerous NGOs for understanding their needs and for providing assistance to overcome the critical shortages of food in their country.

The author consulted numerous publications about Cambodia and by and about CIAP. Some specific publications and sources of further reading are listed below.

Nesbitt, H. (1997) *Rice Production in Cambodia*. Cambodia-IRRI-Australia Project, Phnom Penh, Cambodia and IRRI, Los Baños, Philippines.

"*Cambodia*" Encyclopædia Britannica Online. [Accessed 13 May 2001].

"*Cambodia – Beauty and Darkness*" on the Internet provided useful background information and lists many references.

Findlay, Trevor. *Cambodia: the Legacy and Lessons of UNTAC*, SIPRI Research Report No. 9, Oxford University Press (Internet summary accessed 2001)

Maclean, M.(1998). *Livestock in Cambodian Rice Farming Systems*. Cambodia-IRRI-Australia Project, Phnom Penh, Cambodia

'*The Impact of Agricultural Research for Development in Southeast Asia*.' Proceedings of an International Conference held at the Cambodian Agricultural Research and Development Institute, Phnom Penh, Cambodia, 24-26 October 2000. Edited by Peter Cox and Ros Chhay.

Various analyses and reports of CIAP, such as the *CIAP-NGO Impact Study* by Courtney Norris (2000); *The Impact of CIAP's Human Capital Development and Information Dissemination Efforts, 1987-1999* by R. T. Raab, (2000); *The Economic Impact Assessment of the Cambodia-IRRI-Australia Project* by D. Young and co-authors (January 2001); and the *Environmental Impact Assessment of the Cambodia-IRRI-Australia Project (CIAP)* by N. Urwin and T. Wrigley (May 2001).

About the Author

Don Puckridge was progressively a farm labourer and university lecturer in Australia and a research leader for the International Rice Research Institute (IRRI) in South and SE Asia. His work with IRRI while based in Thailand for nearly sixteen years involved coordinat-  ing research on deeply-flooded rice ecosystems for collaborative projects extending into India, Bangladesh, Thailand, Myanmar, Cambodia and Vietnam. From 1986 he worked closely with government officials and village leaders in Cambodia and provided logistical support from Bangkok to the Cambodia-IRRI-Australia-Project once that project was established in-country.

INDEX

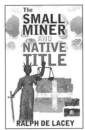

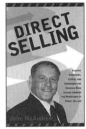

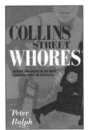

Best-selling titles by Kerry B. Collison

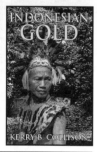

Readers are invited to visit our publishing websites at:
http://www.sidharta.com.au
http://www.publisher-guidelines.com/
http://temple-house.com/

Kerry B. Collison's home pages:
http://www.authorsden.com/visit/author.asp?AuthorID=2239
http://www.expat.or.id/sponsors/collison.html
http://clubs.yahoo.com/clubs/asianintelligencesresources
email: author@sidharta.com.au